The Poetry of Marcia Belisarda

A Bilingual Edition

Medieval and Renaissance
Texts and Studies

Volume 545

The Poetry of Marcia Belisarda

A Bilingual Edition

Transcribed and translated by
Connie L. Scarborough

Dando a conocer estos versos su legítimo autor
So you will know the legitimate author of these verses

Arizona Center
for Medieval &
Renaissance Studies

Tempe, Arizona
2019

Arizona Center
for Medieval &
Renaissance Studies

Published by ACMRS (Arizona Center for Medieval and Renaissance Studies)
Tempe, Arizona
© 2019 Arizona Board of Regents for Arizona State University.
All Rights Reserved.

Library of Congress Cataloging-in-Publication Data
Names: Belisarda, Marcia, active 17th century, author. | Scarborough, Connie
  L., 1954- transcriber, translator. | Container of (work): Belisarda, Marcia,
  active 17th century. Poems. | Container of (expression): Belisarda, Marcia,
  active 17th century. Poems. English.
Title: The poetry of Marcia Belisarda : a bilingual edition / transcribed and
  translated by Connie L. Scarborough.
Description: Tempe, Arizona : ACMRS (Arizona Center for Medieval and
  Renaissance Studies), 2019. | Series: Medieval and renaissance texts and
  studies ; volume 545 | Includes bibliographical references and index. | In
  English and Spanish.
Identifiers: LCCN 2019011721 | ISBN 9780866986038 (hardcover : alk.
  paper)
Subjects: LCSH: Spanish poetry--17th century--Translations in to English. |
  Spanish poetry--17th century--History and criticism. | Belisarda, Marcia,
  active 17th century. | Poets, Spanish--Classical period, 1500-1700--
  Biography. | Women poets, Spanish--Biography. | Nuns as authors--Spain.
Classification: LCC PQ6279.B395 A2 2019 | DDC 861/.3--dc23
LC record available at https://lccn.loc.gov/2019011721

Cover Image:
Rutilio Manetti, *Santa Caterina che scrive*
Su concessione del ministero dei Beni e delle Attività culturali. Polo Museale della
Toscana. Foto Pinacoteca Nazionale di Siena.

∞
Printed on acid-free paper in the United States of America

Table of Contents

Acknowledgments	v
Introduction	1
BNE ms. 7469	2
Sor María de Santa Isabel/Marcia Belisarda	3
Scholarship to date	6
Edition and Translation	17
Norms of Transcription	18
Abbreviations in Footnotes	19
Text and Translation of Biblioteca Nacional Española (Madrid) ms. 7469	21
Introductory Poems to the Collection	22
The Poems of Marcia Belisarda	36
Index of Poems	371
Bibliography	381

Acknowledgments

I would like to acknowledge my colleagues in the Department of Classical and Modern Languages and Literatures of Texas Tech University for their support of the present project. I also thank the staff of the Biblioteca Nacional Española for facilitating my access to a very fragile manuscript. I acknowledge, too, the services of the Interlibrary Loan Department at Texas Tech University. Finally, a thanks to my husband, Charles, for his ongoing encouragement and patience.

Introduction

Sor María de Santa Isabel, writing under the pseudonym Marcia Belisarda,[1] was one of the most prolific female poets of seventeenth-century Spain. The body of her known work is preserved in one manuscript in the Biblioteca Nacional Española (Madrid),[2] ms. 7469, prepared for publication but never published.[3] Belisarda has received some critical attention; she is represented in a number of anthologies of women's writings from Iberia, and a Spanish edition of her poems appeared in 2015.[4] The present edition of Belisarda's work was prepared from the unique manuscript and, for the first time, makes these poems accessible to an English-speaking audience. As happens with other poets, anthologies that include poems by Belisarda publish the same poems, usually copying from an earlier anthology or transcription, often without consulting the original manuscript to check for errors in transcription or other anomalies.[5] Belisarda's most-cited poems have, in general, been favorably viewed by critics, but, since the entirety of work has been, until recently, unavailable for study, she has not received the same degree of scholarly attention enjoyed by other women poets of the Golden Age, such as María de Zayas y Sotomayor, Catalina Clara Ramírez de Guzmán, Luisa de Carvajal y Mendoza, and Sor Marcela de San Félix. The present edition is not an exhaustive critical study of Belisarda's work, but rather it provides students and researchers with a faithful transcription of BNE ms. 7469 together with an English translation for those interested in women's writing from the early modern period but who are not trained as Hispanists.

---

[1] This is an anagram of her name as pointed out by María Dolores Martos Pérez, "Receptores históricos y consciencia autorial en paratextos de impresos poéticos femeninos (1600–1800), *Criticón* 125 (2015), 89.

[2] Hereafter, BNE.

[3] On the intention of Marcia Belisarda to publish her poetry, see Martos Pérez, "Receptores históricos," 88–89.

[4] This is the edition prepared by Martina Vinatea Recoba, *María Fernández López (Marica Belisarda): Obra poética completa* (New York: Instituto de Estudios Auriseculares, 2015).

[5] While I have found few errors in the transcriptions of Belisarda's poems as they presently appear in anthologies, I have been able to make corrections, and these are noted in footnotes to the transcription.

BNE ms. 7469

This edition is particularly timely as access to the Belisarda manuscript is currently restricted due to its deteriorating condition. There is a digital copy available from the BNE, but it presents several problems including the illegibility of certain words, words not captured by the digital images due to the manuscript's tight binding, and the fragile nature of some pages that result in poor photographic quality. Physically, the manuscript measures 21 x 86 cm with 88 folios; the last four folios are badly damaged from moisture and parts of these pages are missing entirely. The binding is typical of the nineteenth century,[6] and the binding does not always respect margins. As a result, some words bound on either the extreme right or left of the folio are only partially legible, and trying to more fully expose them could risk further damage to the manuscript or the binding. In such instances, I have tried to render illegible or missing words from the letters available, relying on both meaning and rhyme-scheme for the most probable reading. The manuscript is a clean copy in that there are very few obvious errors and only a very few minor corrections. The poems attributed to Belisarda are in one hand, so we can assume that these were penned by the author or entrusted to one copyist. The introductory poems to the collection, written by other authors, are in different hands. I studied the manuscript over three summers (2012–2014), and the present transcription is a faithful rendition of the contents together with accompanying explanatory notes and English translations for all poems.

All critics agree that ms. 7469 was prepared with the intention of publication as evidenced by the poet's initial prologue addressed to her readers (folio 2r) and inclusion at the beginning of the manuscript of eight encomiastic poems by other authors in praise of Belisarda's volume. We do not know the reason why the poems were never published and any theories regarding the matter are pure speculation. We know that the book was prepared for the censors, a necessary step toward publication, but the manuscript appears to have never reached their hands. Amy Katz Kaminsky suggests that Belisarda's death may have interrupted the process or that "her confessor or mother superior forbade her to continue with such a profane project."[7] However, I have found no concrete evidence, whatsoever, to uphold either of these suppositions. Other nuns of the period wrote on religious as well as secular topics and were published,[8] so we cannot assume that her vows alone prevented the manuscript from being published.

---

[6] Cerezo Soler, Juan, "El *Libro de poesías* de Marcia Belisarda: Notas al ejemplar autógrafo de la Biblioteca Nacional." *Manuscrt. Cao*, 13 (2012), n. pag.

[7] Kaminsky, *Water Lilies/Flores de agua: An Anthology of Spanish Women Writers from the Fifteenth through the Nineteenth Century* (Minneapolis: University of Minnesota Press, 1996), 372.

[8] For example, Sor Violante do Ceo (Lisbon), Doña Ana Francisca Abarca de Bolea, Sor María de la Antigua, and Sor Marcela de San Félix (illegitimate daughter of Lope

Sor María de Santa Isabel/Marcia Belisarda

Sor María de Santa Isabel, whose pseudonym was Marcia Belisarda, was born in the area of Toledo,[9] probably at the beginning of the seventeenth-century. Manuel Serrano y Sanz and almost all subsequent commentators on Belisarda confirm that she professed as a nun in the Royal Convent of the Conception in Toledo, housed in part of the Palacios de Galiana. Belisarda herself tells us in a poem dedicated to Saint John the Evangelist, found on folio 6r, that she began to write when she was twenty-seven years old. If we speculate that she entered the convent probably in her late teens and that ms. 7469 dates from ca.1640, we can approximate her date of birth at around 1613 and that she probably professed in or around the year 1632. A title of another poem (no. 138) bears the date 1646, indicating that she was still alive at that date, but we do not know the exact dates of either her birth or death. From the prologue Belisarda authored for her collection, we know that the poet wanted her work published as a collection. Kaminsky contends that "Sor María reveals in her prologue a sophisticated understanding of the importance of collecting her works and publishing them together so they might be judged not individually, but rather each in relation to the others, and as the product of a single pen."[10]

Recently Martina Vinatea Recoba has determined that the Palacios de Galiana in Toledo housed two different orders: the Concepcionistas and the Comendadoras de Santiago. Her search in the archives of the Comendadoras reveals that a nun by the name of Sor María de Santa Isabel professed in this convent during the years that correspond to the time frame for the life of Belisarda. A document of "limpieza de sangre"[11] for María Fernández López was found to correspond to the nun who took the name of Sor María de Santa Isabel upon entering the convent of the Comendadoras.[12] Although this new line of investigation is worthy of consideration, the content of the manuscript seems to point more towards Belisarda's association with the Concepcionistas.[13] Belisarda dedi-

---

de Vega).

[9] We learn this from one of the laudatory poems by an individual identified as Licenciado Montoya, found on folio 4r.

[10] *Water Lilies*, 371.

[11] Literally "clean blood," a document that stipulated that her family had not converted to Catholicism from Judaism. It was necessary to prove that one was a "cristiano viejo" (old Christian) to be an acceptable candidate to enter the order.

[12] Vinatea Recoba, *María Fernández López*, 60–61.

[13] There exists in the archives of the Convent of the Concepcionistas a manuscript known as the *Primer libro de la Fundación de la Orden* or *Libro de Registro Antiguo*. Pedro de Quintanilla, in 1660, wrote an introduction to this manuscript, an index, and notes, giving it the title *Libro y Registro antiguo del Convento de Religiosas de la Inmaculada Concepción de María Señora y Abogada nuestra, de la ciudad de Toledo, cabeza de esta esclarecida*

cates three poems to the Concepcionitas' founder, Doña Beatriz de Silva (1424–1492) and at least eight poems to the Virgin emphasizing the purity and singularity of Mary—the very foundational beliefs for an order dedicated to the Immaculate Conception of the Virgin.[14] In addition, Belisarda wrote four poems to commemorate the profession of nuns in the convent of the Concepcionistas and one for the visit of the Provincial of Castile to the convent. It is also worth noting that Belisarda dedicates more poems to St. John the Evangelist and St. John the Baptist than to Santiago (St. James). If she had been a nun in the order of the Comendadoras de Santiago, it seems likely that she would have written more poems about the saint to whom the order was dedicated. Furthermore, the convent of the Concepcionistas was badly damaged during the Spanish Civil War, and most of its records were lost at that time.[15] While preparing the present study, I spoke personally with the Reverend Mother of the convent, who made a thorough search of the surviving convent records, but she was unable to locate any more data about Sor María de Santa Isabel.

The figure of Beatriz de Silva was held in particular esteem by Belisarda as a nun dedicated to the Immaculate Conception of the Virgin. Beatriz served as a lady-in-waiting at the court of Juan II of Castile (1405–1454). Juan's second wife, Isabel of Portugal (1428–1496), was jealous of Beatriz's beauty and imprisoned her in a locked box in the palace with the intent of murdering her. But Beatriz survived the ordeal, she believed, through the intercession of the Virgin Mary. She reported that, while imprisoned in the trunk, the Virgin Mary, carrying the infant Jesus in her arms, appeared to her in a blue and white habit and told her to form a religious order devoted to the Immaculate Conception. From that point on, Beatriz dedicated herself to religious life[16] and set about to found a convent of nuns devoted to the Immaculate Conception who would wear the habit she had witnessed the Virgin wearing in her vision. Beatriz first went to live with the nuns of the Royal Convent of Saint Dominic in Toledo.[17] When Isabel of Castile

---

Orden, de quien es fundadora la Santa Madre Beatriz de Silva (Balbina Martínez Caviró, *Conventos de Toledo: Toledo, Castillo interior*, Madrid: Ediciones de Viso, 1990, 279. Quintanilla states that 303 women professed as nuns between 1496 and 1658 (Balbina Martínez Caviró, *Conventos de Toledo*, 281–82).

[14] Although not proclaimed as dogma by the Roman Catholic Church until 1854, the belief that Mary was conceived free of the taint of original sin had been circulating among Christians since the fourth century.

[15] Due to its proximity to the Alcázar, and the site's intense shelling, almost the entire archives of the convent were lost with the exception of the papal bull for the foundation of the order (Manola Herrejón Nicolás, *Los conventos de clausura femeninos de Toledo*, Toledo: Diputación Provincial, 1990, 60). Martínez Caviró states that the sisters had to abandon the convent and take refuge in a nearby house when the Alcázar was shelled (*Conventos de Toledo*, 275).

[16] Although she did not profess as a nun.

[17] Belisarda dedicates a poem to St. Dominic, no. 54.

ascended to the throne, she learned of Beatriz's piety and, together with her confessor Hernando de Talavera and her advisor Cardinal Mendoza, became patrons of Beatriz and donated an old palace in Toledo to her for the founding of her new convent.[18] In 1484 the new house began with Beatriz, her niece, and eleven other women. Beatriz dedicated the new order to the Immaculate Conception, and, in 1489, the pope gave his approval for the new order. The nuns were granted a distinctive habit that they still wear today—it includes an image of the Virgin Mary on a white scapular on the chest and right shoulder, a blue mantle, and a rope belt similar to that used by the Franciscans. In 1494 the order was placed under the Rule of Saint Clare,[19] and a constitution was later drawn up that included the nuns' strict enclosure. The Concepcionistas is the only religious order in Spain, before the mid-sixteenth century, created by a woman.[20]

All evidence suggests that Sor María de Santa Isabel was from a family with enough resources to send her to a convent in Toledo patronized by King Ferdinand and Queen Isabel. It is evident that she had received a good education as her poetry displays knowledge of a variety of verse forms, includes frequent reference to figures of Greek and Roman mythology, and uses some Latin phrases or Latinized words in Castilian. She was also well-read in hagiography with poems dedicated to martyrs and key Christian figures such as Saint John the Baptist, Saint John the Evangelist, Saint Sebastian, Saint Catherine of Siena, Saint Teresa, Saint Dominic, and Saint James (Santiago, patron of Spain), among others. She also dedicated poems to Beatriz de Silva, as noted.[21] Sainz de Robles cites the encomiastic verses penned by a Master Montoya[22] at the beginning of Belisarda's manuscript to conclude that Belisarda was from a prominent family.[23]

---

[18] Martínez Caviró identifies this palace as the Palacios de Galiana that included the capilla de Santa Fe. "Por eso se llamó en un principio convento de la Concepción de Santa Fe" (*Conventos de Toledo*, 259).

[19] Belisarda writes a poem dedicated to Saint Clare (no. 3).

[20] Information about Beatriz de Silva and the founding of the Concepcionistas is from Elizabeth Lehfeldt's *Religious Women in Golden Age Spain: The Permeable Cloister* (Alderhot, UK and Burlington, VT: Ashgate, 2005).

[21] Martínez Caviró in her detailed study, *Conventos de Toledo*, attributes to Belisarda verses dedicated to Beatriz de Silva as preserved in *La margarita escondida*, a work written in 1661 by Catalina de San Antonio. *La margarita* is a record of saintly women in the Convent of the Concepcionistas, and the poem to Beatriz found at the end of the manuscript is usually attributed to Catalina, but Martínez Caviró deems it more logical to ascribe it to Belisarda (*Conventos de Toledo*, 278). Vinatea Recoba also attributes the *Vida de María Bautista* to Belisarda (*María Fernández López*, 62–64).

[22] Sainz de Robles falsely identifies this individual as Moya. *Ensayo de un diccionario de la literatura, Tomo II: Escritores españoles e hispanoamericanos* (Madrid: Aguilar 1973), 1,118.

[23] See folio 4r.

Scholarship to date

Modern scholarship on Marcia Belisarda began in 1905 when Manuel Serrano y Sanz published his *Apuntes para una biblioteca de escritoras españolas desde el año 1401 al 1833*.[24] Under the heading, "Santa Isabel (Sor María de)," Serrano y Sanz made an inventory of BNE ms. 7469. He transcribed, in whole or in part, a number of poems, and, to this day, these are the ones most often included in anthologies of Golden Age poetry or of women writers from Spain. While Serrano y Sanz's work continues to be a valuable introduction to Belisarda's work, there are errors in the inventory and some in the transcriptions. I have also identified seven poems in the manuscript that he failed to mention in the inventory for a total of 145 compositions.[25] He speculates that Belisarda may have entered the convent due to "desengaños amorosos" [disappointments in love], but he presents no evidence to support this claim other than the fact that several of her profane lyrics treat this theme.[26] He also deemed her profane poetry far superior to her verses on religious subjects, and this evaluation continues to be repeated by most critics.[27]

---

[24] Manuel Serrano y Sanz, *Apuntes para una biblioteca de escritoras españolas desde el año 1401 al 1833* (Madrid: Tipografía de la *Revista de archivos, bibliotecas y museos*, 1903–1905), 362–78.

[25] Vinetea Recoba's edition has 148 poems since she separates the "coplas" [stanzas} from poem 130 when actually it forms part of a *villancico* [carol] dedicated to Santiago. Similary, she cites the "coplas" as poem 140, when actually they form part of the *villancico* for the Feast of the Ascension she lists as poem 139. Also, she separates the "coplas" from the *villancico* written for the profession of a nun in San Clemente in Toledo, which she cites as poem 144.

[26] Kaminsky rightly points out that Belisarda's frequent treatment of the theme of failure in love should not be seen as autobiographical. "They rely on such familiar set pieces as the disenchanted lover, and they are remarkable not for the way in which they reveal the deepest reaches of the poet's soul, but for the fluidity of the poetic voice. . . ." (*Water Lilies*, 371–72).

[27] Angel Flores and Kate Flores in their *Poesía feminista del mundo hispánico (desde la edad media hasta al actualidad): Una antología crítica* (México, DF: Siglo Veintiuno, 1984) contend that disillusionment with love was the motive for Belisarda to take the veil (55). Ana Navarro in *Antología poética de escritoras de los siglos XVI y XVII* (Madrid: Castalia, 1989) claims that Belisarda's profane poems are more emotional and sincere than her religious poetry (54). Navarro also states that "La diferencia de inspiración entre los poemas religiosos y los profanos, a favor de los últimos, permite suponer que libre de las limitaciones impuestas a este tipo de obra por el claustro, al que posiblemente no llegó por vocación, 'Marcia Belisarda' hubiera sido una de las poetisas más vehementes e interesantes de nuestro siglo XVII" (55) [The difference in inspiration between the religious and the profane poems, in favor of the latter, permits one to suppose that, free of the limitations placed on profane poetry by the cloister, which she may not have entered with a true vocation, Marcia Belisarda would have been one of the most vehement and interesting female

Largely due to Serrano y Sanz's *Apuntes,* Sor María de Santa Isabel began to receive some critical attention in the first half of the twentieth century. For example, Margarita Nelken in *Las escritoras españolas,* first published in 1930, follows Serrano y Sanz's lead in praising Belisarda's profane verses over those she wrote on religious topics, calling the latter "anodina" [unremarkable or dull].[28] Nelken also opines that Belisarda might have been a poet of great renown if she had not been a nun and sees in her verses a certain melancholy that could imply a lack of sincere religious vocation.[29] Federico Sainz de Robles, without any evidence other than the existence of Belisarda's secular poetry (which he also deems superior to her verses on religious themes), affirms that our poet did not have a true religious vocation and that "siempre guardó en su corazón afectos mundanos" [she always harbored worldly affections in her heart].[30]

A significant step forward in scholarship about Belisarda and ms. 7469 was the publication in 1993 of the first edition of Julián Olivares's and Elizabeth Boyce's *Tras el espejo la musa escribe: Lírica femenina de los Siglos de Oro.*[31] In the introduction, they discuss Belisarda's profane poetry and identify the topics she most often addresses. These include women's complaints (including criticisms of men), courtly love motifs (sometimes composed in the voice of a man), and dedications to novels and other literary works penned by others. Olivares and Boyce classify Belisarda's religious poetry, according to subject matter, including poems dedicated to the Immaculate Conception, Christ's humanity (poems about Christmas, for example), the Holy Eucharist, and female mystical experience. Their anthology includes Belisarda's introductory prologue directed to her readers ("A quien leyere estos versos") [To whomever reads these verses] and thirty-four poems, divided into two sections—secular and religious poetry (twenty-three secular and eleven religious). They modernize Belisarda's spelling and provide punctuation, and I have followed their lead in this regard in preparing

---

poets of the seventeenth century]. Cristina Ruiz Guerrero also contends that Belisarda may have entered the convent after being disappointed in love since we find echoes of these sentiments in her poetry (*Panorama de escritoras españolas,* Vol. 1, Cádiz: Universidad de Cádiz, 148). Ruiz Guerrero notes the influence of Góngora on Belisarda's work and praises her verses on secular subjects over those that treat religious ones, calling the former "más sincereas, atrevidas y cálidas" [more sincere, daring, and enthusiastic] (*Panorama de escritoras españolas,* 148). Without critical comment, Clara Janés includes five of Belisarda's poems on secular subjects in her *Las primeras poetisas en lengua castellana* (Madrid: Endymion, 2000).

[28] Margarita Nelken, *Las escritoras españolas* (Madrid: horas y HORAS, 1930), 147.

[29] Nelken, *Las escritoras españolas,* 147–48. She specifically cites the ballad that begins "Pensamiento, si pensáis" [Thought, if you plan] (Melancholic Ballad, poem 56). She follows the transcription given by Serrano y Sanz (*Apuntes para una biblioteca,* 367) of only the first thirty-two verses (the poem in its entirety is comprised of forty-three verses).

[30] Sainz de Robles, *Ensayos de un diccionario,* 1118.

[31] Madrid: Siglo Veintiuno, 1993.

my present edition. However, we should note that, in the manuscript, Belisarda does not separate her secular poems from the ones on religious topics, and the two types of verse are intermingled throughout the manuscript. Since, in the heading to the first poem, the poet indicates that it is the first poem she wrote, the mixture of religious and secular verses may indicate a chronological ordering by date of composition.

In 2012, Olivares and Boyce published a second edition of *Tras el espejo la musa escribe*.[32] This version of their anthology includes more authors and fewer poems by Belisarda than the first edition. The second edition includes her prologue to readers, ten poems on secular topics, and six on religious topics. All poems included in the second edition, previously appeared in the first. I indicate in footnotes in the Spanish transcription, the poems that Olivares and Boyce anthologize as well as those found in Serrano and Sanz's inventory.

Another widely-circulated, bi-lingual anthology of Spanish women writers that includes poems by Belisarda was edited by Amy Katz Kaminsky and appeared in 1996. In her *Water Lilies/Flores de agua: An Anthology of Spanish Women Writers from the Fifteenth through the Nineteenth Century*,[33] Kaminsky reproduces eight of Belisarda's poems, all of which originally appeared in Serrano y Sanz's inventory. Amanda Powell provides an English translation for the poems in Kaminsky's anthology as well as a translation of the poet's prose introduction to the manuscript.[34] All of the poems included in this anthology are of a secular nature, and Kaminsky provides a two-and-one-half-page introduction to Belisar-

---

[32] Madrid: Siglo Veintiuno, 2012

[33] Minneapolis: University of Minnesota Press, 1996.

[34] Kaminsky includes the following selection: A quien leyere estos versos [To the Reader of these Poems] (374); Romance, Procurad memorias tristes [Poem in Ballad Meter, Make your attempt, sad memories] (375); Otro, dándome el asunto, Escapé de tus cadenas, entregándome a sosiego [Another Ballad, on a Topic That Was Given to Me, I gave myself to rest and peace/and slipped your heavy chains] (375–76); A una gran señora, casada, a quien aborrecía su marido [To a Noble Married Lady, Whose Husband Shunned Her] (376–77); Décimas para una novella, Fatigado corazón [Verses for a Novel, My heart, so sadly vexed and weary] (377–78); Décimas escritas muy de prisa, en respuesta de otras en que ponderaban la mudanza de las mujeres, Hombres no deshonréis [Verses Written in Great Haste, in Reply to Others, Which Considered the Inconstancy of Women, You men must no dishonor do] (378–79); Décimas para cantadas, dándome el asunto, Juré, Filis, de no verte [Verses to be Sung, on a Topic That Was Given to Me, I swore, my Phyllis, not to see you] (379–80); Romance para una novela, Pues gustas, mi dueño hermoso [Poem in Ballad Meter: For a Novel, Since you are pleased, my lovely lord] (380–82); Soneto, dándome por asunto cortarse un dedo llegando a cortar un jazmín, Filis, de amor hechizo soberano [A Sonnet, Having Been Given the Topic of Cutting One's Finger in Reaching to Cut a Jasmine, Phyllis, sublime enchantment of love's powers] (*Water Lilies/Flores de agua*, 382). I here give Powell's translations of these titles.

da's work. In her succinct introduction Kaminsky makes several salient points. First, she notes that Belisarda, in the poems in which she complains about love, is remarkably fluid with regard to the poetic voice; sometimes the voice is masculine, in other poems it is feminine and, at times, of indeterminate gender. She also is accurate in stating that Belisarda does not usually directly complain to the beloved but rather complains about the nature of love itself and often about the absence of love.[35] Kaminsky stresses that Belisarda's work does not indicate that she was isolated from the world outside the convent: "Her poems reveal not only that she was familiar with the poetic conventions of the day, but also that she kept current with the political and cultural events of the period."[36] She knew the work of other poets as evidenced by her glosses on the works of others, and she praises other writers of the period. We know, too, that she wrote many poems in replies to requests from others and participated in poetic competitions as revealed in many of the titles and introductions she gives to her poems.[37] Gwyn Fox claims that local and national *certámenes* (literary contests) in the sixteenth and seventeenth centuries were "a legitimate outlet for women's verse and hence opportunities for officially sanctioned fame."[38] Since Belisarda also wrote poems in praise of novels and other literary works, we can conclude that much of her poetry was intended for an audience well beyond the other nuns of her convent.[39] But, as noted, our poet did compose a number of poems specifically dedicated to novices who professed in her convent and in other religious houses. Kaminsky contends that Belisarda reached the height of her fame between 1643 and 1646 since these are the dates given for poems sung in the churches of Seville and Toledo during these years.[40]

The important issue of gender and the poetic voice is the subject of an essay by Amanda Powell, Kaminsky's collaborator for the translations of Belisarda's poems in *Water Lilies*. Powell examines how Belisarda adopts, at times, a male voice while in other poems she clearly speaks as a woman. In her study, "'¡Oh qué diversas estamos,/dulce prenda, vos y yo!' Multiple Voicings in Love Poems to Women by Marcia Belisarda, Catalina Clara Ramírez de Guzmán, and

---

[35] Kaminsky, *Water Lilies/Flores de agua*, 371–72.
[36] Kaminsky, *Water Lilies/Flores de agua*, 372. On this point, see also Elizabeth A. Lehfeldt, *Religious Women in Golden Age Spain: The Permeable Cloister* (Aldershot, UK and Burlington, VT: Ashgate, 2005). Although Lehfeldt bases her work on archival records from convents in Valladolid, many of her conclusions can be generalized to other locales in the same period.
[37] "Dándome el asunto" [Giving me as the topic], for example.
[38] Gwyn Fox, *Subtle Subversions: Reading Golden Age Sonnets by Iberian Women* (Washington, DC: The Catholic University of America Press, 2008), 158. In citing Fox, I use the English translations that she provides in her book.
[39] Kaminsky, *Water Lilies/Flores de agua*, 372.
[40] Kaminsky, *Water Lilies/Flores de agua*, 372.

Sor Violante del Cielo,"[41] Powell examines how "women poets redirected Petrarchan conventions in order to critique gender inequalities and to discard the mute, passive role assigned to women on and off the page."[42] She summarizes the arguments for and against these poems as expressions of homoeroticism and concludes that love poems written by women to women, whether adopting a male grammatical voice or not, play on the ambiguity inherently present when women adopt the conventions of male love poetry. Powell bases her analysis on Belisarda's secular poems as anthologized in the 1993 edition of Olivares's and Boyce's *Tras el espejo la musa escribe*. For example, she studies the *décima*[43] beginning "Hombres, no deshonoréis" [Men, do not dishonor] (Poem 104) in which "Belisarda counters the misogynist canard of women's inconstancy with the concluding suggestion that changeableness on the part of men (who, worse than mutable, are mendacious) would be an improvement."[44] Powell examines how Belisarda continues her questioning of masculine privilege in "Para una novela" [For a Novel, that begins "Baste el injusto rigor" [Enough of unjust rigor] (Poem 112). In this poem, the speaker, grammatically identified as a man, addresses the beloved as "lord" or "master" [dueño], thus adopting a position in which a male poetic voice addresses the object of his affections as the poet's superior. By speaking as a male, Belisarda asserts that not all men occupy a place of power and that hierarchies are more nuanced than simply one of men positioned in a superior status to women. Gwyn Fox analyzes the sonnet, also entitled "Para una novela" [For a Novel] (Poem 97), in which Belisarda adopts a complaining male voice. Fox contends that, although the poetic voice bemoans the loss of Clori to another man, Belisarda here plays with the usual scheme of the woman as the "ingrata" [ingrate] and suggests that both the man and woman may be at fault in this failed relationship.[45] Belisarda alludes to the Sermon on the Mount[46] when she quotes "porque bien no se sirve a dos señores" [because it is impossible to serve two masters] near the end of the sonnet, and I believe that she is alluding to Clori's (potential) interests in two men—one represented by the complaining (male) poetic voice and the other the one who caused him to become jealous. But Fox contends that Clori in this poem occupies a place of inferiority rather than the traditional role usually assigned to women in *amor cortés* poetry, i.e., a mistress who has control over the suffering male lover. She states that "Marcia Belisarda exposes the

---

[41] In *Studies in Women's Poetry of the Golden Age*. Coord. Julián Olivares (Woodbridge, UK: Tamesis, 2009), 51–80. I give Powell's translations of the poem titles as they appear in her essay.

[42] Powell, "'¡Oh qué diversas estamos, dulce prenda, vos y yo!,'" 51.

[43] A poem with ten octosyllabic lines rhyming abbaaccdde.

[44] Powell, "'¡Oh qué diversas estamos, dulce prenda, vos y yo!,'" 60.

[45] Fox, *Subtle Subversions*, 216–17.

[46] Matthew 6:24.

masculine love complaint as a rhetorical sham and women as simply pawns in political, economic, and familial alliances."[47]

Fox analyzes another example of Belisarda writing in a male voice in the sonnet, "A consonantes forzosos sobre que habían escrito sonetos con asuntos diferentes diferentes personas, diéronme por asunto no desmayar a vista de un desdén"[48] [In set rhyme, about how different people having written sonnets on different matters, I have been given the topic of not swooning in the face of a rebuff] (Poem 32). In this poem, Belisarda uses a masculine "yo" [I] to justify her appeal to reason and "determines to employ reason as a cure for the ills of disdain and the passions of love."[49] Fox argues that Belisarda, although relying on the motif of the hapless lover imprisoned by love, concedes that reason alone will only go part way in extinguishing passions (221–22). What this critic stresses most is Belisarda's "artfulness" in this sonnet in which the poet examines the powers of the soul in a manner similar to religious meditation technique but here employed in the play of courtly love.[50]

Powell, in her analysis of "Escapé de tus cadenas" [I escaped from your chains] (Poem 10), identifies how Belisarda uses the "self-positioning" of the male voice to speak as a martyred courtly lover. The poet complains to Cupid himself and curses his misfortunes in love. Powell also points out that in many poems, Belisarda refuses to identify the speaker by gender. These include the sonnet, "Cuando borda de perlas el aurora" [When the dawn borders with pearls] (Poem 45) in which the "yo" [I] introduced in the first tercet is ambiguous since, while it appears to be a courtly lover complaining of his lover's disdain, there is no indication that Belisarda is not speaking as a woman who has suffered rejection.[51] In "En suspiros y llanto arroje el pecho" [Let my breast hurl forth sighs and weeping] (Poem 97), Belisarda plays the role of a jealous male suitor who complains that his beloved Clori has abandoned him for another. At the same time, however, she subtly hints that Clori may have been justified in leaving him because her former lover shows himself to be faithless and vengeful, proposing ultimately "to forget her by cultivating the taste for another."[52] Playing with gender roles, vis-à-vis grammar, is clearly seen in the ballad "Bella pastorcica de oro" [Beautiful little shepherdess of gold] (Poem 106). Here, according to Pow-

---

[47] Fox, *Subtle Subversions*, 218.

[48] This poem is also briefly analyzed by Dianne Dugaw and Amanda Powell on pages 133–34 of their chapter "Baroque Sapphic Poetry: A Feminist Road Not Taken" in *Reason and Its Other: Italy, Spain, and the New World*, ed. David R. Castillo and Massimo Lollini (Nashville: Vanderbilt University Press, 2006), 123–44.

[49] Fox, *Subtle Subversions*, 221.

[50] Fox, *Subtle Subversions*, 222.

[51] Powell, "'¡Oh qué diversas estamos, dulce prenda, vos y yo!,'" 65.

[52] According to Powell, in this sonnet, "Knowing a woman is writing, we are meant to question who speaks" ("'¡Oh qué diversas estamos, dulce prenda, vos y yo!,'" 66).

ell, Belisarda employs "stock pastoral imagery" but, by making "almas" [souls—a feminine word] the subject for those who adore the "bella pastorcica," she may imply that the souls of young men yearn for the beautiful shepherdess; by the use of a feminine term, we can also read the verses to mean that young women are equally in love with her.[53] In conclusion, Powell contends that "In seemingly conventional guise. . . Belisarda's love poems to women, in their range of voicings set about upsetting gender arrangements that are exposed as fictively stable."[54]

Gwyn Fox analyzes other aspects of Belisarda's poetry in *Subtle Subversions: Reading Golden Age Sonnets by Iberian Women*.[55] According to Fox, Belisarda does not use the sonnet to explore a single theme, such as love, but uses this verse form as a vehicle for topics ranging from literary criticism to female friendship. For example, in "Alabáronme me un soneto tanto que le pedí con instancia, aunque después de leído no entendí nada y respondí el siguiente confesando mi poco saber" [They so praised a sonnet to me that I demanded to read it, although having read it I could not understand it at all and responded as follows, confessing my lack of understanding],[56] Fox shows how Belisarda "mocks the sonnet form itself, while also lampooning the other poet's gongorism, but the message is concealed in well-composed admiration and self-denigration."[57] This poem appears to deride the sonnet as a verse form or to complain about poets who willfully obscure their meaning while in other sonnets Belisarda skillfully subverts the Petrarchan model and its love motif. For example, in "Dándome por asunto cortarse un dedo llegando a cortar un jazmín"[58] [Giving me for a topic cutting one's finger reaching to cut a jasmine] (Poem 145), prepared for a poetic competition, Fox contends that Belisarda undercuts the common pastoral mode since she portrays Phyllis, not as the enamored and enchanting shepherdess, but as silly and somewhat vain: "Marcia Belisarda converts the sonnet into an anti-Petrarchan admonition concerning human vanity appropriate to the nun's calling."[59] She finds that the sonnet actually has little to do with love and does not, as is usual in the Petrarchan model, portray the meeting of the young girl with the flower as a motif to examine the inextricable march of time and its effect on waning beauty.[60] But Fox's supposition that Belisarda is here writing in protest of the triviality of young women's lives "denied education, and bound to the home, the *estrado*

---

[53] Powell, "'¡Oh qué diversas estamos, dulce prenda, vos y yo!,'" 67.

[54] Powell, "'¡Oh qué diversas estamos, dulce prenda, vos y yo!,'" 68.

[55] See footnote 38.

[56] Poem 72. Fox misidentifies the sonnet as appearing on folio 42v; it appears on folio 41v.

[57] Fox, *Subtle Subversions*, 155.

[58] I here correct Fox who does not precede "jazmín" with "un," which is clearly visible in the manuscript.

[59] Fox, *Subtle Subversions*, 202.

[60] Fox, *Subtle Subversions*, 202.

[ladies' parlor], their embroidery, and empty conversation until they are married off to husbands chosen by their fathers"[61] seems a bit strained. If Belisarda was writing as part of a poetic exercise or joust, she certainly, cleverly manipulates the motifs of the white jasmine flower and red blood of Phyllis's cut finger (the colors were probably the theme assigned for the poem), but to suppose that she meant this sonnet as a protest about young women's limited opportunities does not, to my reading, seem supported by the text itself.

Belisarda also uses the sonnet to write an encomium for a woman whom Fox presumes to be a fellow poet. "Fatal rigor, ejecutando aleve" [Harsh fate, treacherous, cunning] (Poem 109)[62] is an ode to Anarda, who has died. Fox contends that our poet not only wants to immortalize the dead woman but that she also finds solace in the fact that Anarda's perfection has assured her eternal life as evidenced in the last line of the sonnet: "gloriosa vida en un morir preciso" [in death, a more glorious life].[63] The presumption that Anarda was a poet who Belisarda knew is based on Fox's analysis of the verses in which Belisarda characterizes the dead woman as possessing "gala, entendimiento" and "ingenio" [brilliance, perception and wisdom]. Fox contends that this verse "implies that the dead woman may have been a contestant in the convent's poetic jousts . . . . This would make the loss of a companion who shared and perhaps equaled her intellectual interests and capacities particularly poignant."[64]

While we cannot be certain of the identity of Anarda or her exact relationship with Belisarda, the poet dedicates other poems to the theme of female friendship and companionship, especially among nuns. For example, in "A una religiosa que lloraba sin medida la muerte de otra que la había criado" [To a religious who cried uncontrollably for the death of another who had raised her] (Poem 80)[65] Belisarda tries to console a friend named Virena upon the loss of one who had been like a mother to her.[66] Our poet also composed poems dedicated to women who professed in her own convent and in other religious houses in Toledo. These imply that Belisarda probably personally knew the women who were entering religious orders and wanted to commemorate the occasion for them. In her analysis, Fox singles out the sonnet, "A la profesión de Doña Petronila de la Palma en la Concepción Real de Toledo, siguiendo la metáfora de la palma" [On the profession of Doña Petronila de la Palma in the Royal Conception of Toledo,

---

[61] Fox, *Subtle Subversions*, 202.
[62] Fox misidentifies the sonnet as appearing on folio 57v; it appears on folio 67r.
[63] Fox, *Subtle Subversions*, 186.
[64] Fox, *Subtle Subversions*, 187.
[65] This is a *romance* [ballad], not a sonnet but Fox includes it in her analysis. Fox misidentifies the poem as appearing on folio 45r; it appears on folio 48r.
[66] Fox, *Subtle Subversions*, 188.

following the metaphor of the palm] (Poem 4).[67] Belisarda wrote both a sonnet and a *décima* for Doña Petronila, so one may assume that she was either well-known or esteemed by our poet. Fox thoroughly examines Belisarda's reliance on the multi-faceted metaphorical meanings of the "palm" in this poem, including classical and biblical antecedents from both the New and Old Testaments that allude to this plant.[68] By cleverly playing on the nun's name (de la Palma), Belisarda links the nun to the concept of the *hortus conclusus* as symbol of virginity and female enclosure,[69] and she portrays God as the divine gardener who will nourish this new plant (palma) or bride of Christ in the garden/convent.[70] Fox further concludes that Belisarda emphasizes that this "new bride of Christ is not just a passive recipient of God's fertile power, but an intelligent rational woman who chooses this life of her own volition."[71]

Fox also discusses Belisarda's pair of sonnets between a *galán* [young man] and a *dama seglar* [secular woman] found on folio 17v, Poems 30 and 31.[72] These paired poems are a scholastic-type exercise in which similar terms are used to argue the same point from opposite sides.[73] Again, Fox sees in the response of the *dama* Belisarda's appeal to reason, i.e., that the woman's "voice" is superior in that it invokes the rational soul whereas the *galán* argues for satisfaction of sexual desire (expressed in terms of the appetite).[74] Fox contends that "the *dama* expresses the philosophical view that contemplation is preferable to action, particularly when the pursuit is purely for physical satisfaction . . . . The *dama* ignores the body to privilege the mind and intelligence, and does not shrink from expressing her own preference for the Christian ideal of containment toward which a rational man should naturally strive . . . ."[75] By subverting the common association of the body and bodily desire with women, the poet argues that women possess the power to reason on a par with that traditionally attributed to men.

A significant study of ms. 7469 appeared recently in 2015—Martina Vinatea Recoba's *Obra poética completa* of Marcia Belisarda.[76] This transcription, study, and notes is the most complete to date. It contextualizes Belisarda with other

---

[67] Fox states that this sonnet is found on folio 8v, but it actually appears on folio 7v. Fox also here cites Belisarda's manuscript as ms. 4169, when, in fact, it is BNE ms. 7469.

[68] Fox, *Subtle Subversions*, 170–71.

[69] It should be noted that the *hortus conclusus* was also a metaphor for the perpetual virginity of Holy Mary.

[70] Fox, *Subtle Subversions*, 171.

[71] Fox, *Subtle Subversions*, 172.

[72] "Soneto de un galán a una dama seglar" and "Encoméndoseme la respuesta y fue por los mismos consonantes [sic]".

[73] Fox, *Subtle Subversions*, 227.

[74] Fox, *Subtle Subversions*, 228.

[75] Fox, *Subtle Subversions*, 231.

[76] See footnote 4.

known women writers from Toledo as well as important new, possible biographic information about the poet. She analyzes the poems' stylistics as well as the different lyric forms and strophic patterns that Belisarda employs in her work.[77] This is an invaluable contribution to the study of Belisarda's poetry but, unfortunately, scholars who do not read Spanish, especially those in fields of comparative literature or women's studies, cannot take advantage of Vinatea Recoba's analysis.

While the work of Vinatea Recoba, Powell, and Fox present the most thorough analyses of Belisarda's work to date, Ann Craig Befroy includes an examination of our poet in her 2009 PhD dissertation, "The Flesh Made Word: Writing Women in the Poetry and Prose of Late Medieval and Early Modern Spain."[78] In her fourth chapter, "Poets Incarnate: The Female-Authored Self-Portrait," Befroy cites Belisarda's defense of women writing as found in the prose prologue she composed to introduce her collection of poetry. She points out that our poet posits that, since women may be mothers, they are more capable than men of producing poetry because God did not grant to men the ability to reproduce.[79] Befroy relies on the poems transcribed by Serrano y Sanz and those that appear in the first edition of Olivares and Boyce. She specifically cites those poems that "treat female authority within the constructs of Petrarchan poetics."[80] She analyzes, Poem 145, "Dándome por asunto cortarse un dedo llegando a cortar un jazmín" [Giving me for a topic cutting one's finger reaching to cut a jasmine][81] as an example of Belisarda critiquing the Petrarchan code. Befroy concludes: "The metaphorical dismemberment and disintegration that Laura suffered at the hands of Petrarch's poet/lover here moves beyond the metaphor. Filis is actually cut, her hand possibly severed from her body. Belisarda, it seems, recognizes the cruelty of both the Petrarchan strategies and the lovesickness that inspired his verses" (270). Befroy also cites the poem "Persuadiendo a una dama que amase . . ." [Persuading a lady to fall in love . . .] (Poem 131) in which Belisarda responds to the gloss of four male poets in the voice of a lady. Our poet's conclusion that it is better to love oneself than the male suitor, according to Befroy, implies that Belisarda sees heterosexual love as a trap for women.[82] Befroy also includes Belisarda's burlesque ballad, Poem 95, the self-portrait that she sends to an unidentified lady. She points out that Belisarda here paints herself as a vibrant woman and eschews the formula of the woman as the inaccessible object of male desire.[83]

---

[77] This work is based on her 2013 Ph.D. dissertation for the Universidad Nacional de Educación a Distancia (Madrid), under the directorship of Nieves Baranda.
[78] New York University, 2009.
[79] Befroy, "The Flesh Made Word," 266.
[80] Befroy, "The Flesh Made Word," 267.
[81] I cite the translation as it appears in Befroy's dissertation.
[82] Befroy, "The Flesh Made Word," 271.
[83] Befroy, "The Flesh Made Word," 273.

Belisarda's work has not gone unnoticed in other, more generalized studies of female poets in Spain. For example, in an article, "Femenismos prevalecientes: hacia una nueva historia del siglo XVII" [Prevailing Feminisms: Toward a New History of the Seventeenth Century][84] published in 2007, Teresa Langle de Paz uses two of Belisarda's poems as examples of the poet's advocacy for autonomy of the female poetic voice. She specifically cites, as does Befroy, the *décima* "Persuadiendo a una dama que amase, escribieron cuatro poetas glosando esta copla, y yo respondí sobre la misma glosa por la dama, conforme a su dictamen" [Persuading a lady to fall in love, four poets wrote glossing a couplet and I responded to the same gloss for the lady according to her dictate] (Poem 131) and argues that Belisarda announces with her title that her intention is to give the female subject of the poem her own voice. Langle de Paz contends that Belisarda's poem is feminist in that she responds to four, supposedly male, poets' glosses, allowing the woman to protest men's inability to love truly and concluding that she prefers to love herself rather than be the object of men's fickle affections.[85] This critic also includes the "Romance Burlesco" [Burlesque Ballad] that begins "¡Oh, cómo intenta Leonida" [Oh, how Leonida tries] (Poem 57) as another example of Belisarda's "feminist consciousness," but she does not analyze it in detail.[86]

---

[84] Teresa Langle de Paz, "Femenismos prevalecientes: hacia una nueva historia del siglo XVII," *Edad de Oro* 26 (2007), 147–58.

[85] Langle de Paz, "Femenismos prevalecientes," 156–57.

[86] Other critics who allude to Belisarda's poetry include Isabel Colón Calderón in her article, "El lenguaje de Fabo" (*eHumanista* 3 (2003), 91–104). She singles out for study Belisarda's response to the courtier, Poem 52 which begins "No podrán, discreto Fabio" [They cannot, discrete Fabio] (94–95). Dianne Dugaw and Amanda Powell in their article "Baroque Sapphic Poetry: A Road Not Taken," (in *Reason and Its Other: Italy, Spain, and the New World*, ed. David R. Castillo and Massimo Lollini, Nashville: Vanderbilt University Press, 2006, 123–44) briefly discuss Belisarda's sonnet, "Si no impide mi amor el mismo cielo" [If heaven does not impede my love] (Poem 32). Lisa Vollendorf mentions Belisarda among the poets included in her article "Transatlantic Ties: Women's Writing in Iberia and America" (in *Women, Religion, and the Atlantic World (1600–1800)*, ed. Daniella Kostroun and Lisa Vollendorf, Los Angeles: The Regents of University of California, 2009, 79–110) but does not cite any of the poet's poems specifically. Nieves Baranda Leturio in her *Cortejo a lo prohibido: Lecturas y escritoras en la España moderna* (Madrid: Arcos/Libros, 2005) cites Belisarda among other female poets who did not limit their writings to circulation within a convent, but interacted in literary circles outside the convent walls. She also briefly discusses Belisarda in connection with other poets such as Leonor de la Cueva and Violante do Ceo who openly write in a woman's voice but appropriate many of the same motifs used by male poets to express amorous sentiments. Bárbara Mujica in her well-known anthology, *Women Writers of Early Modern Spain: Sophia's Daughters* (New Haven and London: Yale University Press, 2004), makes only brief note of Belisarda in her introduction (lxxiii–lxiv) as a prolific poet whose poetry had not yet been published.

Edition and Translation

The present edition is a transcription of BNE ms. 7469, prepared from personal consultations of the manuscript, and includes all the known poems attributed to Marcia Belisarda. By luck of circumstance the manuscript of her poetry found its way into the Biblioteca Nacional Española, but the librarians there were unable to find any information about how or when the manuscript came into their collection. I provide English translations for all the poems, and I have tried as much as possible to align the translation with the original ordering of the verses in Spanish so that readers can easily compare the two. With this goal in mind, the syntax is, at times, hyperbatic, but, I believe, this captures part of the esthetic of seventeenth-century verse. At times, I have had to choose between one or more possible readings due to the ambiguity of antecedents or grammatical inconsistency. The poems that are lettered A–I are introductory poems to the collection written by other poets, except for B which is Belisarda's prose introduction to her collection. The numbered poems represent the works of Marcia Belisarda, unless otherwise indicated.

Norms of Transcription

Manuscript	**Modernized**
ç	z or c (voçes = voces)
f initial or lack of initial consonant	h
x	j (monxe = monje)
ss intervocalic	s
b (bilabial)	v (biento = viento)
i initial	y (io = yo)

Other notes:
"por que" is often substituted for modern "para que" + subjunctive.

When an antecedent or reference is unclear in the English translation, I supply a clarification in brackets. When there is an obvious misspelling in the Spanish transcription, I indicate it with [sic]. All other oddities in the original Spanish are explained in footnotes.

Brackets are also used to indicate lines of refrains when, after a first occurrence, subsequent appearances of the lines of the refrain are indicated, usually, by "etc." in the manuscript. I supply the completed refrain each time its repetition is indicated.

Parentheses indicate that parentheses occur in the manuscript.

I indicate with a series of commas those places where the paper is torn and parts of the lines are therefore missing. Feasible reconstructions when these are possible are indicated in italics.

In order to give readers a picture of the format of the manuscript, folios written in more than one column, are indicated as First and Second Column. Folios where there is no indication of columns are written in a single column.

Abbreviations in Footnotes

Olivares and Boyce, 1st ed. = Olivares, Julián and Elizabeth S. Boyce, eds. *Tras el espejo la musa escribe: lírica femenina de los Siglos de Oro.* 1st ed. Madrid: Siglo XXI de España, 1993.

Olivares and Boyce, 2nd ed. = Olivares, Julián and Elizabeth S. Boyce, eds. *Tras el espejo la musa escribe: lírica femenina de los Siglos de Oro.* 2nd ed. Madrid: Siglo XXI de España, 2012.

Serrano y Sanz = Serrano y Sanz, Manuel. *Apuntes para una biblioteca de escritoras españolas desde el año 1401 al 1833.* 2 vols. Madrid: Tipografía de la *Revista de archivos, bibliotecas y museos*, 1903–1905. Serrano y Sanz's entry, "Santa Isabel (Sor María de)," appears in Vol. 2 on pages 363–78.

BNE MS. 7469

[Introductory Poems to the Collection]

A. Décima al autor.[1] 1r

Si por su infeliz suerte
el cisne, en canto fatal
celebra estando mortal
las exequias de su muerte,
mejor cisne en ti se advierte,
Belisa, pues cuando escribes
vida inmortal te apercibes;
luego ser mejor, se infiere,
pues él cuando canta muere,
y tú cuando cantas vives.

1v [Blank]

B. A quien leyere estos versos. 2r

Siento pasión natural amar los hijos (aun sin ser hermosos, mayormente los del entendimiento), no se extrañará que éstos del corto mío recoja mi amor. Porque desperdiciados cada uno por sí se exponen a padecer injustos naufragios en el crédito de las gentes, y juntos podrán más bien valerse unos con otros, por cuanto la cadencia y las voces de ellos darán señas suficientes de ser, no hijos de muchos padres, sí de uno sólo tan honrosamente altivo que antes morirá de necesidad que buscarla socorro, estimando en más parecer pobre que valerse de prestado caudal para ostentar lúcidamente rico. Ociosa satisfacción para los que con discreta y urbana atención o intención bien advertirán que quien dio alma a la mujer le dio al hombre, y que no es de otra calidad que ésta aquélla, y que a muchos concedió lo que negó a muchos. Y si dando a conocer estos versos su legítimo autor (por serles en todos sus defectos parecidos) no bastare para que se dude, la gloria que en la duda le adquirieren se deberá a Dios, y cuando no, la [sic] goce no le falte la de su cielo que es la que desea y pretende.[2]

---

[1] Serrano y Sanz, 363.

[2] Serrano y Sanz, 362; Olivares and Boyce, 1st ed., 329; Olivares and Boyce 2nd ed., 248.

Introductory Poems to the Collection

A. **Décima[1] to the author.**

If, for his sad fate
the swan, in fatal song,
celebrates being mortal
the funeral of his death,
one notices that you are a better swan,
Belisa, since when you write
you perceive immortal life;
thus, being better, one infers
that he, when he sings, dies
and, you, when you sing, live.

B. **To whomever reads these verses.**

Since it is a natural passion to love one's children (even if they are not beautiful, especially those of the intellect), it should not seem strange that these of my little wit should receive my love. Because thrown out, each one on its own, they are exposed to suffer unjust shipwrecks in peoples' opinion, and together they can better be valued, comparing one to another, for which their rhythm and words will give sufficient signs of being, not the children of many parents, but of one so honorably proud who will die from want rather than ask for help, thinking it better to appear poor than take advantage of a fortune on loan in a show of ostentatious wealth. Pointless satisfaction for those that, with discreet and urbane attention or intention assert that He who gave a soul to women, gave it also to men, and one [soul] is not of a different quality than the other, and what is conceded to many women may be denied to many men. And, knowing the legitimate author of these verses (for all their apparent defects), may cause one to doubt, but do not doubt that any glory she acquires is owed to God, and may not be denied the joy of heaven which is what she most desires and seeks.

---

[1] A décima is a poem with strophes of ten, eight-syllable lines, usually rhyming *ab-baaccddc*.

C. De el [sic] padre Jacinto Quintero de los Clérigos Menores,[1] 2v
a estas obras de María de Santa Isabel. Décimas.

FIRST COLUMN
Ese aliento que te inspira
alguna oculta deidad
siendo en tu ingenio verdad
es en tu sexo mentira.
Los acentos de tu lira
resuenen de polo a polo,
pues, vence tu plectro sólo
por más que su gloria excusas
todo el aire de las Musas
y todo el fuego de Apolo.

SECOND COLUMN
Tu nombre asegura fiel
lo canoro a tu armonía
entre la voz de María
y el acento de Isabel.
Pues, el labio de clavel
y tu sonora garganta
en cuantas piedades cantar
prevenidamente anima
una y otra cuerda prima,
una y otra prima santa.

---

[1] Author of a treatise on rhetoric, *Tenplo de la eloquencia castellana en dos discursos. Aplicado al uno al uso de los predicadores* (Sevilla: Rodrigo Calvo, 1629). See Jaime García Galbarro, "Hacia una catalogización de las retóricas españolas más importantes del siglo XVII. Modelos, tendencias y canon poético" in *El canon poético en el siglo XVII: IX Encuentro Internacional sobre Poesía del Siglo de Oro (Universidad de Sevilla, 24–26 de noviembre de 2008)*, ed. Begoña López Bueno (Sevilla: Grupo PASO, Universidad de Sevilla, 2010), 84. In the Biblioteca Nacional Española in Madrid there are two printed works attributed to Jacinto Quintero: *Discursos evngélicos de Quaresma: para sus tres principales días, domingo, miércoles y viernes* (Madrid: Imprenta de Gregorio Rodríguez a costa de Juan de San Vicente, 1651, and *Panegíricos sagrados para festivades varias de Santos* (Madrid: Greogrio Rodríguez a costa de Juan de San Vicente, 1652. There are also two manuscipts of Quintero in the BNE: *Fiestas de Cristo* (ms. 3465) and *Homilías de Cuaresma y Adviento para domingos, miércoles y viernes* in two volumes (ms.7059, v. 1 and ms.7060, v. 2).

C. **By Father Jacinto Quintero of the Clerics Minor, to these works of María de Santa Isabel. Décimas.**

This breath that inspires you,
some hidden deity,
for in your talent truth
is belied by your sex.
The accents of your lyre
resound from pole to pole,
since your plectra alone conquers,
more than your glory shuns,
all the air from the Muse
and all the fire of Apollo.

Faithfully your name assures
your melodious harmony
between the sound of María
and the accent of Isabel.
From the lip of the carnation
and your sonorous throat
singing of such mercies
are destined to enliven
one and another primary chord,
one and another saintly prime.[1]

---

[1] One of the canonical hours.

D. No elogio sino deuda a estas obras divinas. De Doña Juana de Bayllo, monja en Santa Isabel el Real de Toledo.[1]

Si fatal parasismo
te aclama el mundo de las Musas, cuando
en proceloso abismo
queda el oído con tus obras, dando
en corto espacio breve,
veneno mucho en que su ruina bebe.
Que pluma por sonora
no repite los riesgos de su vida
pues, nada se mejora
si no es con el silencio suspendida.
Que intentar tu alabanza
solo tu ingenio el mérito se alza.
Viva eterno tu nombre,
Amarilis bizarra, pues, te alienta
tu discurso elegante a tal renombre
de la común lisonja vive exenta,
mirando ya difusa
la gloria en ambos polos de tu Musa.

E. Al mismo asunto, si con menos acierto, con más afecto agraviando en la insinuación tanto lo sonorio [sic] relevante de estas obras como lo [inmenso][2] del sentir de quien los alaba de esta manera.

FIRST COLUMN
Pluma osada y atrevida
tu vuelo no se remonte
porque como otro Faetonte
fatal será tu caída.
Mas, si perdiendo la vida,
crédito puedes ganar,
no te dejes de asestar,
que el triunfo de una victoria
cambiando por pena, gloria

---

[1] According to Serrano y Sanz, Juana de Bayllo was a nun in the convent of Santa Isabel in Toledo. She was active as a writer around the mid-seventeenth century. He attributes this poem to her as well as claiming that she is the author of "Décima a una monja que le dio un desmayo," not Belisarda (vol. 1: 154).

[2] "Inmenso" is my probable reconstruction as most of this word is illegible due to the tight binding of the manuscript.

D. Not a eulogy but a debt to these divine works. By Doña Juana de Bayllo, nun in Santa Isabel the Royal of Toledo.

> If fatal paroxysm
> the world of the Muses proclaims you, when
> in stormy abyss
> the sound of your works remains, giving
> in a brief, short space
> much poison in which to drink their ruin.
> A pen so sonorous
> does not repeat risks in its life
> because it can make no improvement
> unless it is cut off by silence.
> To try to praise you
> is worthy given your ingenuity.
> May your name live eternally,
> brave Amaryllis,[1] may your elegant discourse
> strengthen your renown
> that lives exempt from common flattery,
> seeing now widespread
> the glory of your Muse from pole to pole.

E. On the same topic, if with less success, with more affection, offending by hinting at the sonorous quality of these works that merit my tremendous admiration and praise.

> Daring and adventurous pen
> do not soar too high in flight,
> because like another Phaeton[2]
> your fall would be fatal.
> But, if by losing your life
> you can gain credit,
> do not stop aiming;
> the triumph of a victory
> to exchange pain for glory

---

[1] In Greek mythology, Amaryllis was a woman who fell in love with Ateo who loved flowers. Amaryllis pierced her heart with an arrow and a beautiful flower bloomed from her blood, thus winning Ateo's love.

[2] Son of the sun-god, Helios.

al gozo te ha de alentar.
Aunque expuesta a que ingeniosos
cuando agudos los comentos
desbaraten mis intentos,
yo los imploro piadosos
porque en todo gananciosos
hoy puedan quedar ufanos
de haber sido más que hermanos.
Pues, a un divino pensar
que elogio ha de ponderar
tus conceptos tan soberanos.

SECOND COLUMN
Sólo con insinuar
lo activo de mi deseo
lo estimaré por trofeo
puesto que no he de llegar
a lo excelso ni acertar
el término de alabarte.
Pero bien puedes gloriar
que tu ingenio el orbe aclama
y que ha de aprestar la fama,
mil lauros que tributar.
Yo por más afición a da[r],
te los quisiera blandir
pues siempre observo seguir
la opinión más acierta,
y desde hoy de liberada
me ofrezco al servicio,
cuando de este afecto arguye
me proceden muchos creces
pues viendo lo que merece
crédito en el gusto incluye.

let joy encourage you.
Even though ingenious
as well as sharp comments,
thwart my intentions,
I beg mercy for them
because, though in all profitable,
today they may be proud
of having been more than beautiful.
It is divine to think
and praise to ponder,
your sublime concepts.

Only by hinting at
my ardent desire
will I deem it ugly obstinacy,
since I have come
to the sublime without
sufficiently praising you.
But you can well bask in the glory
of your genius that the world proclaims
and your fame will be recognized by
a thousand laurels in tribute.
I, to show you more affection,
would like to praise you,
since I always try to follow
the most exact opinion,
and from today on, liberated,
I offer myself to your service.
Of this affection one could argue
many proceed and far exceed me
seeing that what deserves
credit is included in the pleasure.

F. **Elogio de veras en el sentimiento, aunque en chanza al decir** 4r
al libro y dueño. Del Licdo. Montoya,[1] **opositor de los curatos.**

Ingeniosa toledana,
yerra quien tu libro abona
si no te llama Elicona
y aun alabanza es muy vana.
Hoy mi musa de la rana
con voz ronca no confusa,
dice que el decir no excusa
viendo a su dueño empeñado
que a Musa no has estudiado
y has entendido la Musa.

G. **A mi Sra. Da. María de Ortega porque me condujo este libro**
teniéndole yo muy deseado.

A ti, Amarilis, hermosa
agradezco este buen rato,
pues, me le doy de barato
por mostrarte gananciosa
la estimación es forzosa
y voluntaria también.
Pero, ¿qué puede dar quien
es en todo tan señora
sino, como siempre, ahora
comunicar todo bien?

H. **A las nunca bien encarecidas ni bastamente alabadas varias** 4v
poesías de este libro. Soneto.

El nombre de María nos explica
atributos de gracia en quien se emplea;
y, si atendemos a la lengua hebrea,
Isabel abundancia significa.

---

[1] Not identified.

F. **True eulogy in sentiment, even though in jest, to the book and its owner. By the Licenciado[1] Montoya, candidate for the exam of curate.**

Ingenious Toledan,
one errs who gives credit to your book
if he does not call you Helicon[2]
and even praise is very vain.
Today my muse is a frog
with an unconfused but hoarse voice
that says speaking does not excuse
seeing its determined owner
has not studied the Muse,
but you have understood the Muse.

G. **To my lady Doña María de Ortega because she sent me this book, since I so desired to have it.**

To you, Amaryllis, beautiful
I am grateful for this fine moment
and I consider it insufficient
to show you winning;
esteem is compulsory

and also voluntary.
But, what can one give to one
who is in all ways a lady
except, as always, now
to send you all good wishes?

H. **To the never sufficiently extolled or praised poems in this book. Sonnet.**

The name of María explains for us
attributes of grace in whom they are found;
and, if we take into account the Hebrew language,
Isabel means abundance.

---

[1] Title given to one who has graduated from a university; one holding the equivalent of a BA or BS degree.

[2] Mountain in Greece where the pool that Narcissus saw his reflection in is located.

Estos dos nombres hoy en vos duplica
naturaleza sabia que desea
que en su atención el universo vea
que todo su saber en vos aplica.
Vuestro talento a todo el mundo asombra
y la fama, oh Belisa, voladora
dilate con sus lenguas por el mundo,
un ingenio tan digno de renombre
que en cuanto ciñe el orbe y el sol adora,
no puede haber al vuestro otro segundo.

I. **Elogio a lo espirituoso y elegante de los versos de aqueste libro. De un religioso francisco.**[1] 5r

¿Cuyas sois?, que aún no recelo
el dueño, obras peregrinas
pero el veros tan divinas
publica que sois del cielo;
no hay razón para extrañar
al notar vuestra elocuencia,
la sentencia,
porque solo pudo hablar
tan alto una inteligencia.
Aquesta sola instrucción
de vuestro dueño he tenido,
y es que no la han conocido
voluntad ni inclinación;
mas yo a vosotras atento
hallo que fuera en verdad
un portento
que tuviera voluntad
quien es toda entendimiento.
Digna admiración consagro
hoy a vuestra erudición,
que afectos debidos son
los asombros a un milagro;
al ser de mujer, zozobras
allá el genio en lo que os ven,

---

[1] Serrano y Sanz, 363 transcribes up to verse 9 on folio 5v. The phrase "De un religioso francisco" is in a different hand from that of the title of the poem.

These two names today in you
wise nature duplicates for she desires
that by her service the universe may see
that all her knowledge applies to you.
Your talent astonishes the whole world,
and your fame, oh Belisa, as though in flight
expands by word of mouth throughout the world,
a wit so worthy of renown
that encompasses the world and is adored by the sun
could not measure up to yours.

I. **Praise for the spirituality and the elegance of the verses of this book. By a Franciscan religious.**

Are these yours? For still I do not suspect
who might be the owner, strange works;
but seeing you so divine
shows that you are from heaven;
there is no reason to wonder
upon noticing your eloquence,
the judgement,
because only a great intelligence
could speak so highly.
That education alone
I have had from your master,
and they have not known
either will or inclination;
but I, attentive to you,
find that it was truly
a wonder,
that one who had the will
is one who possessed all understanding.
I consecrate worthy admiration
today to your erudition,
to whose affects are due
the wonders of a miracle;
and being a woman, you upset
those who see the genius in you,

pero, ¿quién
esperará malas obras
de ardor que piensa tan bien?
Ya a las damas los poderes
negaban leyes confusas
de hablar, como si las Musas
no hubieran sido mujeres;
mas hoy los altos renombres
que les gana vuestro ser,
da a entender
que aprender pueden los hombres
a escribir, de una mujer.
Que es religioso, adivino,
obras de unas letras, y otras
vuestro autor, pues, en vosotras
hasta lo sumario es divino.
Reverencio su talento,
pues, me obliga vuestra suma,
que presuma
muy agudo pensamiento
para tan delgada pluma.
Quien quiera, pues, que seáis
ángel, que aquesto escribís,
pues, como pensáis, decís,
no calléis lo que pensáis.
Viva tan ardiente llama
hasta que en mayor victoria
la memoria,
sus plumas pida a la fama
para escribir vuestra gloria.

but who
would expect bad words
from a spirit who thinks so well?
And women to whom power
to speak is denied by confused laws,
as if the Muses
had not been women;
But today the great renown
that you have gained
makes one understand
that men can learn
to write from a woman.
I suppose that the author of these works
is a religious from the content of some and others
since, in the poems,
even the summary is divine.
I hold in reverence her talent,
your sum obliges me
to presume
very sharp thinking
for such a delicate pen.
Whoever you may be,
angel, who wrote this,
as you think so do you speak
and do not keep quiet what you are thinking.
Long live such an ardent flame
until in great victory,
memory
ask fame for her pens
to write of your glory.

[The Poems of Marcia Belisarda]

1. Al evangelista San Juan. Romance que fue el primero que
   escribí a los 27 años de mi edad.

FIRST COLUMN
El regalado de Cristo,
el benjamín[1] de su pecho,
amigo fiel en sus penas
y archivo de sus secretos,
el águila caudalosa
cuyo remontado vuelo
llegó a penetrar el sol,
rayo a rayo los misterios
sin que hoy le ofenda el rigor.
De Domiciano soberbio,
fénix renace en la tina,
enamorado y suspenso,
gallardo cuanto animoso.
Busca el daño, sigue el riesgo
bebe el cáliz deseado,
echando de amante el resto;
pero ya, con nuevas glorias,
triunfa del voraz incendio
y en fe de que es inmortal
sale libre del tormento.
Quedó el oro de su amor
acrisolado en el fuego,
Cantándole están la gala
en acordes instrumentos.
Atended a su armonía
mientras le digo estos versos:

SECOND COLUMN
el farol con nueva luz,
y Juan, con lauros de eterno
cumplió con la obligación
de discípulo, de deudo,
de amante y de agradecido,

---

[1] A "Benjamín" is the youngest child.

Poems by Marcia Belisarda

1. To the Evangelist Saint John. The first ballad that I wrote when I was 27 years old.

>   The rewarded by Christ,
>   the favorite child of his bosom,
>   loyal friend in His pains,
>   and keeper of His secrets,
>   the mighty eagle
>   whose soaring flight
>   managed to penetrate the sun,
>   ray by ray the mysteries
>   today without harshness offending him.
>   Of a proud Domitian,[1]
>   a phoenix is reborn in the cauldron,
>   enamored and in suspense,
>   genteel as well as courageous.
>   He looks for danger, seeks out risk,
>   he drinks from the desired chalice,
>   as a lover, pouring out the rest;
>   but now, with new glories
>   he triumphs from the voracious fire
>   and in a faith that is immortal
>   he comes out free from the torment.
>   The gold of his love remained
>   crystalized in the fire,
>   The celebration is singing for him
>   on fine-tuned instruments.
>   Listen to the harmony
>   while I recite these verses:
>
>   the lantern with new life,
>   and John with laurels eternal
>   met his obligation
>   as disciple, as relative,
>   as lover and a grateful one,

---

[1] Roman emperor from A.D. 81–96 who severely persecuted Christians and Jews.

imitando a su maestro
tantos actos positivos
hace de amoroso y tierno
que enseña ciencia de amar.
Por ser de todas espejo
amagos tiene de Dios,
pues, tiene de Dios efectos,
mas no es mucho, si le hizo
hijo de su entendimiento.
Del esplendor soberano
es Juan divino reflejo,
que desterró las tinieblas
con *in principio erat verbum.*
Es dulce imán de las almas;
es Dios de amor tan supremo
que cautiva corazones
y enamora hasta los cielos.
toquen las campanitas,
toquen a fuego,
que se abrasa de amores
es amor mismo.

2. **A Señor Santiago. Endecha.**[1]

Atended y veréis, españoles,
que girando su luz arreboles,
rompe los aires, destierra las nubes,
entre escuadras de hermosos querubes,
el mártir más fino, el sacro farol,
del cielo la gala y de España el sol.

FIRST COLUMN

Invencible Diego,
divino patrón
de España, por quien
glorias mereció.
Rayo de la guerra
que causando horror
las lunas moriscas
tu nombre rindió.

---

[1] A sad song or lament, usually in stanzas of four verses with each line consisting of six or seven syllables.

imitating his master.
So many positive acts
he performs with a love and tenderness
that he teaches the science of love.
By being for all a mirror
signs he has from God,
since his effects come from God,
but there is more, since He made him
a child of His understanding.
Of sovereign splendor
John is a divine reflection
who destroyed the darkness
with Him who in the beginning was the Word.
He is a sweet magnet for souls;
God's love is so supreme
that it captivates hearts
and even makes the heavens fall in love.
let the bells ring out,
play as if on fire
for one who is burning from love
is love itself.

2. **To our lord, Saint James. Lament.**

<blockquote>
Pay attention and you will see, Spaniards,
spinning with a red glow,
breaking through the air, banishing the clouds,
among squadrons of beautiful cherubs,
the finest martyr, the sacred light,
the celebration of heaven and the sun of Spain.
</blockquote>

Invincible James,
divine patron
of Spain, who
glories deserved.
Lightning bolt of war
who caused horror
in Moorish moons,
that surrendered to your name.

Purísima antorcha
cuyo resplandor
tanta luz esparce
que te aclama sol,
deslucir pretende
tu inmenso esplendor

SECOND COLUMN
con mortal eclipse,
fiera emulación.
Más bizarro amante,
imitando a Dios,
de la vida ofreces,
víctima a su amor.
A la muerte buscas,
grande es tu valor
que humano no temes
lo que Dios temió.
Alegre te espera
la triunfante Sión
porque de su honra
fuiste defensor.

3. **A Santa Clara. Romance.**

FIRST COLUMN
Hoy las flores de un jardín
el triunfo feliz celebran
de la milagrosa Clara,
cándida y pura azucena.
Plantóla Dios de su mano
y quiere que espejo sea
en cuyo candor se miren
para imitar su pureza.
Si flor, la aplauden las flores,
divina aurora las perlas
con que bordó los pensiles
sacrosantos de la iglesia;
el religioso valor
deben asta aurora excelsa
que, aunque pobre, fue tesoro
de virtudes y excelencias.

Purest torch
whose splendor
spreads so much light
that the sun acclaims you,
and tries to reduce
your immense splendor

with a mortal eclipse
of ferocious envy.
But brave lover,
imitating God,
you offer your life
as a victim of love.
You look for death,
so great is your valor
that you fear no man
who feared God.
You wait with joy
for the triumphant Zion
because, of her honor,
you were the defender.

3. **Ballad to Saint Clare.**

Today the flowers of the garden
celebrate the happy triumph
of the miraculous Clare,
white and pure lily.
God planted her with his hand,
wanting her to be a mirror
on whose brightness one looks
in order to imitate her purity.
If a flower, the other flowers applaud her,
and the divine pearls of dawn
with which she embroidered beautiful gardens
sacred to the Church;
religious valor
they should proclaim her sublime dawn
who, although poor, was a treasure
of virtues and excellent qualities.

En la noche de la vida
salió cual la luna bella,
las estrellas ilustrando
con la luz de su elocuencia.
De su esplendor adornadas
que bien guiadas dan muestra
que cuando a ser luna falta,
es norte que las gobierna.

SECOND COLUMN
Hoy celebran las flores
una azucena,
y a la aurora y la luna
perlas y estrellas.
No menos fue, si se advierte,
fuente clara que alimenta
con licor dulce y suave
la caridad y pobreza.
Los hijos que han merecido
beber el divino néctar
de tu doctrina hallan fácil
el yugo de la obediencia.
Fue paloma que antes que
su castidad adolecía
amorosa a Dios consagra
la vida, el alma y potencia.
En su alabanza las aves,
que por madre la festejan,
cantan con dulce porfía
y armónica competencia.
Hoy celebran las flores
una azucena
y a la aurora y la luna;
perlas y estrellas
las aves cantan
a la casta paloma,
a la fuente clara.
Todas se alegran:
flores, perlas, estrellas,
aves y fuentes.

In the night of life,
she appeared like a beautiful moon,
enlightening the stars
with the light of her eloquence.
Adorned with her splendor,
they well guide us
when there is no moon,
for she is the guide who steers them.

Today the flowers celebrate
a white lily,
and the dawn and the moon
pearls and stars.
If you but notice, she was none less
than a clear fountain that nourishes
with sweet and delicate nectar
of charity and poverty.
The children who deserved
to drink the divine nectar
of her doctrine find easy
the yoke of obedience.
She was a dove and before
her chastity could suffer,
lovingly she consecrated to God
her life, her soul, and her power.
In praise of her, the birds,
who celebrate her as a mother,
sing with sweet persistence
and harmonious competency.
Today the flowers celebrate
a white lily,
and the dawn and the moon;
pearls and stars
the birds sing
to the chaste dove,
to the clear fountain.
All are happy:
flowers, pearls, stars,
birds, and fountains.

4. **A la profesión de Da. Petronila de la Palma, en la Concepción Real de Toledo, siguiendo la metáfora de la palma. Soneto.**

En este real jardín, ¡oh palma hermosa!,
os plantó vuestro dueño soberano.
Dispuso y cultivó su sacra mano
para que deis la fruta milagrosa,
no ingrata vegetal, si generosa,
racional. Producid de amor temprano
dulces efectos con intento sano,
mudando el ser de planta en él de esposa.
Advertid, pues, que el dueño es infinito,
abreviada y finita vuestra vida,
pagas de esposa fiel frutos del alma
elogios, no, verdades os remito.
Sed siempre palma a Dios agradecida
gozaréis en su gloria eterna, Palma.

5. **A la misma: décima.**

FIRST COLUMN
Tu nombre mismo acredita
el premio justo que alcanza,
Palma, tiene la esperanza
del premio que solicita
sólo el temor la limita,
que no hay horror que la asombre.
Mil veces palma se nombre,
la que en méritos del alma
tres veces la dan la palma:
virtud, profesión y nombre.

6. **Otra. Dándome que glosar, rimo [sic], pie y el asunto.**

SECOND COLUMN
Si mi corazón, señora,
sus afectos te ocultara,
la venganza no extrañara
que en parte tu amor desdora.
Pero, si tan sola un(a) hora
jamás los quiero ocultar,
¿Cómo puedes tú dudar?
Es ofensa de mi amor,
el decir con tal rigor:
pene, pues, hace penar.

4. To the profession of Doña Patronila de la Palma, in the Royal Conception of Toledo, using the metaphor of the palm. Sonnet.

In this royal garden, oh beautiful palm!,
your sovereign master planted you.
His sacred hand arranged and cultivated you
so that you might give miraculous fruit,
not as an ungrateful plant, but rather a generous one
and rational. Produce from this early love
sweet effects with healthy intent,
from a plant transforming you into his bride.
Take notice then that your master is infinite,
and that life is short and finite,
as a wife, you repay with the faithful fruits of your soul
the praises, no, the truths that I send to you.
Be always a palm grateful to God
and you will enjoy His eternal glory, Palm.

5. To the same woman: décima.

Your name itself confirms
the just prize that the palm
deserves who hopes
for the prize that she solicits;
only fear could limit her,
but there is no horror that alarms her.
She is named Palm a thousand times,
she who by merits of her soul
three times receives the palm:
virtue, profession, and name.

6. Another, charging me with a rhyme scheme and the subject.

If my heart, my lady,
its affections hides from you,
it would not surprise that revenge
should, in part, tarnish your love.
But, if for only an hour
I ever wish to hide them,
How can you doubt?
It is an offense to my love,
saying with such rigor:
be in pain, which makes me suffer.

7. **Décima de Da. Juana de Baíllo, monja de Santa Isabel el Real a otra que le dio un desmayo.**[1]

FIRST COLUMN
Desmayada vi una flor
mas no amancilló lo hermoso,
que en su imperio poderoso
lugar no tuvo el dolor.
Ay, Anarda,[2] qué rigor.
en un paréntesis breve
ver, si no ajada la nieve,
con amagos de atrevida
la Parca, porque su vida
dice que muertes la debe.

8. **Respuesta mía por los consonantes mismos [sic].**[3]

SECOND COLUMN
Desde hoy me introduzco a flor
aunque mendigue lo hermoso,
sin temer el poderoso,
desmayó de algún dolor.
Porque cuando su rigor
de la muerte me haga en breve
trasunto de helada nieve,
confiada, no atrevida
pediré a tu ingenio vida,
pues, darla en los versos debe.

9. **Procurad, memorias tristes . . .**[4]   8v

FIRST COLUMN
Procurad, memorias tristes
divertir mi sentimiento
con penas que siempre son

---

[1] N.B., this is not a poem by Belisarda as the author is clearly identified in the poem's title.

[2] According to Virgil, sister of Dido. See also "Mandas, Anarda, que sin llanto asista" of Sor Juana Inés de la Cruz.

[3] "Consonantes" in this title, and in others, refers to consonant rhyme scheme in which all consonants and vowels are identical after the last accented syllable of the final word of each line.

[4] Serrano y Sanz, 364; Olivares and Boyce, 1st ed., 349; Olivares and Boyce, 2nd ed., 252–53.

7. Décima by Doña Juan de Bayllo, nun at Saint Isabel the Royal to another [nun] who gave her a fright.

> I saw a flower in faint
> but her beauty was not stained,
> for its imperious power
> gave no place to pain.
> Ay, Anarda, what rigor
> in a brief pause
> to see the snow not melted
> with threats of the brazen
> Parca,[1] because life
> she claims owes her deaths.

8. My answer with the same consonants.

> From today I introduce myself to a flower
> even though her beauty begs,
> without fearing the powerful,
> she fainted from some pain.
> Because when the rigor
> of death made me briefly
> a reflection of frozen snow,
> confident, not brazen,
> I will ask your wit for life,
> for your verses give life.

9. Try, sad memories...

> Try, sad memories,
> to amuse my feelings
> with pains that are always present

---

[1] In Roman mythology, one of the Fates that holds lives by a thread.

y no con gustos que fueron.
Representadme pesares,
dejad pasados contentos,
que son figuras de humo
en el teatro del viento.
Muy bien entiendo las voces
de vuestro mudo silencio,
que mal concertadas suenan
que acordes fueron un tiempo.
De mis muertas esperanzas
clamor parecen sus ecos,
o que se cantan endechas
a mi perdido sosiego.
Si con inciertos favores
olvidáis agravios ciertos,
guerra armáis al corazón
no menos que a sangre y fuego.
No me deis en vaso de oro
disimulado veneno,
creyendo así lo que dice
quien no cree lo que siento.

SECOND COLUMN
Memorias, dejadme ya
o acabad mi vida luego,
que no hay fuerzas en el alma
para tan crueles tormentos.

10. Otro, dándome el asunto.[1]

Escapé de tus cadenas
entregándome al sosiego,
amor, porque siempre al rostro
salen tus pesados hierros.
Cuando juzgué que me hallaba
libre de tu cautiverio,
con otros nuevos me oprimes,
fatigándome de nuevo.
¿De qué sirve atormentarme,
amor loco, niño ciego,

---

[1] Serrano y Sanz, 304; Olivares and Boyce, 1st ed., 350.

and not with pleasures that have gone away.
Sorrows represent me,
leave off past contentment
that are but figures of smoke
in the theater of the wind.
I understand very well the voices
of your mute silence
that disharmoniously sound
what was once in harmony.
Of my dead hopes
their echoes seem a clamor,
or the singing of dirges
to my lost serenity.
If with uncertain favors
you forget certain grievances,
you make war on the heart
no less than with blood and fire.
Do not leave for me in a vessel of gold
dissimulated poison,
thus believing what one says
who does not believe what I feel.

Memories, leave me now
or later end my life,
for there are no forces in my soul
to counter such cruel torments.

10. Another, charging me with the subject.

I escaped from your chains
giving myself over to serenity,
love, because always before me
your heavy chains appear.
When I judged myself
free from your captivity,
with other new ones you oppress me,
wearing me down again.
What does it serve to torment me,
crazy love, blind child,

si ya me doy por vencido
a tus arpones soberbios?
Montes de dificultades
se oponen a mis deseos;
mas como te ves gigante,
me animas[1] al vencimiento.
Nací con honra y sin dicha;
a mundo obliga un respeto
y mucho más el amor.
¿Qué haré, pïadosos cielos?
Mi infeliz suerte maldigo,
del hado injusto me quejo;
pues muero de lo que callo
y de lo que digo muero.
Ni mi voluntad se logra,
ni en lo que callo merezco,
ni se cree lo que digo
por no asistir lo que quiero.
Mártir de amor muere el alma,[2]
pues cuando obligar pretendo,
con el silencio no obligo
ni con las palabras muevo.

---

[1] Olivares and Boyce, 1st ed., 350, reads "anima" but the manuscript says "animas." Here I agree with Serrano y Sanz, who also gives the transcription as "animas."

[2] This final strophe is missing in Serrano y Sanz's transcription (350) but is supplied in Olivares and Boyce (both editions) and verified by my reading of the manuscript.

if I already declare myself defeated
by your sharp arrows?
Mountains of difficulties
oppose my desires;
but since you see yourself as a giant
you spur me on to defeat.
I was born with honor but no luck;
the world deserves respect
and more so does love.
What shall I do, merciful heavens?
I curse my unhappy luck,
I complain of my unjust fate;
thus I die from what I do not say
and from what I say, I die.
Neither my will can obtain
nor do I deserve what I keep quiet,
nor is what I say believed
because what I want does not appear.
Martyred, the soul dies from love,
for when I try to refuse
with silence I do not refuse
nor do I move with words.

11. Alabando al Rvo. Joan Peréz Roldán[1] la ciencia de músico compositor. Soneto.

Si la pluma de Ovidio mereciera,
y si Apolo su lira me prestara,
tus obras describiera y discantara
y que pude alabarte presumiera.
Tu ingenio sube a la mayor esfera,
tu ciencia se prefiere a la más rara;
quien alabanzas tuyas intentara,
que alcanzar imposibles no emprendiera.
Vive nuevo Anfión y Dafne, esquiva
Benigna te corone de laureles.
Darás timbre a tu nombre, al mundo gloria,
y, en tanto en bronce o láminas le escriba
la fama, con buriles o pinceles,
porque eterna se observe tu memoria.

12. Alabanza al Evangelista San Juan. 9v

El que en cuerpo al alcázar supremo
llega y al Rey se presenta triunfante.
¿Quién es, señores,
que sus resplandores
abrasan de amores
y doran el aire?
Es quien muere de amor y, en su fuego,
fénix divino a sus cielos renace.

---

[1] Born in Calahora in 1604. In his youth, he served as magistrate in the cathedrals of Toledo and Segovia. He was also "Maestro de Capilla" at various times in the convent of the Descalzas Reales in Madrid, the Convent of the Encarnación in Madrid, as well as in the cathedrals in León and Zaragoza. He was painted by Velázquez when he succeeded Carlos Patiño as director of the Royal Chapel in Madrid. He wrote zarzuelas [operettas] and villancicos [carols] and was also the author of *Laura de la música eclesiástica, nobleza y antiguedad de esta sciencia y sus profesores,* dated 1644 but not published until 1875. Belisarda probably knew Pérez Roldán from his years serving the cathedral in Toledo (1634–1642) (www.melomanodigital.com). However, a note pasted to a copy of the *Laura de la música*, housed in the BNE, claims that Pérez Roldán was Prior of the Colegiata de Berlanga (Soria) in 1644, that he was born in Segovia and that he also served as Maestro de Capilla in the cathedral of León. The information about the Colegiata de Berlanga appears to be correct since the subtitle of the *Laura de la música* identifies the author as "Prior en la Santa Iglesia Colegial de Verlanga."

11. **Praising the Reverend Juan Pérez Roldán, a composer of the science of music. Sonnet.**

If the pen of Ovid I was deserving,
or if Apollo lent me his lyre,
I would describe and write verses about your works
and I could presume to praise you.
Your genius rises to the highest sphere,
your science is preferred to the most rare;
whoever tries to sing your praises
would find it impossible even to try.
Amphion and Daphne live again, elusive
Benigna crowns you with laurels.
You will give timbre to your name, glory to the world,
and, may much be written on bronzes and engravings
with burins and brushes of your fame
to preserve your memory forever.

12. **In praise of the Evangelist Saint John.**

He who in body to the supreme castle
arrives and to the King presents himself,
who is it, gentlemen and ladies,
whose splendors
burn from love
and gild the air?
It is he who died from love and, in its fire,
is reborn a divine phoenix in the heavens.

Éste es Juan, éste es Juan,
el amante y amado de Cristo,
que al mundo dio luz de su divinidad.

BEGINS FIRST COLUMN OF TWO
Este cándido jazmín,
esta azucena fragrante,
¡Oh rayo que brota luces!
¡Oh sol que nieblas deshace!
¿Quién puede ser sino Juan,
aquél a todos amable
que desmintiéndose humano,
ostentó divinidades.
El principio de la vida,
que con elocuencia grande,
mostró en efectos del hijo
propia voluntad del Padre.
El que fino se acredita
con blasones de diamante,
y tanto el amor se encumbra,
que a Dios y a Juan hizo iguales.

SECOND COLUMN
Aquel águila famosa,
que haciendo de lince alarde,
a tanto excelso misterio
dieron sus ojos alcance,
hoy del cielo en cuerpo y alma
rompe estrelladas celajes
que allí Dios le deposita
y todos su triunfo aplauden.

13. **A Señor Santiago, Patrón de España.**

FIRST COLUMN
Españoles, soldados,
al arma, al arma.
Resistid valerosos
furias contrarias.
Seguid a Diego,
que lidiando os infunde
valor y esfuerzo,
por el honor de su Rey,

This is John, this is John,
the lover and beloved of Christ
who gave the light of His divinity to the world.

This white jasmine,
this fragrant white lily,
Oh ray that pours forth light!
Oh sun that vanquishes the fog!
Who can it be but John,
he who was kind to all
and denying his humanity,
flaunted divinities.
The principle of his life
with great eloquence
showed in the effects of the Son
the true will of the Father.
He whose worth is recognized
with diamond blazons,
and with so much love was exalted
that God and John were made equals.

That famous eagle,
making such a shrewd show,
that such a lofty mystery
was displayed before his eyes,
today from heaven in body and soul
he breaks through the starry clouds of sunset
where God deposits him
so that all may applaud his triumph.

13. To Lord Saint James, Patron of Spain.

Spaniards, soldiers,
to arms, to arms.
Bravely resist
contrary furies.
Follow James,
who fighting infuses you
with valor and strength
for the honor of his King,

estableciendo su ley,
peleó con gran fineza
hasta perder la cabeza;
y tanto, tanto ha vencido
que el horror de la muerte
venció en sí mismo.
Fieles soldados del rey,
que al militar ejercicio
exponéis los corazones,
armados de amantes bríos,
los que en continua vigilia
celáis del fiero enemigo
la ciudad porque, a sus fuerzas
no contrastan sus arbitrios.
No temáis aunque bisoños
que hoy Diego para instruiros,

SECOND COLUMN
de enamorado y valiente,
actos hace positivos.
Vencer errores intenta
con argumentos divinos,
glorias vinculando al Rey
en créditos de infinito.
Viendo, pues, que la verdad
no imprime en pechos inicos,[1]
deja en carácter de acero
su valor con sangre escrito,
a todo sentir de amante,
el cuello ofrece al cuchillo,
cuando cáliz le contempla
con que le brindó su primo.
Pelead y venceréis;
pues Diego es norte y caudillo,
mil muertes en cada giro,
blandid sin miedo el acero
que en vuestro favor, al filo
da en privilegios de sangre,
calidad de ejecutivo.

---

[1] Probably a mistake for "inicuos."

establishing his law,
he fought with great elegance
until he lost his head;
and so much, so much has he conquered
that the honor of his death
vanquished death itself.
Faithful soldiers of the King,
who to military exercise
you expose your hearts,
armed with beloved zeal,
those who in constant vigilance
keep a watchful eye out for the fierce enemy
of the city against whose forces
there will be no arbitration.
Do not fear, even if you are novices,
for James will instruct you

to be enamored and valiant,
making all your acts positive.
He strives to overcome errors
with divine arguments,
glories bound to the King
in infinite credits.
Thus, seeing that the truth
will not imprint on wicked hearts,
he leaves, with a character like steel,
his valor written in blood,
with all the feelings of a lover,
his neck he offers to the blade,
when he contemplates the chalice
with which his cousin toasted him.
Fight and you will conquer;
James will be your guide and leader,
a thousand deaths at every turn,
brandish without fear the sword
that, in your favor, the blade
gives privileges in blood,
and exquisite worth.

FIRST COLUMN
En vida y muerte os enseña
a librar de los peligros,

SECOND COLUMN
viviendo a la vida muerto,
muriendo a la muerte vivo.

14. **Al Santísimo Sacramento. Vejamen.**[1]

FIRST COLUMN
Señor, galán disfrazado,
si oír verdades le agrada,
escúcheme ahora algunas
o sean dulces o amargas.
No se esconda, por mi vida,
amantísimo del hampa;
atienda que por Dios vivo
le he conocido si basta.
¿No es quien la paz de los hombres
llorando solicitaba,
y en medio de estos cuidados
dicen se durmió en las pajas?
¿Cómo tan oculto viene
el que en pública batalla
se le dejaron desnudo
por amores de una dama?
Tan grande como su Padre
dicen era y que clamaba
"Padre mío," articulando
"¿por qué así me desamparas?"
Jesús, que colores muda,
como a una rosa encarnada

10v

---

[1] Transcribed in full in Olivares and Boyce, 1st ed., 387–88. Serrano y Sanz, 365, transcribes the first six lines and also lines 13–16. In a footnote on p. 388, Olivares and Boyce provide the following definition for "vejamen": "En los certámenes y funciones literarias es el discurso festivo y satírico en que se hace cargo a los poetas u otros sujetos de la función de algunos defectos o personales, o cometidos en los versos" [In competitions and literary functions it is festive and satirical discourse in which the poets or other participants in the function point out the others' personal defects or shortcomings in their verses].

In life and death he shows you
how to liberate yourself from danger,

living dead to this life,
dying alive to death.

14. For the Holy Sacrament. Satire.

Sir, disguised as an elegant young man,
if it pleases You to hear truths,
listen to some now
whether they be sweet or sour.
Do not hide, by my life,
beloved of the underworld;
pay attention for, by the living God,
it suffices that I have known You.
Is it not You who peace solicits
for mankind, sobbing,
and in the midst of woes,
they say You slept on straw?
Why so hidden comes
the one who in public battle,
let Himself be disrobed
for the love of a woman?
As great as His Father
they say He was and that He cried out
"My father," saying
"Why have you abandoned me?"
Jesus, who changes color
like a red rose

SECOND COLUMN
le puso el amor un día
y hoy a la nieve se iguala.
Tenga paciencia, pues todos
dicen sabe tener tanta
que tal vez a los azotes,
¿no les volvió las espaldas?
Si es Rey, ¿por qué a sus criados
tanto los honra y ensalza
que cuanto son más humildes,
tanto más con ellos trata?
Al que es Todopoderoso,
supremo Rey y Monarca,
¿abrevian en esta forma
con solas cinco palabras?[1]
Dígame, ¿es seña de paz
la que trae divisa blanca,
o viene armado de vidrios
a emprender grandes hazañas?
Y no entiendo sus misterios
de amante si no le alaban,
y por mi fe que ahora creo
debe de ser toda gracia.
Mucho se precia de mí
y a todos llama sus almas;
sin rebozo puede verlas
que ni me importa ni agravia.
A todas las enamora
y de todas se recata;
devoto de toda reja,
galán de toda ventana.
No es amante de este siglo
quien tanto silencio[2] guarda,
que todos de engaños cultos
pertrechan sus esperanzas.
La que es todo fiesta
va de alabanzas
al manjar de mi gusto,
vida del alma.

11r

---
[1] Hic est Jesus rex Iudeaorum (Mateo 27:37)
[2] Olivares and Boyce, 1st ed., 388 reads "silencia," but this word clearly ends in "o" (silencio) in the manuscript.

given by love one day,
today is white as snow.
Be patient, for all
say that He knows so much
that perhaps to the whip
He should not have exposed his back?
If He is King, why does He give to His servants
so much honor and exaltation;
for those who are so humble,
why does He spend so much time and energy?
To Him who is All Powerful,
Supreme King and Monarch,
How can He be summed up
With just five words?[1]
Tell me, is it a sign of peace
when one brings a white emblem
or does He come armed with crystal
to do great deeds?
I do not understand His mysteries,
or why they do not praise Him as a lover,
and, by my faith, I now believe
that He is full of grace.
He esteems me,
and He calls all souls;
for He sees them all openly,
which neither matters to me nor offends me.
He loves them [souls] all
and He acts discreetly with all;
He is the devoted one at the doorway,
the gallant one at every window.[2]
He is not a lover of this world
who keeps so silent,
that all learned deceits
He supplies with hope.
All that is festive
goes praising,
to eat at my pleasure,
this life for the soul.

---

[1] Jesus, King of the Jews (Matthew 27:37).
[2] A reference to courtship when young men and women spoke at the barred windows of the woman's house.

15. A San Jerónimo. Romance.

FIRST COLUMN
El príncipe de las ciencias,
raro por su erudición,
docto por antonomasia,
valiente por su fervor,
la luz que alumbra el mundo
en el más puro farol
a desafiar los rayos
sube del astro mayor.
No bien llegaba a su esfera
cuando las armas rindió
el sol material a quien
la fe por sol aclama.
Gloria es darse por vencido
del que con tanto valor

SECOND COLUMN
venció protervos infieles,
y a sí mismo se venció.
En el cielo de la iglesia
ningún ingenio salió
brillante sin ser primero
de sus rayos girasol,
a la elocuencia y doctrina
de Jerónimo debió
el más sabio sus aciertos
y la iglesia, su esplendor,
la virtud con la nobleza
en tanto grado igualó
que, si ambas no se compiten,
no tendrán competidor.

FIRST COLUMN
Del propio amor se desnuda,
y con tanta perfección,
que, a fuer de gran penitente,
de carne se desnudó.

15. Ballad to Saint Jerome.

The prince of sciences,
rare in his erudition,
wise par excellence,
valiant in his fervor,
the light that illuminates the world
in the most pure lantern
to defy the rays,
he climbs to a higher star.
No more than arriving to his sphere,
than the sun surrendered
its material to him whom
faith acclaims a sun.
It is glorious to surrender
to one who with such valor

defeated stubborn infidels,
and, also, conquered himself.
In the church in heaven
no genius shone forth
so brilliantly without being first
a sunflower to his rays,
for the eloquence and doctrine
owed to Jerome
who is the wisest
and the church, in splendor,
with truth and nobility,
equal to such a degree
that if both did not compete,
there would be no other competitor.

For love he disrobes,
and with such perfection,
that, as a great penitent,
also strips himself of his skin.

SECOND COLUMN
Por Dios dejó dignidades,
y riquezas despreció,
y, en pago de sus finezas,
con glorias le premia Dios.

ONE CENTRAL COLUMN
Atended a las aves
que con dulce voz,
aunque voz no articulan,
piden atención.
Escuchad, escuchad,
que entre voces divinas
vuelven a cantar,
diciendo alegres,
pues, que siempre venciste.
¡Viva quien vence!

16. **Villancico a la Natividad de Cristo entre cuatro.**[1]

FIRST COLUMN
1º Hola, zagalejos, hola,
romped la prisión del sueño,
y de espíritus divinos
veréis escuadrones bellos.
2º Venid, zagales, a ver
las luminarias del cielo,
luces que bordan la noche,
voces que pueblan el viento.
3º Venid, zagales, oiréis
que en repetidos acentos
cantan con dulce armonía
la paz al hombre en el suelo.

SECOND COLUMN
4º ¿Quién da voces, pastores?
Pasito quedo.
1º ¿Quién se opone a mi orgullo?
4º Que está durmiendo.
2º ¿Quién suspende mis voces?

---

[1] Olivares and Boyce, 1st ed., 389–90. The four parts to be sung are as indicated in the manuscript and do not agree in all cases with Olivares's and Boyce's indications.

He gave up dignity for God,
and he rejected wealth,
and, in payment for his elegance,
God rewards him with glories.

Listen to the birds
that with a sweet voice,
even though not a word do they articulate,
ask for attention.
Listen, listen
for among divine voices
they sing again,
voicing happiness
because you always won.
Long live he who conquers!

16. **Christmas Carol for four voices.**

1st Hello, boys and girls, hello,
break out of the prison of sleep
and of divine spirits
you will see beautiful squadrons.
2nd Come, all of you, to see
the stars in the heavens,
lights that embroider the night,
voices that populate the wind.
3rd Come, boys and girls, you will hear
in repeated accents
how they sing with sweet harmony
peace to men on earth.

4th Who is shouting, shepherds?
Shhh, quietly.
1st Who opposes my pride?
4th He is sleeping.
2nd Who suspends my voices?

4º Pasito quedo.
3º ¿Quién impide mi pasos?
4º Que está durmiendo.
1º, 2º, 3º ¿Quién es el que duerme
que pides silencio?
4º Es un niño amante;
es un rey supremo;

FIRST COLUMN
un Dios disfrazado
con humano velo.
1º, 2º, 3º Dinos, pues, zagal,
dónde le hallaremos,
y antes nos declara
prodigio tan nuevo.
4º Bien cerca hallaréis
en un portalejo,
apenas nacido,
el infante tierno.
Mas entrad callandico,
pasito quedo;
no despierte mi niño
que está durmiendo.
Éste que hallar deseáis
es el humanado Verbo,
del Padre eterno engendrado
con su voz y entendimiento,
para rescatar al hombre
del injusto cautiverio
en que la culpa le puso,
baja del trono excelso.
De María virgen nace,
llorando injurias del tiempo,
sujeto a humanas miserias,
indignas de tal sujeto.

SECOND COLUMN
Y porque no se dilate
el lograr vuestros deseos,
lo que resta aquí no digo;
Juan lo dirá en su evangelio.

4th Shhh, quietly.
3rd Who impedes my steps?
4th He is sleeping.
1st 2nd. 3rd Who is he that is sleeping
and for whom you ask silence?
4th He is a child lover;
he is a supreme King;

God disguised
behind a human veil.
1st 2nd 3rd Tell us then, fellow,
where we can find Him,
and quickly tell us
of such a new wonder.
4th Very near you will find
in a portico,
just recently born,
the tender infant.
But enter very quietly,
stepping lightly;
do not wake up my baby
who is sleeping.
He who you want to find
is the Word made flesh,
engendered of the Father eternal
with His voice and His understanding
to rescue mankind
from unjust captivity;
placed there by his own fault,
He comes down from the exalted throne
and is born of the Virgin Mary,
crying for the injustices of time,
subject to human miseries
undignified for such a one.

And so that there be no delay
in complying with your desires,
of the rest here I will not say;
for John will tell all in his gospel.

17. Otro.[1]

Alma mía, despertad
que no es hora de dormir.
Ved, como en brazos de alba,
nace el sol con rayos mil.
Si al letargo del deleite
os rendisteis, infeliz,
viendo un rey que amante os vela,
más bien os podéis rendir,
para obligar con finezas
que se transforma, advertid,
en niño pequeño un Dios
cuya grandeza es sin fin.
Si de hermosura fingida
os llevasteis sin sentir,
ved la suya y sentiréis
el engaño en que vivís.
No a su albura compararse
puede el cándido jazmín,
ni a lo encarnado igualar
del clavel lo carmesí.

FIRST COLUMN 12v
A la vista desempeños
ceda el pincel más sutil,
porque presumir pintarla
fuera vano presumir.
(Ahora) no a su albura compararse
puede el cándido jazmín,
ni a lo encarnado igualar
del clavel el carmesí.
Si entre las flores el gusto
os procura divertir,
en el niño reducidas
se miran las del abril.

[1] Olivares and Boyce, 1st ed., 373–74; Olivares and Boyce 2nd ed., 264–65.

17. Another.

Awake, my soul,
now is not the time for sleeping.
See how on the arms of the dawn
the sun is born with a thousand rays of light.
If to the delight of lethargy
you give in, unhappy one,
seeing a King who is waiting for His lover,
you should rather surrender,
to oblige with courtesies
He who transformed, be warned,
a little child into God
whose greatness is without limit.
If by feigned beauty
you are carried away without thinking,
see it as such and you will know
the deception in which you are living.
To compare itself with His purity
the white jasmine cannot,
nor to His redness[1] equals
the crimson of the carnation.

At the sight [of God], carrying out this task
the most subtle paintbrush cedes,
because trying to paint it [the image of God]
is vain presumption.
To compare itself to His purity
the white jasmine cannot,
nor to His redness equals
the crimson of the carnation.[2]
If among flowers pleasure
you want to enjoy,
reduced in the form of the Child
you will see the flowers of April.

---

[1] "Encarnado" can mean redness or incarnate, and here the poet is playing with the double meaning in reference to God incarnate as man in Christ.

[2] The repetition here of verses 17–20 follows the manuscript. Olivares and Boyce, 2nd ed. note this without comment (265), but I believe it may be an internal refrain.

SECOND COLUMN
Y si riquezas buscáis,
sus ojos son de zafir [sic],
oro su cabello y perlas
éstas que llora por mí.
¡Velad, alma!, pues Dios vela.
Gozaréis si no os dormís,
cuando no un pensil ameno,
un eterno Potosí.[1]
Mas, si a Dios sois ingrata,
y del bien huís,
¡Ay de vos, y qué pobre
vendréis a morir!

18. **Ensalada de Navidad.**[2]

FIRST COLUMN
Forman escaramuzas
copos de blanco armiño
embarazando el paso
al viento fugitivo;
globos de niebla y hielo
bajan haciendo giros
a contrastar los rayos
de dos soles divinos
pueblan la baja esfera,
celestes paraninfos,
que dan noticia al hombre
de Dios recién nacido.

SECOND COLUMN
De diversas naciones
llegan al portalillo
y entre pajas adoran
el amante prodigio,
sujeto como humano
al rigor enemigo,

---

[1] A reference to the silver mines of Potosí in Bolivia.

[2] In this poem, Belisarda mimics, or imitates, in Spanish how a Portuguese and an Ethiopian would speak for humorous effect. I have transcribed it as written. Other poets, including Sor Juana Inés de la Cruz, used similar devices in their villancicos. My thanks to my colleague, Sara Guengerich, for this fact. Many sixteenth and seventeenth century Mexican villancicos and Christmas ballads share the same poetic tropes as this poem.

And if you are looking for riches,
His eyes are of sapphire,
His hair is of gold and pearls
are the tears He sheds for me.
Keep watch, my soul! For God keeps watch.
You will enjoy, if you do not fall asleep,
not only a beautiful garden,
but an eternal Potosí.[1]
But if you are ungrateful to God,
and you flee from His goodness,
woe to you and how poor [in spirit]
you will come to death!

18. Christmas Salad.

Skirmishes form
flakes of white ermine
hindering the pass
of the fugitive wind;
spheres of mist and ice
fall turning about
to contrast the rays
of two divine suns
populating the sphere below,
the celestial assembly halls,
that give notice to man
of God recently born.

From diverse nations
they arrive at the door
and in the straw they adore
the prodigious lover,
subject to human form
and to hostile rigor,

---

[1] Name of the town in Bolivia where the world's largest and richest silver mine existed in the sixteenth and seventeenth centuries. The word now figuratively in Spanish, means "a huge fortune."

pagan tributos en perlas,
sus hermosos zafiros.
Y a vista de su llanto
de amores derretido
un Portugués Fidalgo
de aquesta suerte dijo:

FIRST COLUMN
Si naçerais meo nino
ala en Purtugal
eu se que naon façeira
o frio, chorar.
Ay, ay, ay,
naon choreis, meo amor,
que esas pelrras saon frechas
de meo coraçaon.
Si frio tenedes
chega a vos lamais
que aunque o pecho enebe
calor prestara.
Naon choreis meos ollos
que os mote faran
de poco balente
si vos bein tembrar.
Ay, ay, ay naon choreis
[meo amor,
que esas pelrras saon frechas
de meo coraçaon.][1]
Esto decía cuando
en traje peregrino
dos etíopes llegan
de gozo dando indicios;
y al son de unas sonajas
con donairoso brío
ambos bailan y cantan
esta letrilla al niño:

13r

---

[1] Belisarda writes "etc." to imply a repetition of the refrain which I supply here in full in brackets. This indication for repeated refrains is common and I render the full refrains where these are abbreviated.

they pay tribute in pearls
and beautiful sapphires.
And at the sight of His weeping,
madly in love
a Portuguese gentleman
in this way said:[1]

If You had been born, little child
over there in Portugal
I know that You would not
be crying from the cold.
Ay, ay, ay,
Do not cry, my love,
that those pearls are arrows
in my heart.
If You are cold
I will give You some wool
for even though it may scratch Your chest
it will give You warmth.
Do not cry, my eyes,
for they will make fun of You
for having little courage
if You tremble.
Ay, ay, ay, do not cry
[my love,
that those pearls are arrows
in my heart.][2]
He way saying this when
in pilgrim garb
two Ethiopians arrived
giving indications of great joy;
and to the sound of timbrels,
lively and spirited
both danced and sang
this song to the child:

---

[1] For each national/language group the original Spanish is written not in another language, but rather in a semi-phonetic imitation of other languages. For the translation, however, I have opted for the most probable, logical meaning rather than trying to imitate the linguistic humor of the original.

[2] Between brackets indicates a refrain that is abbreviated in the manuscript.

SECOND COLUMN
Aguediya y Frasico benimo
a verlo siquito de Santo Tomé
y a lo son de la sonatiya
alegre bailamo así solo Manue:
Usie, usie,
y a lo son de la sontiya
alegre bailamo así solo.
Yega frasico plimera
a besa así quita epe
y si e fosico branquea.
Y o tanbu lo beçare.
Yamalo de çeñolia
que he branqui yo a bona fe
y se sona pol Guinea
que a de benimo ase rey.
Disen que no ay neglo aca
y a lo que yegamo a ver
una dança ven formada
tu ropore mostasse.
Usie, usie
Y a lo son de la [sonatiy
alegre bailamo.]

19. **A Santa Teresa. Romance.** 13v

FIRST COLUMN
Hoy que ufana el labio aplica
la fama al sonoro bronce,
y, en vez de remos, el viento
sulca[1] con plumas veloces.
Hoy que la circunferencia
navega de todo el orbe,
porque a tu aplauso se inclina
y a tus fiestas se convoque.
Hoy que solo en repetir,
Teresa, insigne tu nombre,
aumenta gloria a tu patria
y, a tu nobleza, blasones.

---

[1] For "surca."

SECOND COLUMN
Agatha and Francis we come
to see the little child of Saint Thomas
at the sound of the timbrel
Manuel happily dances alone:
Your Lordship, your Lordship,
and to the sound of the timbrel
happily he dances alone.
Francisco arrives first
to kiss His feet
and if an animal bellows
I will also kiss him.
Call Him Your Honor
I heartily shouted
and sounded as far as Guinea,
for He shall be King.
They say there is a black man here
and from what we see
they are forming a dance
to show off their robes.
Your Lordship, your Lordship
and to the sound of the timbrel
[happily he dances alone.][1]

19. Ballad for Saint Theresa.

Today how proudly lips speak
of her fame and the sonorous trumpet sounds,
and wind is plowed, not by oars,
but by swift pens.
Today they sail round
the whole world
to draw near to your acclaim
and convene your festivals.
Today only by repeating,
Theresa, your illustrious name,
the glory of your homeland grows
and coats of arms proclaim your nobility.

---

[1] See footnote 16.

Préstame tu ingenio en tanto
que el afecto mío logre,
si no elogios, que te cuadren
a alguna virtud conformes.
Casta Diana, que exiges
templos al Dios de los dioses,
por dar realce a su culto,
o, porque el mundo se asombre.
Esposas suyas congregas
a quien dan tus esplendores
rayos con que se defiendan
de nocturnos anteones.[1]

SECOND COLUMN
Ave fenicia, abrasada
de tu esposo en los amores
tan otro Elias renaces,
que a padecer te dispones.
Símbolo de la paciencia,
fuiste de la envidia al golpe
de una [sic] crisol que la afina
para otra, escudo de bronce.
Oveja del buen pastor
que, cuando le reconoces,
tu amor pasos apresura
para alcanzarle en el monte.
Oh, cuán amante le sigues
y cuán fervorosa rompes
entre abrojos la piel blanca
que esmaltan de sangre noble.
Sapientísima causa
de admiraciones,
sólo un ángel merece
cantar tus loores.

---

[1] An "anteón" is a "baranda," a plant with hook-like thorns.

Lend me your genius so that
my affection may produce,
if not praises worthy of you,
some virtue with which you may be content.
Chaste Diana, you demand
temples from the God of the gods
to give splendor to your cult
so that the world may be astonished.
You consecrate brides
to whom your splendors give
lightning bolts so that they may defend themselves
from nocturnal snares.

Phoenician bird, burned up
in love of your spouse
like another Elijah[1] you are reborn,
you have the resolve to suffer,
a true symbol of patience,
you are a blow to envy,
a crucible that refines it
for another, shield of bronze.
Sheep of the Good Shepherd
who, when you recognize Him,
your love quickens your feet
to reach Him on the mountain.
Oh, what a lover You follow,
and how fervently is pricked
your white skin by the thistles
that are enameled with noble blood.
Wisest of causes
of admiration,
only an angel deserves
to sing your praises.

---

[1] Elijah was an Old Testament prophet of the ninth century B.C. who was known as a wonder-worker: he raised the dead, brought down fire from heaven, and upon his death was taken up to heaven in a chariot of fire.

20. A la profesión de una monja Bernarda que la hice en día de la degollación del Baptista estando el Santísimo Sacramento descubierto y su nombre Paula.

Si admiráis en este día
ver que a la pompa funesta,
desvanece el regocijo
mezclando bodas y obsequias.
Sabed que el supremo Rey
sus desposorios celebra
con hija del gran Bernardo,
timbre y honor de la iglesia.
Para alegrar a la esposa,
sale de color de perla
y los lutos del palacio
conmuta en blancas libreas.
El padrino es el Baptista
que solo de su grandeza
fió el mayor lucimiento
en caso de tanta esencia.
Galante y bizarro Juan,
viste una costosa tela
que la verdad de rubíes
bordó con mil excelencias.
Por acreditarse fino,
hace la corta a la mesa
y en solos dos platos cifra
con comida opulenta.
Y como es primo del Rey,
y aun dicen que se sospecha,
ser su devota la novia,
padrino y galán se muestra.
Un cordero ofrece a Paula
que, si con gracia y limpieza
le come, purificada
queda de humanas miserias.
Sazonada, en vez de clavo,
le da la mejor cabeza

20. For the profession of a nun, Bernarda, on the day of the beheading of the Baptist with the Holy Eucharist present, taking the name of Paula.

If you think on this day
to see doleful pomp,
joy will dispel it
mixing weddings and gifts.
Know well that the supreme King
is celebrating His betrothal
to a daughter of Bernard,
seal and honor of the church.
For the joyful bride
comes out dressed in the color of pearl
and the mourning of the palace
is changed into white livery.
The godfather is the Baptist
who alone in his grandeur
gives credit to the greatest brilliance
in the case of such an essence.
Gallant and brazen John,
wears a rich cloth
truly of rubies
embroidered with a thousand excellences.
To prove his renown,
he sets the table

and on only two plates he places
opulent food.
And, since he is the cousin of the King,
and they say that most probably
the bride is his devotee,
thus making him both godfather and suitor,
he offers a lamb to Paula
who, with grace and chastity
eats it, and is purified
of all human miseries.
Seasoned, not with clove,
but with the best head[1]

---

[1] In other words, the lamb as Body of Christ, the Eucharistic food is "seasoned" by the sacrifice of the beheaded John the Baptist.

con los claveles que brota [sic]
a manos de una inclemencia.
Con retórico silencio
la persuade y enseña
que, si imitare su vida,
será esposa verdadera.
Y las aves sonoras coros alternan
y en el aire se oyen voces diversas:
¡oh, qué bien cantan,
celebrando gozosas fiesta tan alta!

21. A la Concepción de Nuestra Señora. [1]

FIRST COLUMN

A la azucena más pura,
que fue escogida *ab eterno*[2]
para reina de las flores
o para gala del cielo.
La que preservó entre todas
con singular privilegio
de aquella ley general
para madre suya el Verbo.
La que hollando la cabeza
al enemigo soberbio
a la vida de la gracia
restituye al hombre muerto.
A[3] la perfecta paloma
que el esposo en dulces versos
llama hermosa amiga mía,
de mi amor divino espejo.
A María, de Dios madre,
que es su mayor epíteto,
cuya feliz concepción
celebra el mundo universo.
Una zagala devota,
obligada de su celo,
aquesta letra le canta
al compás de un instrumento:

---

[1] Olivares and Boyce, 1st ed., 375–76.
[2] Desde la eternidad.
[3] "A" is missing in Olivares and Boyce, 1st ed., 375.

with carnations[1] that sprout
as result of inclemency.
And with rhetorical silence
he persuades her and teaches her
that, if she imitates his life,
she will be his true bride.
And the sonorous birds alternate in choruses
and in the air diverse voices are heard:
Oh, how well they sing,
joyfully celebrating such a fine feast!

21. To the Conception of Our Lady.

To the most pure white lily
who was chosen from time eternal
to be queen of the flowers
and the celebration of heaven.
She who was preserved among all women
with singular privilege
from the general rule,
so that she might be the mother of the Word.
She who tread on the head
of the arrogant enemy[2]
to a life of grace
restores fallen man.
To the perfect dove
whom the Bridegroom with sweet verses
calls His beautiful friend,
a mirror of divine love.
To Mary, Mother of God,
her greatest epithet,
whose happy conception
the whole world celebrates.
A devoted young woman,
chosen by heaven
for whom this song is sung
to the rhythm of an instrument:

---

[1] Often metaphorically a reference to the wounds of Christ or, in this case, to the wounds of John the Baptist.

[2] The devil.

SECOND COLUMN
Norabuena sin culpa
sois concebida,
para ser de los cielos reina divina.
De la culpa y pecado
Dios os preservó,
porque vos podáis sola
ser madre de Dios.
Del pincel soberano
sois desempeño,
y de Dios el más propio
retrato bello.
Pues en vos, atesora
Dios tanta gracia,
¡enriqueced, Señora,
todas las almas!

22. **Al baptismo [sic] de Cristo.**[1]

FIRST COLUMN
¡Oh, cuán alegre ha salido
hoy el enero escarchado,
logrando de primavera
cuanto presume de mayo!
Su gala ostentando, el sol
parece que borda a rayos
la tela de plata verde
de que está vestido el campo.
Del Jordán en la ribera
vi la gloria en breve espacio,
producir la tierra flores,
llover el cielo milagros.
¡Zagalejos, venid al Jordán!,
veréis maravillas que yo miré allí;
querubes que pueblan de plumas and voces
vistosas y dulces el viento sutil.
¡Venid, venid, el paso animad!,
y veréis a los pies del Bautista
postrada de Cristo la majestad.
¡Llegad a admiraros!

---

[1] Olivares and Boyce, 1st ed., 377–78.

congratulations to her who without sin
was conceived,
to be the divine Queen of Heaven.
From guilt and from sin
God preserved you,
because you alone
were to be Mother of God.
Of the sovereign paintbrush
you are the product,
and of God the most faithful
beautiful portrait.
For in you, God amasses
so much grace,
enrich, My Lady,
all souls!

22. **To the Baptism of Christ.**

Oh how happily departs
frosty January today,
with Spring arriving
as if it were already May!
Showing off its finery, the sun
seems to embroider with rays
the silvery green cloth
in which the countryside is dressed.
On the shores of the Jordan
I saw glory in a small space,
produce flowers on earth
and rain down miracles from heaven.
Lads and lasses, come to the Jordan!,
you will see marvels that I saw there;
cherubs populate with plumes and voices
brilliantly and sweetly the subtle wind.
Come, come, hurry up!,
and you will see at the feet of the Baptist
the majesty of Christ prostrated.
Come and admire!,

Que de verlo los cielos y tierra
suspensos contemplan prodigio tan raro.
Juan, que aún antes de nacido
fue de Dios santificado;
la gracia que en él vincula,
rompió el límite a lo humano.

SECOND COLUMN
Tan valido es de su Rey
que entre los demás vasallos
privilegios del mayor
le dio con gajes de amado.
En premio de su humildad,
de sus finezas en cambio,
hoy le prefiere a sí mismo,
dándole lugar más alto.
Tanta deidad acredita
Juan en sí que es necesario
que el Padre eterno asegure[1]
que no es Juan su mayorazgo.

23. **Otro.**

Serranos de estas cumbres,
pastores de estos llanos
venid al Jordán todos.
Veréis que se transforma
el enero escarchado,
sin límite del tiempo,
en un florido mayo.
Veréis que en la presencia
del lucero más claro
porque brillen sus luces
que oculta el sol sus rayos.

FIRST COLUMN
Veréis pues al baptista
que, si bien es vasallo,
es tan grande que el Rey
a sus pies ha postrado.
Venid, veréis el [a]siento

15v

---

[1] Olivares and Boyce, 1st ed., transcribes "asegura," but manuscript reads "asegure."

seeing heaven and earth
stop to contemplate such a rare wonder.
John, who even before he was born
was sanctified by God;
the grace that was bestowed on him
broke all human limits.

He is such a loyal minister to his King
that, among all His vassals,
privileges of the favorite
He gave as a token of His love.
As a reward for his humility,
in exchange for his gallantry,
He today prefers him [John] to Himself,
giving him [John] the higher place.
So much divinity is credited
to John that the Father
must affirm
that John is not His first-born.

23. **Another.**

Highlanders of these peaks,
shepherds of these plains
all come to the Jordan.
You will see how frosty January
is transformed,
beyond the limits of time,
into florid May.
You will see that in the presence
of this brilliant star
He shines so brightly
that He blocks the rays of the sun.

You will see the Baptist
who, even though a vassal,
is so great that the King
prostrates Himself at his feet.

hecho real palacio
de tantos como asisten
celestiales cortesanos.
Veréis que de la gracia
el autor soberano,
hoy de Juan la recibe
que es de gracias milagro.
Y que Juan, más que Cristo,
tiene de Dios amagos
y más que Dios parece
pues, viene a estar más alto.

24. Otro.

FIRST COLUMN
Hoy que floridos los campos
ufanos se ven lucir,
volviendo mayo el enero,
en competencia de abril,
aquel excelso lucero
que explayando rayos mil
tanto iluminan que pueden
con los del sol competir.
A vista del sol ostenta
un lucero tan feliz

SECOND COLUMN
que en créditos del mayor
sol le pueden presumir.
De Cristo la majestad
a Juan se llegó a rendir
que es bien si un grande se humilla
sublimarle el Rey así.
El cordero que a su pecho
de tusón[1] pudo servir
puesto a sus plantas indicia
de Juan grandezas sin fin.

---

[1] Reference to the Golden Fleece.

Come, you will see the place
become a royal place
for in attendance are so many
celestial courtiers.
You will see the grace
that the sovereign author,
today receives from John,
who is a miracle of graces.
And that John, more than Christ,
has signs from God
and more than God appears,
in his exalted state.

24. Another.

Today how the florid fields
proudly show off,
changing January into May,
in competition with April,
that excellent bright star
who extends a thousand rays
that can illuminate
and compete with those of the sun.
At the sight of the sun shines forth
so happily a bright star

that shining more brilliantly [than the sun],
they presume it to be the sun itself.
Christ's majesty
is surrendered to John
since it is well if a great one humbles himself
to thus exalt the King.
The lamb that at his breast
could serve as a golden fleece,
now placed at his feet to show
that John enjoys boundless grandeur.

Más parece Juan que Dios
pues superior se ve allí,
y solo el Padre pudiera
cuál era Dios discernir.
La gala al baptista cantan
y yo me atrevo a decir
que si le canta, le emula
el más puro serafín.
Pues le cantan la gala
a Juan los cielos,
celebrando sus dichas,
todos cantemos.
El tesoro franquea
Dios de la gracia,
porque de ella mendiga,
no muera el alma.

FIRST COLUMN
Como es grande en su corte
el baptista Juan,
con la llave de gracia
le ha querido honrar.
Siendo Dios todo [sic] gracia
a Juan la pide
porque en pedirle gracia,
todos le imitan.

SECOND COLUMN
Precursor soberano
grande es tu poder,
pues, el verbo humanado
se humilla a tus pies.
En pedirte el baptismo
Dios manifiesta
los inmensos quilates
de tu grandeza.

John seems greater than God
since he stands above Him,
and only God the Father would be able
to discern which of the two was God.
They sing the glory of the Baptist
and I dare to say
that if one sings to him, one emulates
the purest of seraphim.
The heavens sing
praises to John,
celebrating his joys,
and let us all sing.
God gives the
treasure of grace
so that, through grace, we may beg
for the soul not to die.

Since great in His court
is John the Baptist,
with the key of grace
He wanted to honor him.
God, being all grace
asks John for grace
so that in asking for grace,
all may imitate him.

Sovereign precursor,
great is your power,
the Word taking human form
humbles Himself at your feet.
In asking you for baptism,
God manifests
the refined purity
of your greatness.

25. **Soneto trovando uno de Lope de Vega muy celebrado.**[1]

Si yo las flechas del amor tuviera,
de Vos a todo mundo enamorara;
y si fuera posible, le obliga
a que después, mi Dios, no os ofendiera.
El hombre que os quisiera tanto hiciera
que de otro ningún bien se le acordara;
su pensamiento a vuestra cruz atara
porque sólo a seguiros atendiera.
Y si pudiera yo, con una llave
cerrara su deseo presuroso
cuando en la juventud, dulce y suave,
se pierde por hallar todo lo hermoso,
y en Vos no busca en todo hermoso y grave
con que su amor tuviera fin dichoso.

26. **Alabando la fábula de Hércules y Deyanira**[2] **de D. Jerónimo Pantoja, vecino de Toledo, escrita en octavas elegantes.** 16v

Observe eterna lámina de oro
la que cantas Jerardo Deyanira
en metro que a tu fama aliento inspira
en voces cultas de metal sonoro.

---

[1] Olivares and Boyce, 1st ed., 369; Olivares and Boyce, 2nd ed., 262.
[2] The third wife of Hercules, known in Greek as Heracles.

25. **Sonnet, imitating a very celebrated one by Lope de Vega.**[1]

If I had arrows of love,
I would make all the world fall in love with You;
and if it were possible, I would oblige everyone
afterward, my God, to never offend You.
Any man who would love You so much
would never think about any other good thing;
his thoughts would be bound to Your cross
because he would only strive to follow You.
And if I could, with a key
I would lock away hasty desire
when in one's youth, sweet and mild,
one loses himself trying to find beauty,
and does not seek in You all that is beautiful and lofty
so that one's love might find a fortunate end.

26. **Praising the fable of Hercules and Deianira, written in elegant octaves, by Don Jerónimo Pantoja,[2] a citizen of Toledo.**

May an eternal engraving in gold
set forth what you, Jerardo, sing of Deianira
in a meter that inspires and imbues with fame
in learned words of sonorous metal.

---

[1] Olivares, 1st ed., 369. This sonnet is a sacred version on a theme from a sonnet by Lope de Vega that appears in his play, *Lo cierto por lo dudoso* (*Certainty for the Sake of the Doubtful*), spoken by Don Enrique in Act 3, Scene 4.

Si yo las fleches del amor tuviera,	If I had the arrows of love,
de vos a todo el mundo enamorara,	I would make the whole world fall in love with you,
y en torres de diamantes os guardara,	and I would keep you in diamond towers,
porque después de amaros nada os viera.	so that after loving you no one would see you.
Que tanto me quisiérades hiciera,	You would love me so much that I would make
que de otro ningún se os acordara;	it so that you could not remember anyone else;
el pensamiento a una cadena atara,	I would imprison your thoughts with a chain,
y la imaginación se suspendiera.	and I would suspend your imagination.
Y si pudiera yo, con una llave	And if I could, with a key
cerrara el tiempo el curso presuroso	a would lock up time's hasty course
en esa dulce juventud suave,	in that sweet and mild youth,
porque jamás en ese rostro hermoso	so that your beautiful face would never
la edad pusiera cosa menos grave,	experience with age anything less lofty,
ni yo pudiera ser menos dichoso.	nor make me any less fortunate.

[2] I have not been able to find any further biographical reference to this individual.

Cuanto de ellas alcanzo cuanto ignoro
émula aplaudo, siempre en ti me admira
facundia que alabar mi genio aspira
tácitamente atento a tu decoro
en la que a Alcides[1] das, te apropias gloria;
la envidia en causa tanta vida adquiere,
si opinión de discreto el envidioso
canta, pues, perpetúa tu memoria,
que, cuando más la envidia te ofendiere,
más te aumenta atributos de famoso.

27. Octava.

Desaires de tu amor mi amor recibe
cuando llamas tormento su fineza,
porque si a cuenta de las penas vive
el amor, el huirlas es flaqueza
de tu valor, si me amas, te apercibe
a pagar de mi amor tanta nobleza
que en el penar por ti tiene más gloria
que en buscarla del gusto en tu memoria.

28. Alabando las novelas de D. Pedro de Paz,[2] vecino de Toledo y de ingenio lucidísimo.

17r

Alabaros, Don Pedro, no es mi intento
ni el ingenio a pluma ha concedido
saber encarecer el que ha excedido
a todo estilo de encarecimiento;
ni a mi corta energía el sentimiento
se atreviera a fiar lo que ha sentido,
ni menos de la ajena ha permitido
que me valga mi altivo pensamiento.
Es delirio intentar vuestra alabanza,
humildad, mendigar de ingenio rico
elogios que me nieguen proprio [sic] dueño;
y, pues, confieso mi desconfianza
y que a ajenos conceptos no me aplico
libraré en mi deseo el desempeño.

---

[1] Another name for Hercules.
[2] The only person of note by this name was a sixteenth-century sculptor, but I have found no author thus identified.

Even though I understand some of your words but not others
I applaud you, and in my admiration for you
my wit aspires to praise your eloquence
tacitly I put your decorum at risk
in what you tell of Alcides, you gain glory for yourself;
but you also cause great envy in others
and if the opinion of a discreet person, an envious one
sings, it only perpetuates your memory,
when envy might most offend you,
it makes you all the more famous.

27. Octave.

My love receives only rebuff from your love
when you call torment elegance,
because if love lives by an accounting of its pains
fleeing from them is a weakness
in your valor, if you love me, it warns you
that so much nobility is payment of my love,
for suffering because of you brings more glory
than looking for it happily in your memory.

28. Praising the novels of Don Pedro de Paz, a neighbor of Toledo with very lucid wit.

To praise you, Don Pedro, is not my intent
nor has my wit conceded to my pen
knowing how to praise one who has exceeded
in all manner of exaltation;
nor, due to my lack of energy, my sentiment
would dare to trust what I have felt,
and even more alien to admit
that haughty thoughts might help me.
It is madness to try to praise you,
humility, to beg from a rich wit
eulogies that a proper master denies me;
and, I confess my lack of confidence
and applying myself to other things
I will liberate myself from the task.

29. **Octava a una señora que con pocas razones enamoraba y decía pesares con gran discreción.**

Hanme dicho, señora, que pasmado
sientes el corazón; la causa ha sido
el entrar en un baño casi helado
y extrañando el efecto he presumido
que sin duda temió verse abrasado;
y para estar a riesgo prevenido
hurto la propiedad a las razones
conque si abrasas, pasmas corazones.

30. **Soneto de un galán a una dama seglar.**[1]   17v

Mal haya un apetito refrenado,
un disimulo y un encogimiento,
un recato, un temor, un desaliento,
para que se interprete un hombre honrado.
Si en el tiempo fatal se halla el cuitado
hecho Tántalo al husmo del contento,
agresor general de pensamiento,
sin que a la parte se le dé traslado.
Yo por huir de aqueste inconveniente
digo que sois el norte de mi vida;
sois el incendio que mi amor inflama
y en consecuencia de los antecedentes
esta alma alborozada se convida
a ser la mariposa de esa llama.

31. **Encoméndoseme la respuesta y fue por los mismos consonantes [sic].**[2]

Bien haya un apetito refrenado,
que en ocasiones el encogimiento
no es cobardía menos desaliento,
cuerdo reparo sí de un hombre honrado.
Presumo que de juicio está menguado
aquél que a ejecuciones el contento
atribuye, si ya de pensamiento,
no es del mismo apetito vil traslado.
Para mi gusto es este inconveniente

---

[1] Serrano y Sanz, 366. I have included this poem among those attributed to Belisarda because she does not identify the "galán," supposedly the author of the sonnet, and it may indeed be an invention of our poet in order to construct her response.

[2] Serrano y Sanz, 366.

29. **Octave to a woman who foolishly fell in love and recounted her woes with great discretion.**

I have been told, my lady, that your heart
has been stunned; the cause has been
on entering a nearly frozen bath
and not expecting the effect I presumed
that without doubt your heart was in fear of being burned;
and being forewarned of the risk
I steal the property of reason
so now you know if you scald, you stun hearts.

30. **Sonnet by a gentlemen to a lady.**

It is bad to refrain the appetite,
a dissimulation and a resignation,
a demureness, a fear, a discouragement,
if a man is to be considered honorable.
If in fatal times one finds worry
made a Tantalus[1] looking for contentment,
general aggressor of thought,
without letting him move.
I to flee from this obstacle
and say that you are the guide of my life;
you are the fire that inflames my love,
and as a consequence
this jubilant soul is invited
to be the moth to that flame.

31. **Charging me with the response using the same consonants.**

It is well to have a moderate appetite,
since occasionally restraint
is not cowardice but rather refraining
is wise judgment for an honorable man.
I presume that one's judgment diminishes
when one equates performance
with happiness or considers
a vile move the same as appetite.
To my way of thinking this problem

---

[1] Tantalus made fun of the gods when invited to dine with them. He cut up his son and fed him to the gods. When his crime was discovered, he was banished to Tartarus, the deepest part of the underworld where he stood in a pool of water under a fruit tree, with both the fruit and the water forever just out of his reach.

y es conveniente, pues, para la vida
de mi amor que le templa y no le inflama
esto supuesto de lo antecedente
no vive, a lo primero se convida
y al fin de noble amor solo se llama.

32. **Soneto a consonantes forzosas sobre que habían escrito sonetos con asuntos diferentes, diferentes personas, dieronme por asunto no desmayar a vista de un desdén.**[1]

Si no impide mi amor el mismo cielo,
no bastarán cuantos rigores miro
a ponerle del alma en el retiro,
porque en razón fundado toma vuelo.
Y aunque cansarte en porfiar recelo
y en querer porfiar de mí me admiro,
la causa del dolor porque suspiro
no admite de temor prisión de hielo.
Si mi gusto no logra sus antojos,
por negarles tus ojos luces bellas,
y, en vez de amor me pagas con enojos,
no formaré de algún rigor querellas,
sino, sólo, Jacinta, de tus ojos,
puesto que están conformes las estrellas.

33. **A la Asunción de Nuestra Señora.**

FIRST COLUMN
Triunfante llega María
al celestial hemisferio
donde todos la reciben
con aplausos festejos.
Reina la apellida el Rey
a sus cortesanos bellos,
madre y esposa la aclaman
de su Dios y autor supremo.

SECOND COLUMN
Todos los que el triunfo aplauden,
habitantes de aquel reino,
le dan gracias por la gloria
que por su gracia adquirieron.

---

[1] Olivares and Boyce, 1st ed., 332.

is not problematic for the life
of my love should be temperate rather than inflamed
and we can summarize from the above
that one does not live, if at first invited,
for, in the end, it will be called noble love.

32. Sonnet with pre-ordained consonants used by various people to write about different topics, taking as my subject not despairing when one encounters an affront.

If heaven does not impede my love,
all the rigors I see will not be enough
to put my soul to rest,
because founded on reason it takes flight.
And even though I fear wearying you with my insistence
I admire in myself this stubbornness in love,
the cause of my pain and why I sigh
does not admit fear of an icy prison.
If my pleasure does not achieve its whims,
by denying that your eyes are beautiful lights
and, instead of love, you repay me with anger,
I will not complain in the face of such harshness,
but only, Jacinta, of your eyes,
since they are so like the stars.

33. For the Assumption of Our Lady.

Mary arrives triumphant
to the celestial sphere
where all receive her
with festive applause.
The King names her Queen
and His beautiful courtiers
acclaim her Mother and bride
of her God, the supreme author.

All those who her triumph applaud,
inhabitants of that kingdom,
thank her for the glory
that they acquire through her grace.

María, tierna y gozosa,
logra de amante el deseo
que rindió su vida cuando
rompió a la muerte los fueros.

34. A la misma fiesta de la Asunción de Nuestra Señora, otra. 18v

FIRST COLUMN
Entre querubes hermosos
rompe el cendal de zafir [sic]
María, a cuya deidad
ministran de mil en mil.
Bizarramente lucidos
pueblan el viento sutil
de adulaciones de pluma
con lisonjero matiz.
Copia de fulgentes rayos
sirve diáfano feliz
a la que cándida aurora
fue del sol de su zenit.
A su luz se abrasa amante
cual mariposa feliz
que muere en su incendio cuando
posa en él para vivir.
Flor de sus rayos le sigue
en el celeste pensil
donde superior a todas
más vistosa ha de lucir.
La flor, reina de las flores,
espejo ha de ser allí,
cuyo cristal terso y puro
fue de su *agnus dei* viril
y el ángel más perfecto
y puro serafín
que es más perfecta y pura
no cesa de decir.

Mary, tender and joyful,
fulfills the desire of the beloved
who surrendered His life
and destroyed the bonds of death.

34. For the same festival of the Assumption of Our Lady.

Among beautiful cherubs
she breaks through the sapphire-like gauze,
Mary, to whose divinity
thousands and thousands attest.
Brazenly shining
they populate the subtle wind
with plumed adulations
in flattering shades.
An image of brilliant rays
serves happily and clearly
she to whom the bright dawn
was the zenith of the sun.
The lover burns in her light
like a happy moth
who dies in its fire when
he alights on it to live.
The flower of her rays follows her
in the celestial garden
where superior to all women
more brightly she must shine.
The flower, queen of all flowers,
she must be the mirror
whose crystal surface, smooth and pure,
was for the virile Lamb of God
and the most perfect angel
and purest seraph,
the most perfect and pure
never ceases to proclaim.

35. Otro a San Francisco de Paula.

Si es Francisco el trono mismo
de sus triunfos de su fama,
hoy, coronado por ellos,
serán sus glorias más altas.
Farol le aplauden las luces,
planta las flores le aclaman
que unas, fervoroso enciende
y otras penitente esmalta.
Juntas, pues, flores y luces
amorosas cuanto ufanas,
en dos coros divididas
de aquesta suerte le cantan.
1º No tenemos las luces dicha más alta
que encendernos, Francisco, luz soberana.
2º No tenemos las flores gloria más rica
que esmaltarnos, Francisco, planta divina.
1º2º Viva su gala,
pues, la tierra le admira,
farol y planta.
Viva de Paula la tierra,
por el orbe venerada,
pues, a Francisco produjo
planta de virtudes tantas.
Viva el que menor se nombra
cuando grande se levanta

FIRST COLUMN
desde la tierra hasta el cielo,
en hombros de sus hazañas.
Viva el que más humilde
en la esfera empírea[1] campa,
acreditando en él glorias
la deidad más encumbrada.

---

[1] I here corrected an obvious spelling error; the manuscript reads "ympirea."

35. Another to Saint Francis of Paola.[1]

If Francis is the throne itself
of his triumphs and his fame,
today, crowned by them,
his glories are of the most high.
Stars applaud him as a bright light,
the flowers proclaim him a plant
for some he sets alight with fervor
and others he adorns with penitence.
Together, then, flowers and stars
in love and proudly,
divided in two choruses
sing in this fashion.
1st We stars do not enjoy greater fortune
than that you, Francis, give us sovereign light.
2nd We flowers do not enjoy richer glory
than that Francis, divine plant, adorns us.
1st 2nd Long may he be celebrated
by the earth that admires him
as light and plant.
Long live the land of Paola,
venerated by the whole world,
that produced Francis,
a plant of such virtues.
Long live he who calls himself "less"
when he is raised on high

from the earth up to heaven,
on the shoulders of his deeds.
Long live he who most humbly
in the celestial sphere encamps,
gaining glories for himself
as a most exalted deity.

---

[1] St. Francis of Paola (1416–1507) was an Italian mendicant friar who founded the Order of Minims, also known as the Hermit Friars of St. Francis of Assisi.

36. A San Clemente entre dos.

1º ¿Quién es aquél cuyas plantas
dominan signos y astros
y, a su luz, la del mayor,
parias le tributan en rayos?
2º Aquél, docto como ilustre,
el clarecido romano,
que en folio pontifical
dio a su fama timbres sacros.
1º Golfo de zafir [sic] navega
entre bajeles a lados
cuyos matices de pluma
florecen azules campos.
2º El protector de la fe
que alista caudillos sabio,
defensores que la ilustran
si antes la fueron contrarios.

SECOND COLUMN
1º ¿Quién será que, si no escribe,
pinta con lucientes rasgos
la copia de su grandeza
en transparentes espacios?
2º Otro Moisés que consuela
a los sedientos soldados
con la fuente que le indica
el cordero soberano.
1º No entiendo. ¿Quién es? 2º Escucha,
que ya no podrás dudarlo,
pues, al compás de instrumentos
que al viento los ecos impiden el paso.
Celestiales voces alegres,
que viva Clemente, repiten cantando.
2º Pues, el cielo concede este día
al mártir insigne festejos y aplausos,
imitando en la tierra su gozo,
que viva Clemente, mil veces digamos.

36. For Saint Clement, in two voices.[1]

1st Who is that under whose feet
dominates constellations and stars
and, at his light, even the brightest
rays pay him tribute?
2nd That one, so wise and illustrious,
the acclaimed Roman
who in pontifical writ
gave sacred timbre to his fame.
1st He sails the sapphire gulf
amid ships on all sides
whose plume-like wakes
flower like blue fields.
2nd The protector of the faith,
the wise one who enlists generals,
defenders who will uphold it
even though formerly contrary to it.

1st Who can it be, for he does not write,
but rather paints with brilliant strokes
an image of his grandeur
in transparent spaces?
2nd Another Moses who consoles
thirsty soldiers
with the fountain shown to
by the sovereign Lamb.
1st I do not understand. Who is he? 2nd Listen,
for now you cannot doubt it,
because the beats of instruments
impede the echoes of the passing wind.
Happy celestial voices,
repeat, singing: long live Clement.
2nd For heaven concedes this day
festivities and applause to this exemplary martyr,
imitating on earth its joy,
long live Clement, a thousand times we say.

---

[1] Pope Clement I (d. 99) who was martyred by being thrown from a boat into the Black Sea.

De Clemente la doctrina
produce efectos cristianos
y el tirano porque cese
hoy le arroja al mar infausto

FIRST COLUMN 19v
con el áncora que lleva,
se promete salir salvo,
que en ella afianza logros
de su esperanza y cuidado,
retira el mar la corriente
y por temor o agasajo
veneraciones le rinde.
Templo le erige de mármol,
a su valor, el cristal
se reconoce vasallo,
que es Clemente cristal fino
de roca firme labrado.
Pues el cielo concede [este día
al mártir insigne festejos y aplausos,
imitando en la tierra su gozo,
que viva Clemente, mil veces digamos.]

37. **Décima.**

Pensamientos engañados,
¿dónde me lleváis la vida?
Discurriendo un homicida,
laberinto de cuidados,
remedios bien excusados
son los que le proponéis,
si a olvidar no os resolvéis
la causa de sus tormentos;
pero, advertid, pensamientos,
que el olvidar no olvidéis.

38. **Descripción del martirio de San Vicente mártir.**

SECOND COLUMN
Vicente, español insigne,
cuyo valeroso esfuerzo
tanto pudo que hoy la muerte
yace a tus plantas trofeo.
Tú, que alentado te opones

The doctrine of Clement
produces Christian effects
and the tyrant today, to make him desist,
throws him into an ill-fated sea

with the anchor that weighs him down,
but he is promised to arise safely
for he can overcome it
through his hope and care,
the sea restrains its current
and from fear or honor
venerates him.
A temple of marble is erected
to his valor, and crystal
recognizes itself as his vassal,
for Clement is fine crystal
wrought from hard stone.
For heaven concedes [this day
festivities and applause to this exemplary martyr,
imitating on earth its joy,
long live Clement, a thousand times we say.]

37. **Décima.**

Deceptive thoughts,
where, life, are you leading me?
Pondering homicide,
a labyrinth of cares,
remedy rejected
that you propose,
if you do not resolve to forget
the cause of those torments;
but, be warned, thoughts,
not to forget the forgetting.

38. **Description of the martyrdom of Saint Vincent.**

Vincent, exemplary Spaniard,
whose valorous effort
achieved so much that today death
lies at your feet as a trophy.
You, who in the forefront confront

a sus rigores acerbos,
y, venciéndola en batalla,
por inmortal te tuvieron.
Cuando de un leño pendiente,
descoyuntaron tus miembros,
y, en el corazón se admira,
mucho amor y poco miedo.
Cuerda sonora pareces
de aquel inculto instrumento
que templándola el tirano
su voz penetra los cielos.
Tanto a Daçiano enfurecen
de su poder tus desprecios
que, para vengar su agravio,
fulmina rayos sangrientos.
Que a los costados te apliquen
de dos hachas el incendio;
manda, y que garfios o peines[1]
sean colones de tus nervios.

FIRST COLUMN

A todas luces te mira
y, a pesar de sus deseos,
no había viso, amago o sombra
de cobardía en el pecho.
El padecer por amar
hace alivios los tormentos;
gozo brotas que, al tirano,
sirve de mortal veneno.
Y viendo pues en tu vida
mal logrados sus aciertos,
hierros en que se ejecuten,
fragua el vulcano soberbio.
A los ministros ordena
que de metal en un lecho
te inclinen y mansa lumbre
derrita y no abrase el cuerpo.

---

[1] Torture racks.

the harshest rigors,
and, conquering it [death] in battle,
they considered you immortal.
When hung from a beam,
your members disjointed,
in your heart one admires
so much love and so little fear.
You seem a harmonious chord
of that hidden instrument
that when a tyrant tunes it
the sound penetrates the heavens.
Dacian[1] was so infuriated
by your disdain of his power
that, in order to avenge the grievance,
strikes out with bloody flames
that he applies to your flanks;
he commands that hooks and torture racks
be like two points[2] piercing your nerves.

He sees you in all light
and, in spite of his desires,
there was no semblance, image, or shadow
of cowardice in your breast.
Suffering for love
makes relief of torments;
you sprout forth in joy that, to the tyrant
is like a deadly poison,
And seeing in your life
that his efforts came to naught,
he cast irons
in the forge of sovereign Vulcan.
He orders his ministers
that on a metal bed
you recline and a gentle fire
melts it but does not burn your body.

---

[1] Third century Roman Prefect of Hispania and Bética who tortured and killed Saint Vincent of Zaragoza.
[2] The "colon" in Spanish is also called "dos puntos" (two points) and this seems to be the meaning implied here.

Y cual mariposa amante,
que intrépida busca el fuego,
en las llamas a Dios haces
sacrificio de ti mismo.
Puntas de acero tus venas
rompen con rigor tan fiero
que en tu sangre, a ser bajel,
sulcarás[1] un mar de bermejo.
Del tirano los rigores
aún están mal satisfechos,
pues, quiere comer tus carnes,
siendo el lobo, y tú, cordero.
Como diamante en lo duro
te acreditan los efectos,
para labrarte, es diamante
de su rigor en el extremo.
Con tu sangre al fin te labra;
saldrás, Vicente, perfecto
y a buen fiar, que a la costa
que tienes exceda el precio.
Daciano, desesperado
bien que no de su remedio,
pretende que te retractes,
dejando vanos consejos.
Medios inhumanos pone
para conseguirlo, pero
nunca amantes corazones
se avasallaron al riesgo.
Láminas ardientes viste
al que ya mira esqueleto,
mas tú, en vez de retractarte,
revalidas los intentos.
Para eternizar tu fama,
fue Vicente buen acuerdo
fijarte en láminas vivas
porque no la borre el tiempo.

---

[1] For "surcarás."

And like a lover moth
who intrepidly seeks out the flame,
in the flames, to God,
you make yourself a sacrifice.
Your veins by points of steel
are punctured with force so strong
that, in your blood, you could
sail a ship in the waters of a red sea.
The rigors of the tyrant
are still not satisfied,

thus he wants to eat up your flesh,
he being a wolf and you a lamb.
Like a diamond in hardness
the effects confirm
that to carve you is like carving a diamond,
so extreme in its harshness.
And with your blood he carves you;
but you come out, Vincent, perfect
and to good credit, for your worth
has exceeded the price.
Dacian, desperate
for some redress,
tries to make you retract,
giving vain advice.
He imposes inhuman methods
to achieve this, but
lovers' hearts never
are subdued by threat.
Dressed in burning laminate plates
you now look like a skeleton,
but you, instead of retracting
revalidate your intent.
To eternalize your fame,
Vincent, a fine example
set in luminous engravings
so that time may not erase your fame.

FIRST COLUMN
Oh, más que humano varón,
gloria del cristiano imperio,
quien como tú, tan divino,
logra de amor desempeños.
No mueres, no, del dolor
porque sea manifiesto
que antes Dios a tus finezas
gusta de enviarles premio.
Entre tanto que el tirano
arbitra rigores nuevos,
previene cama y regalo
que te disponga al exceso.

SECOND COLUMN
Y, en el interín, el alma
pasa en un divino sueño,
a gozar lauros felices
en los favores eternos.
De la celestial capilla
van resonando los ecos
que a tu valentía cantan
zagalas con dulces versos.
Qué bien cantan tu triunfo
ángeles bellos:
"viva el mártir invicto,"
van repitiendo.
Oh, qué bien cantan
al son de chirimías,
liras y arpas,
diciendo "viva,"
que, en quien muere por Cristo,
la muerte es vida.

39. Al sudario de Cristo. Romance.[1]

FIRST COLUMN
Sudario que, sepultado
de aquel monte en la eminencia,
piadoso a Cristo acompañas,
cuando el hombre cruel le deja.

---

[1] Olivares and Boyce, 1st ed., 381–82; Olivares and Boyce, 2nd ed., 267–68.

Oh, man more than human,
glory of the Christian empire,
who like you, so divine
gives performances of love.
You do not die, not at all, from pain
so it may be made manifest
that God for your elegance
gladly sent you a reward.
Amidst all, the tyrant
introduces new rigors
and allows you neither sleep nor respite
and makes you suffer in excess.

But, meanwhile, your soul
rests in divine slumber,
enjoying happy rewards
of eternal favors.
From the celestial chapel
echoes are resounding;
young girls sing of your bravery
celebrating with sweet verses.
How well they sing of your triumph
the beautiful angels:
"Long live the unconquered martyr,"
they are repeating.
Oh, how well they sing
to the sound of woodwinds,
lyres, and harps,
they say "long life,"
for he who dies for Christ,
death is life.

39. Ballad to Christ's shroud.[1]

Shroud that was buried
on that mount in eminence,
piously you accompanied Christ,
when cruel mankind abandoned Him.

---
[1] The shroud of Turin.

De aquel Dios de amores muerto,
trasunto vivo que enseña
efectos de la pasión
que en amar al hombre ostenta.
Tan propio en ti se figura
que, muerto, le representas
vivo carácter, que imprimes
su dolorosa tragedia.
Lienzo que a la nave Cristo
fuiste favorable vela,
con que a puerto feliz sale
después de injusta tormenta.
Bandera del Capitán
que en la militante iglesia
su triunfo glorioso indicias
con señales manifiestas.
Digno corporal serviste
a la carne y sangre mesma [sic]

SECOND COLUMN
de Dios, que así se consagra
de Su Padre a la obediencia.
Pues, de Cristo la copia
en ti nos queda,
sea la pena gloria;
celébrese en la tierra
que tú le acompañaste
en la mayor empresa.

40. **A la soledad de Nuestra Señora.**[1]

Sola, afligida y llorosa
María la cruz contempla,
que en la batalla de Cristo
os ostentó fatal palestra.
Son los despojos que mira
clavos y espinas sangrientos
que el corazón le destrozan
con repetida violencia.
Sola, pues, de todo alivio,
sólo la acompañan penas

---

[1] Olivares and Boyce, 1st ed., 384; Olivares and Boyce, 2nd ed., 268–69.

Of that God, dead because of His love,
a living image that shows
the effects of His passion
that He suffered for the love of man.
So true on you they show
that, dead, you represent Him
as if alive, and on you is imprinted
His painful tragedy.
Cloth that for Christ's ship
was a favorable sail,
toward a happy port set forth
after unjust torment.
Flag of its Captain
that in the militant church
his glorious victory you indicate
with manifest signs.
You served as a worthy corporal[1]
to the very flesh and blood

of God, who thus consecrated Himself
to obey His Father's will.
Thus the copy of Christ
on you remains,
that pain might be glory;
let the earth celebrate
for you accompanied Him
in His greatest task.

40. **Ballad to the loneliness of Our Lady.**

Alone, afflicted and tearful
Mary contemplates the cross,
that in Christ's battle,
became a fatal arena.
The spoils that she looks upon
are the nails and bloody thorns
that destroyed her heart
with repeated violence.
Alone, bereft of all relief,
only pains accompany her

---

[1] The cloth on which the priest places the host and chalice during mass.

que del verdadero triste
son amigas verdaderas.

FIRST COLUMN
En sí mesma [sic] busca a Dios,
y en Dios se busca a sí mesma [sic];
que vive y muere con Dios
quien a Dios ama con veras.
¡Qué dulcemente suspira!,
amorosamente tierna,
y del rostro la hermosura
anega en un mar de perlas.
Al espejo en su rostro
se ve la luna funesta;
el sol se mira eclipsado
y llorosas las estrellas.
¡Corazón endurecido!,
¿para cuándo te reservas,
si en suspiros no te exhalas,
y en lágrimas no te anegas?

41. Al expirar Cristo en la cruz.[1]

Clavado Cristo en la cruz,
yace rendido dos veces:
a las flechas del amor
y a las iras de la muerte.
El clavel, rey de las flores,
y destroncado parece

SECOND COLUMN
cárdeno lirio entre espinas
que le esmaltan si le hieren.[2]
Torpe y sacrílega mano
turbó la púrpura y nieve
del rostro divino donde
aún lo hermoso permanece.
El libro de siete sellos,

---

[1] Olivares and Boyce, 1st ed., 379–80; Olivares and Boyce 2nd ed., 266–67. The location of this ballad is given as folio 21v; actually it occupies 21v and continues on folio 22r.

[2] Olivares and Boyce, 1st ed., 379, line 8, reads "hiere." Also, in their 2nd ed., 266.

which, of true sadness,
are true friends.

In herself she searches for God,
and in God, she searches for herself;
and she lives and dies with God
she who God truly loved.
How sweetly she sighs!,
lovingly tender,
and the beauty of her face
is drowned in a sea of tears.
In her face in the mirror
one can see the mournful moon;
the sun has been eclipsed
and the stars are weeping.
Hard heart!,
when will you be able to save yourself
if you are not consumed by sighs
and if you do not drown in tears?

41. **Ballad to Christ expiring on the cross.**

Christ nailed to the cross,
surrenders Himself two times:
to the arrows of love
and to the ire of death.
The carnation, king of the flowers,
now appears cut off,

a purple lily among thorns
that adorn Him when they wound Him.
A clumsy and sacrilegious hand
altered the purple and the whiteness
of the divine face where
even now beauty remains.

que hoy los cinco abiertos tiene,
que deshojado se mira,
descuadernado se lee.
Al cargo que Dios te hace,
que con sangre escribe atiende,
alma, a su amor siempre ingrato,
atenta a tus gustos siempre.
Si ha de valerte el descargo,
bien puedes en Dios valerte,
que hasta en el último valor,
vale todo lo que quiere.
Pues ladrón fuiste del tiempo
por dar horas al deleite,
acompaña en ésta a Dios
si ser cual Dimas pretendes.
Muere por Dios, alma mía,
hoy con Dios, pues por ti muere;
y con un *memento mei*
harás que de ti se acuerde.

FIRST COLUMN
Naufragando entre congojas
aquel corazón valiente,
a que perdones te obliga,
perdonando a quien le ofende.

The book of the seven seals,[1]
today five of which have been opened,
shows missing pages,
and is read without its binding.
To the burden that God gives you,
and that is written in blood, pay heed,
soul, always ungrateful of His love,
even though He is always attentive to your needs.
If you want to put your burden down,
you can do so with God's help,
since no matter how weighty the matter
all are worthy of His love.[2]
You were a thief of time,
by giving over hours to delights,
rather accompany God in this life
if you want to be like Dimas.[3]
Die for God, my soul,
today with God, who dies for you;
and with a "remember me"
you will make Him remember you.

Shipwrecked among anxieties
that valiant heart
obliges you to forgive others
since He pardoned those who offended Him.

---

[1] This refers to the seven seals from the Book of Revelation of St. John, chapters 6–8. I agree with Olivares and Boyce who assert that Belisarda associated the earthquake described in the opening of the sixth seal with the earthquake and solar eclipse that occurred at the moment Christ died on the cross described in verses 37–40 later in the poem. These critics also contend that the last strophe of the poem suggests the Final Judgment.

[2] This strophe is extremely hard to translate since the poet is playing with the verb "valerse" which can mean "to avail oneself" but it also means "to have a value or price." Her use of the word "valor" in verse 23 is tricky since it can mean "value" or "courage." Mixed with these double meanings are the words "cargo" that can mean either a "charge" (as in value of something) or "burden," and "descargo" which can mean a "discharge" (as in a receipt) or "unburdening." I have opted for the idea of availing oneself of God's help to put down your burdens in life. Other readings are certainly valid.

[3] A name often given to the thief crucified with Jesus who asked to accompany Christ when He entered His kingdom. The reference in verse 31 to "memento mei" is from the Gospel of St. Luke that records the thief's words in chapter 23, verse 42: "Domine, memento mei cum veneris in regnum tuum."

La vida de un Dios, que es vida,
zozobra entre angustias crueles;
ya se estremece, ya expira,
ya todo el orbe estremece.
Para ahora son, ¡oh alma!,
tantos suspiros ardientes
que corazones inflamen
y que los cielos penetren.

42. A Santa Catalina de Sena.

Aquella que fue de Sena
si[1] honorífico blasón,
flor de las flores más bellas
en que amor la transforma.
De virtudes, maravilla,
que siempre viva asistió
al sol que asistía siempre
a inflamar su corazón.
Flor de sus rayos le sigue
al ara de su esplendor,
de quien Clicie a ser aspira.
En la suprema región,

SECOND COLUMN
gozar este sol desea[2]
por quien de amor muere hoy
Catalina, y dice viendo
dilatar la ejecución:
dile, sol, que amaneces
al sol de mi amor
que le estoy aguardando
que corra veloz.
Dile que vuele;
que el correr, es pararse;
volar, moverse.
Fue, pues, de la penitencia
clavel de purpureo honor
a quien Dios con cinco suyos[3]

---

[1] "si" should probably read "su."
[2] Paper is torn at the end of this line so it may be incomplete.
[3] A reference to the hand and fingers of God.

The life of God, who is life
foundered among cruel anguish;
now He shudders, now He dies,
now all the world shakes.
For now, oh soul!,
may many burning sighs
inflame hearts
and penetrate the heavens.

42. **To Saint Catherine of Siena.**

She who was from Siena
honored in glory,
the most beautiful of flowers
transformed by love.
Of virtues, a marvel,
while living she always accompanied
that sun that was always present
to inflame her heart.
Like a flower she follows His rays
toward the altar of His splendor,
she who aspires to be like Clytia[1]
in the supreme realm,

wants to enjoy this sun
for whom she dies daily for love,
and Catherine says seeing
the performance unfolding:
tell the sun to rise
to the light of my love,
that I am waiting for him,
may he run quickly.
Tell him to fly;
that running is to stop;
flying is to move.
She was for penance
a purple carnation of honor[2]
to whom God with His hand

---

[1] In Greek mythology Clytia was a water nymph enamored of Helios, the Sun, each day she watched him as he ascended and descended in the sky.
[2] Purple as in the color of cardinals' robes.

dio más viva perfección.
Cándida rosa entre espinas,
fue del lirio a imitación
que en la cruz cárdena mira
con tierno, intenso dolor.
El Apolo soberano
en esta esposa influye
ciencia con que luego supo
amar por arte mayor.
A gozar su esposo anhela
y, entre el presuroso ardor
y acelerado deseo,
repite con dulce voz:
Dile, sol, [que amaneces
al sol de mi amor
que le estoy aguardando
que corra veloz.][1]

43. Glosa.

22v

Si en la tierra donde vivo
es do[2] habita mi adversario,
¿cómo he de huir del agravio
que de sus manos recibo?

FIRST COLUMN
Perfecto amor acredita
quien no se rinde al temor,
que amor que en alma habita
en sus riesgos solicita
lucimientos de valor.
Siendo, pues, mi amor activo
vencerá lo executivo
del más tirano poder,
que no me puede ofender
si en la tierra donde vivo.

---

[1] The refrain is indicated by "etc." and I have expanded it here. Other poems follow this pattern as earlier indicated.
[2] Abbreviated form of "donde."

gave the greatest perfection.
Whitest rose among thorns,
an imitation of the lily
who looks upon the deep-purple-colored cross[1]
with tender and intense pain.
The sovereign Apollo
inspires in this bride
wisdom with which she knew how
to love in greatest measure.
To desire to enjoy her husband
and between anxious ardor
and accelerated desire
to repeat with a sweet voice:
tell the sun [to rise
to the light of my love,
that I am waiting for Him,
may He run quickly.]

43. Gloss.

If in the land where I live
my adversary also lives,
how will I flee from the offense
that I receive at his hands?

Perfect love gives credit
to whomever does not surrender to fear,
for love that lives in the soul
in times of risk asks for
shows of valor.
Being active in love
I will defeat the insistence
of the most tyrannical power
that cannot offend me
if in the land where I live
my adversary also lives.

---

[1] A reference to the bloody cross of Christ's sacrifice.

Si es de Dios mi alma cielo
y Dios del alma y potencias
ociosamente recelo,
que el enemigo desvelo
logre astutas diligencias,
porque siendo el alma erario
de Dios, ¿qué poder contrario
contrastará su sosiego,
si en la tierra a que me niego
es do habita mi adversario?

SECOND COLUMN
Prevenido el corazón
de paciencia y caridad
en el mar de tentación
conseguirá en la oración
perpetua tranquilidad,
siendo el amor astrolabio,
el temor piloto sabio,
que en la tormenta enemiga,
antes del riesgo me diga
cómo he de huir del agravio.
Venciendo en fin lo que soy
con pensar quien seré,
libre de peligro estoy
que si venciendo me voy,
mi contrario venceré.
Que aunque la tierra en que estribo
al engaño da motivo,
si prevengo el desengaño,
poca impresión hará el daño
que de sus manos recibo.

44. Décimas a instancia de una monja toledana cuyo amante dejaba un amigo por guarda de su dama.[1]

FIRST COLUMN
Si en un cortés caballero
el ruego halla lugar,
una merced singular
alcanzar de vos espero.

---

[1] Olivares and Boyce, 1st ed., 346–47; Olivares and Boyce, 2nd ed., 250–51.

If my soul is of God's heaven
and the power of God in my soul
I idly distrust,
the watchful enemy,
always astute and alert, may attack
but if the soul is the treasury
of God, what contrary power
can contrast with His serenity
if in the land where I am denied
lives my enemy?

The heart forewarned
by patience and charity
in a sea of temptation
will achieve through prayer
perpetual tranquility,
since love is the astrolabe
and fear a wise pilot
that in the enemy storm
will forewarn of the approaching risk
and tell me how to flee from harm.
In the end I am winning
by thinking about who I will be,
I am free from danger
and if I prevail
I will defeat my adversary.
And even though in the land where I live
there may be reason for deception,
if I foresee the disappointment,
the danger will be minimal
that I receive at his hands.

44. **Décimas requested by a Toledan nun about a lover who left his lady in the care of his friend.**

If in a courteous knight
the plea finds a home,
a singular mercy
I want to win from you.

Ya sabéis, señor, que quiero
bien y, pues, sabéis a quien,
aunque a conocer se den,
os intiman mis recelos,
que Argos de vuestros desvelos
no hagáis a quien quiero bien.
Perdonad el advertiros,
no porque agravio presumo
de él que cortés en lo sumo
atiende sólo a serviros;
pero si habéis de partiros,
y gustáis que os sustituya,
cuando a obediencia atribuya
el que sirva a vuestro dueño,
que ha de hacer con otra empeño
no será mucho que arguya.

SECOND COLUMN
Que aunque de muertas centellas
cenizas no dan calor,
durar puede el de su amor
y hacer otro fénix de ellas;
o puede de las estrellas
que el imperial cielo ostenta,
o curiosa o desatenta,
algunas de vivos rayos
causar en su amor desmayos
y a mi frente dura afrenta.
Todo favor me prometo
de vuestro cortés agrado,
estimándole en el grado
que infunde gran respeto;
y suplid, pues sois discreto,
defectos de gravedad
sin que os cause novedad,
prevención que no asegura
que quien no pica en locura
no pasa de voluntad.

You know, sir, that I love
well and you know whom,
and although it is known,
that you are familiar with my suspicions,
be an Argos[1] in watchfulness
and do not neglect whom I love well.
Pardon me for warning you,
not because I presume a grievance
from him who is courteous in the extreme
and wants only to serve you;
but if you have to leave
and you would like him to substitute for you,
when obedience commands,
as one who serves your master
is determined to have another
there will not be much evidence against him.

Even though from dead sparks
ashes do not give off heat,
her love can endure
and make of them another phoenix;
or from the stars
that in the imperial sky shine forth,
either curious or inattentive,
some of their bright rays
could cause her love to falter
and to my mind, a grave affront.
I promise myself all favor,
I am grateful for your courtesy,
esteeming him to a degree
that inspires great respect;
and I beg, since you are discreet,
serious defects
even though they may not cause anything unexpected,
prevention cannot assure
that one who stings in madness
may not do so willfully.

---

[1] In Greek mythology a giant with one hundred eyes.

45. Dándome por asunto el sentimiento de una persona a un desdén que la hicieron después de una ausencia grande.[1] Soneto.

Cuando borda de perlas el aurora
tapetes que matizan bellas flores,
en lisonjas retornan los favores
con que las enriquece y enamora.
Luego la sigue el sol, que a rayos dora
la variedad vistosa de colores,
a quien las aves repitiendo amores
hacen salva con música sonora.
Así yo, cuando vi la aurora hermosa
del sol que desterró la niebla oscura
de una ausencia, si ya no sol ni ave,
racional la belleza milagrosa,
venero con verdad sencilla y pura,
y el premio fue un desdén severo y grave.

46. A instancia de una dama. Sentimiento de ausencia por ironía que le escribe a una persona por mí.

FIRST COLUMN

Permite a incultos rasguños
de mi pluma formar quejas
cuando materia da el alma
en el sentir de tu ausencia.
De ti no quiero quejarme,
si de mi contraria estrella,
pues, en la orfandad que paso,
aun no me acompañan penas.
De mi pesar no encarezco
cuanto me aflige y molesta
por no hallar en nuestro idioma
término que le encarezca.
De los que arrojo suspiros,
de las que repito endechas
a amor consulto la causa
en mi soledad amena.

---

[1] Serrano y Sanz, 366; Olivares and Boyce, 1st ed., 330; Olivares and Boyce, 2nd ed., 249.

45. Taking as my theme the feelings of a person who is disdained after a long absence. Sonnet.

When the dawn embroiders with pearls
tapestries adorned by beautiful flowers,
in flattery it return the favors
with which it enriches them and makes them fall in love.
Then the sun follows her and in rays makes golden
the spectacular variety of colors,
to whom the birds, repeating love,
make a salute with sonorous music.
As when I saw the beautiful dawn
of the sun that exiled the dark mist
of an absence, if not now sun or bird,
the miraculous rational beauty
of a spring of simple and pure truth,
and the reward was severe and grievous disdain.

46. At the request of a lady. Writing ironically about feelings of absence.

May the unlearned scratching
of my pen form complaints
when material is presented to the soul
about the feelings of absence.
About you, I do not wish to complain,
that due to contrary fate,
I must spend time as an orphan
where even grief does not accompany me.
I do not exaggerate my grief
even though it greatly afflicts and bothers me
for I do not find in our language
a term that makes it more valuable.
For those [griefs] I sigh,
and I write poems,
consulting with love the cause
in my pleasant loneliness.

Bien que duermo a sueño suelto,
y el pensamiento en cadenas,
si comodidad arguye,
dicen que indicia tristeza.
Que estoy triste no te intimo,
sólo diré que me alegra

SECOND COLUMN
la música concertada
de algunas voces diversas.
Que todo instrumento acorde
mis oídos lisonjea
y los que eran chirimías
a cornamutas[1] me suenan.
Comedido el sentimiento
no ha llamado, no, a las puertas
de mis ojos, que llorar
más tamaño no es fineza.
Las lágrimas detenidas
son venenosas saetas
del corazón, y únicamente
de veneno le preserva.
No pido me le remitas,
porque cansarte recela
mi cortesía, ni escribo
más, pues, que sabes mis veras.
Si diamante por lo fino
en esta ausencia te muestras,
yo seré de cristal firme
que es de cristal mi firmeza.
Que, si ausencia causa olvido,
yo hago excepción de su regla,
como verás, pues, me acuerdo
de escribirte esta estafeta.

47. De Navidad. Romance.

FIRST COLUMN
Qué de luces, qué de voces,
qué de plumas de matiz
bordan la noche dichosa,

---

[1] For "cornamusas" or hunting horns or bagpipes.

I sleep well and perhaps dream
and my thought enchained,
for comfort they say,
indicates sadness.
I do not insinuate that I am sad,
I will only say that I am happy

with the harmonious music
of diverse voices.
For every well-tuned instrument
flatters my ears
and those that are wind instruments
sound to me like hunting horns.
Moderate sentiment
has not called, no, to the gates
of my ears, for crying
more loudly is not elegant.
Restrained tears
are poisonous arrows
of the heart, and only
preserve it from poisoning.
I do not ask you to forgive me
because I fear that my courtesy
may bore you, nor do I write
more, since you know my limits.
If you are sharp as a diamond
in your absence,
I will be hard crystal
for my strength is of crystal.
If absence causes forgetfulness,
I make an exception to the rule,
as you will see, since I agreed
to write you this post.

47. Ballad about Christmas.

Light lamps, sing,
what plumes of all hues
surround the fortunate night

pueblan el viento sutil.
A publicar de Dios hombre
del nacimiento feliz,
bellas escuadras descienden
de ese globo de zafir [sic].
En albergue pobre nace
su ser humanando allí
porque extrañezas el hombre
deje ya de repetir,
rústica tropa le asiste
y, pensando divertir,
del hermoso infante el llanto,
un pastor dice así:
"Niño que nacido habéis,
enhorabuena para mí,
más de veinte mil docenas
de mi pebro[1] recibid.
En nombre de los pastores
a hablar[2], señor, vengo aquí
porque todos dicen, cabro,
como un proprio [sic] serafín.

SECOND COLUMN
Que sois muy sabio me dicen
y de la corte venís,
mas no sé hablaros oculto
que al sol a hablar aprendí.
Yo que Pero Gil me nombro
porque, con perdón, nací
cuando me parió mi madre
en sumo del perejil.
Hijo soy del mayoral
alcalde que antaño huí,
y tengo un chocotilla,[3]
más hermosa que Merlín.
Con vos quijera casarla,
porque luego des[de] que os vi,
que seréis hombre de bien

---

[1] For "pueblo."
[2] "Habrar" in manuscipt.
[3] For "chicotilla."

and populate the subtle wind.
To publicize about God made man
of this happy birth,
beautiful hosts descend
from that sapphire-like orb.
In poor lodgings
there He is made human,
and to man's amazement
leaves off repeating,
and a rustic troupe attends,
thinking to gladden
the beautiful crying infant,
a shepherd speaks thus:
"Child, you have been born,
warm welcome I give You
and more than twenty thousand dozen
more receive from my village.
In the name of the shepherds
I come here to speak
because all say, sweet one,
that you are like a seraph.

For they say that You are very wise
and that You come from the court,
but I do not know how to speak to You indirectly
for I learned to speak in the light of the sun.[1]
My name is Pedro Gil
because, pardon me, I was born
when my mother gave birth to me
upon the parsley.[2]
I am the son of the head shepherd,
from whom I fled in days gone by,
and I have a little girl,
prettier than Merlin.
I would like You to marry her,
because ever since I saw You
I knew you were a fine man,

---

[1] In other words, he does not know the "niceties" of court speech and will speak bluntly and directly, since it is the only way he knows.

[2] Notice the clever rhyme between "Gil," the shepherd's last name, and "perejil" meaning parsley.

he llegado a descorrir.[1]
Es como vos, encarnada,
y habéis de quererla, en fin,
pues, dicen su semejante
cada cual suele seguir.
Esposa vuesa[2] ha de ser,
Torivilla,[3] y advertid:
no se entrampe allá en la corte
donde ay trampantojos mil.

FIRST COLUMN
Queredla como a vuestra alma
y que me queréis a mi;
haced cuenta, que lo mismo
creo haréis sin rehortir,[4]
esa cara buenos hechos
promete y aun juro a ti[5]
que habéis de ser buen pastor,
según mi pergenio diz.[6]

SECOND COLUMN
Ea, ea, pastores,
requiebros y amores
al niño decid,
que es hermosa flor de la gracia
y de la gloria, bizarro abril."

48. A la Purificación de Nuestra Señora. Romance.

FIRST COLUMN
En los brazos de la aurora,
el sol más resplandeciente
sale vistiéndola a luces
cuando a perlas la enriquece;
a los rayos de sus ojos
sirve el cristal que disuelven
espejo de su hermosura

---
[1] For "descorrer."
[2] For "vuestra."
[3] For "torbellina," a lively person [?].
[4] Unknown meaning. Perhaps equivalent to "rebatir"?
[5] Manuscript reads "atis."
[6] For "dice."

as I have observed.
she is like you, fleshy[1]
and You will love her forever,
since they say that one should seek
out one's own kind.
Your wife she shall be,
a lively one, but watch out
and do not get ensnared in the court
where there are a thousand tricky deceits.[2]

Love her as you do your own soul
and as You love me;
be aware, that this
I believe, without doubt,
your face promises good deeds
and I even swear to You
that you will be a Good Shepherd,
as all appearances tell me.

Ah, ah, shepherds,
endearments and love
pronounce to the child.
who is a beautiful flower of grace
and of glory, a generous April."

48. Ballad for the Purification of Our Lady.

On the arms of the dawn,
the most resplendent sun
comes out dressed in lights
enriched like pearls;
the rays of her eyes
serve as a crystal that dissolves
the mirror of her beauty

---

[1] The poet is playing with the concept of the incarnate ("encarnado") Christ and the plump girl that the shepherd thinks would be a good match for the baby Jesus.

[2] This is a clever criticism of politics at the royal court when the court actually referred to earlier in the poem is the "court of heaven."

que en cambiantes la encarecen.
Llega al templo, pues, María
que es aunque grande se ostente
corta esfera a tanta aurora,
a mucho sol, cielo breve,
de su esposo acompañada
a purificar se viene.
Que pariedad[1] con María
sólo a Joseph le conceden.

SECOND COLUMN
No puede quedar más pura,
antes la pureza puede
acrisolarse en María,
para ser permaneciente,
Dios para enseñar al hombre
el cumplimiento en sus leyes,
quiere que hombre le reputen,
aunque Dios sedes sospeche
porque no le precipiten
del mundo impulsos luz bebes;
con preceptos le corrige,
con humildades le advierte.
Ya de la región impirea,[2]
hoy de su culto las aras
al primogénito ofrece,
tropas celestes descienden
en el acto a ser ministros
porque a su ser pertenece.[3]

25v

Y entre el golfo vistoso de plumas
que el viento matizan cuando las mueve,
voces suenan, quedan a la aurora
y al sol de justicia, mil parabienes.

---

[1] For "paridad."
[2] For "imperia." At this point in the manuscript, there is an asterisk in the margin, and, above, at the end of the previous poem we find these lines: "hoy de su culto / las aras al primogenitor ofrece," which I have added to the transcription above.
[3] Here the manuscript reads "estribo [estribillo] a la vuelta," i.e., 25v where we find the refrain.

enhanced in ever-changing colors.
Mary arrives at the temple
and even though it is grand, she gives off
so much light that it is brightly illuminated,
as sunny as a brief glimpse of heaven,
accompanied by her spouse
she comes to purify herself.
Such equality with Mary
is only conceded to Joseph.

She could not be more pure
for pureness itself can be
refined in Mary,
for through her permanency,[1]
God shows to man
the fulfillment of His laws,
for He wants man to appreciate her.
even though God anticipates our thirst
because we are in the rush
of our worldly impulses, He gives us light to drink;
and with precepts corrects him [mankind]
and warns with humility.
Now from His imperious domain,
today for His veneration
He offers a dowry to His first-born
and celestial troops descend
to be ministers in the act
because she belongs to Him.

And among the colorful gulf of plumes
that move about blown by the wind,
voices sound, giving to the dawn
and to the sun of justice, a thousand congratulations.

---

[1] In virginity.

49. Al Señor Santiago, patrón de España, villancico.

Pregunta: ¿Quién es aquel capitán
de quien enemigos tiemblan
cuando el eco de su nombre
rinde africanas banderas?
Repuesta: Es el gran patrón de España,
de la fe, muro y defensa
que adquirió gloriosa fama
por las armas y las letras.
Pregunta: Su buena gracia os pregunto
y gracia su nombre sea,
pues la voz de sus hazañas
le da tantas excelencias.[1]
Respuesta: Santiago invicto, rayo de la guerra,
le apellidan los cielos y la tierra:
al arma, al arma, al arma
al arma, guerra, guerra;
que se embisten los campos porque se encuentran . . . .[2]
Coplas: El rayo que brota luces
entre confusas tinieblas
que se opusieron al lastre
de la militante iglesia,
hoy quede un mortal eclipse
triunfa en las sombras funestas
más puro sol se construye
de indeficiente belleza.
La república de luces
a su vista se renueva
bien que de su luz vencidas,
en tanto golfo se anegan.
Girasoles de sus rayos,
si volantes primaveras,
serafines le ministran,
émulos de su pureza.

26r

---

[1] In the right-hand margin next to this strophe, we read "no es mía esta copla" [this strophe is not mine].

[2] Belisarda inserts the comment: "Y no sé cómo decía más que no era mío el estribillo."

49. Carol to Saint James, the Patron of Spain.

Question: Who is that captain
who makes the enemy tremble
when at the sound of his name
they lay down their African banners?[1]
Answer: He is the great patron of Spain,
of the faith, a wall and a defense
who won glorious fame
by arms and by letters.
Question: I ask you about his great grace
and may his name be blessed,
since the renown of his deeds
tells of such excellences.
Answer: Ever-victorious Saint James, lightning bolt of war,
you are called by the heavens and on earth:
to arms, to arms, to arms,
to arms, war, war.
The camps charge and encounter each other . . . .[2]
Verses: The lightning bolt that shoots forth lights
in the confused darkness
that oppose the weight
of the militant church,
today a mortal eclipse
triumphs in the fatal shadows
and constructs the purest sun
of perfect beauty.
The republic of lights
is renewed at the sight of him,
as if conquered by his brighter light
that floods the gulf.
Sunflowers to his rays
flying in the spring,
seraphim minister to him,
rivals of his purity.

---

[1] A reference to Islamic troops from northern Africa.
[2] The phrase: "I do not know how to finish the refrain because it is not mine" occurs here in the poem itself as the next verse. It was obviously meant as an editorial comment.

Tan divino le reputan
que por dar de humano señas
entregando al labio el cáliz,
el cuello al cuchillo entrega,
un corazón tan bizarro
destroza la parca fiera;
muere de amor porque Diego
le hizo blanco de sus flechas.

50. **Décimas a un sujeto bizarro que perdió una canonjía de Toledo por oposición teniendo el día antes de votarse grandes esperanzas de conseguirla.**[1]

FIRST COLUMN
1ª No ya de esperanza alguna,
fiéis la dicha, señor,
que como caduca flor,
nace y expira en la cuna,
a la inconstante fortuna,
en quien siempre he conocido
que la dicha de escogido
con los méritos no iguala,
paga pensión vuestra gala
de los gajes de entendido.

SECOND COLUMN
2ª Aunque logrado no habéis
triunfo tanto en ser premiado,
hoy la gloria de admirado
en la atención poséis
lucir cuanto merecéis,
porque no tenéis segundo;
en aquesta razón fundo
que no os volváis a oponer
que, según llego a entender,
no habrá con quien en el mundo.[2]
3ª La riqueza temporal,
adquirir no habéis podido

---

[1] This poem does not appear in Serrano y Sanz's inventory.
[2] Next stanza in one column at bottom of page. Also, in a box in the left margin, we read "Lloran tres damas de sentimiento del fracaso" [Three ladies mourn your failure].

They deem him so divine
that to prove his humanity
he puts his lip to the chalice,
and his head to the sword;
so brave a heart
destroys cruel death
and dies for love because James
made himself a target for his arrows [of love].

50. **Décimas about a gallant subject. How a Canon of Toledo lost an election when only the day before he had great hopes of winning it.**

1st There is no hope now,
pay heed to this saying, my lord,
that as a flower withers,
dies, and expires in its crib,
so does inconstant fortune
in whom I have always known
that luck does not choose
in equal measure to one's merits
and your performance pays a dividend
from the fees of the learned.

2nd Even though you did not win,
your triumph is justly awarded
by being so admired today
in the attention you have earned,
to shine as you deserve
because there is no one second to you;
I base myself on that reason
that you will not stand for election again,
since, as I understand it,
there is no one in the world who can compete with you.

3rd Worldly riches,
you were unable to acquire

y que no hay, sea conocido,
bien que no venga del mal;
puesto que os dan sin igual
tres albas en perlas solo
más riqueza que de un polo
a otro, el mundo enriquece
que perlas de albas merece
quien se acredita de Apolo.

51. Romance de un cortesano.[1] 27r

FIRST COLUMN
No quiero, discreta Filis,
que me infamen de grosero;
ni del desdén los rigores,
ni del rigor los extremos;
que como sólo procuro
estimar merecimientos,
aunque amante los adoro
sin gusto no los pretendo.
La misma injuria[2] que paso
tan generoso agradezco,
que desmintiendo su agravio,
por favor la lisonjeo.
Como solo amor estimo,
como solo amor me contento,
comedido en la esperanza
y cortes en los deseos,
preceptos guarda el decoro,
tan obediente al respeto,
que le niega de atrevido
licencias al pensamiento.
Dudoso triunfo acredita
en el blasón de tu imperio,
amor, que tiene albedrío
tan obediente a preceptos.

---

[1] Olivares and Boyce, 1st ed., 353–54; Olivares and Boyce, 2nd ed., 253–55. Again, I include this poem among Belisarda's since she may here be playing the role of the "cortesano" who supposedly authored this poem, in order to make her "reply" in the following poem.

[2] "Infuria" in Olivares and Boyce.

but it is well known that
good can come from bad;
since even if they give you
three albs of pearls without equal,
more richness than from pole
to pole, the world will enrich
he who deserves albs of pearls,
he whose worth is approved by Apollo.

51. **Ballad of a courtier.**

I do not wish, discreet Phyllis,
that you defame me as uncouth;
nor the disdain of your harshness,
nor the rigor of your extremes;
since I only want
to esteem your merits,
even though a lover adores them
I do not claim them with pleasure.
For the insult that I experience
I generously thank you,
by denying the offense
I actually delight in it.
For only love do I esteem
and I am only content with love,
moderate in hope
and courteous in my desires,
decorum exacts precepts,
and so obedient to respect,
that it denies to the bold
free license of thought.
A doubtful triumph authorizes
in the honor of your empire,
love, that with free will
is so obedient to your rules.

FIRST COLUMN

Ya de tu desdén despojo,
hermosa Filis, no quiero
negarme al rigor constante
por los peligros del riesgo;
pues, cuando muera esperando,
baste la gloria que tengo
de elección que, a la esperanza,
le rompe los privilegios.
La mudanza en mis desdichas,
ni la busco ni la espero,
que no quiero que me arguyan,
que de cobarde las dejo,
si posible imaginara
que a los males que padezco,
siendo el remedio un favor,
llegar pudiera el remedio.
A esta[1] dicha me negara,
porque con reparo cuerdo
cuando favor no le dude,
le he de imaginar violento,
como del veneno siempre
de tu desdén me alimento,
no basta para matarme
que se repita el veneno.

FIRST COLUMN

Que en todo favor te excuses
disculpada te confieso;
mas negarte agradecida,
si no es malicia, es desprecio;
de tanto rigor el rayo
no deje cenizas hecho
del corazón más rendido
el más noble atrevimiento,
que no es adorarte agravio
en la observancia del duelo,
tan libre que te provoque
a menos precios sangrientos;

---

[1] Olivares and Boyce reads "hasta"

For because of your disdain I must relinquish,
beautiful Phyllis, I do not want
to deny myself your constant rigor
for the dangers of the risk;
for when I die still hoping,
the glory I have will be enough
for I chose it and hope
destroys privileges.
Change in my misfortunes,
I do not look for nor do I expect,
for I do not want to be reproached
for having abandoned them out of cowardice,
if I could but imagine
that for the pains that I suffer,
being the remedy a favor,
I could obtain the remedy.
But this good fortune is denied to me,
because with prudent qualms,
when one does not doubt the favor,
I must imagine it absurd,
for always the poison
of your disdain nourishes me,
but it is not enough to kill me
so I drink of that venom again and again.

For in every favor that you reject
I confess you blameless;
but to deny you gratitude,
if it is not malice, it is scorn;
so mighty a lightning bolt
does not leave any ashes
of the most devoted heart
the most noble boldness,
for it is not a grievance to adore you
in the observance of pain,
so freely given, only provokes in you
bloody contempt;

que tendrás dueño dichoso,
ni lo dudo ni lo temo,
más dichoso le aseguro,
pero amante más no puedo.
No más, Filis, que al dolor
quiero volverme tan presto,
que conozca que le busco
cuando hallándole me pierdo.

RETURNING TO 27R, SECOND COLUMN
52. Mi respuesta por curiosidad por los asonantes [sic].[1]

No podrán, discreto Fabio,
castigarte por grosero
de mi libre voluntad
los rigurosos extremos;
que como el cielo te hizo
rico de merecimientos,
y amante cortés me obligas,
no ser ingrata pretendo.
La nobleza de tu amor
reconocida agradezco,
tanto que mi gusto sólo
con su gala lisonjeo;
de tu proceder bizarro
me satisfago y contento.
Cree, pues, que ya te pagan[2]
grandes sí honestos deseos,
porque tú sólo has sabido
con industrioso respeto
abrir la puerta del alma
para entrar al pensamiento
que un amante comedido
tiene en las almas imperio,
y, en mi opinión, más obliga
cuando obedece preceptos.

---

[1] Belisarda uses the same e-o assonant rhyme-scheme in the even-numbered lines as did the previous poem.

[2] Olivares and Boyce reads "paga."

you will have a fortunate master,
I do not doubt it nor do I fear it,
more fortunate I assure you,
but that lover I cannot be.
Only to the pain, Phyllis,
do I wish to quickly return,
and know that I will look for pain
and when I find it, I will be lost.[1]

52. My response out of curiosity about the assonant rhymes.[2]

They cannot, discreet Fabio,
accuse you as insensitive
to the harshest extremes
of my free will;
since heaven made you
rich in merits,
and as a perfect courtly lover you oblige
me not to be ungrateful.
The nobility of your love
I recognize and I am grateful,
so much so that it is my pleasure
only to praise your gallantry;
of your brave actions
I am satisfied and content.
Trust that you will be rewarded
greatly for your honest desires,
because you alone have known how
with unfailing respect
to open the door of my soul
and enter my thoughts,
for a courteous lover
reigns in souls
and, in my opinion, is more compelling
when he who obeys the rules.

---

[1] The following poem appears side-by-side with the previous "Ballad of a Courtier" as Belisarda's reply.

[2] Rhyming of vowels only in the last word, including and following the accented syllable. In the ballad, the rhyme occurs in the even-numbered lines.

CONTINUED IN SECOND COLUMN 27v
No quiero ser desdeñosa,
ni menos premiarte quiero
con favores que ocasionen
a mi decoro algún riesgo;
que para corresponderte,
precisamente no tengo
necesidad de romper
del recato privilegios.
Perseverancia en tu amor,
no sé si engañada espero;
y atenta a cuanto me obligas,
el crédito libre dejo,
viéndote desconfiado,
tus mismos males padezco,
porque piadosa quisiera
darles alivio o remedio;
mas tan discreto te admiro
que en todo reparo cuerdo,
como dices, no estimarás
favor que juzgues violento.
Bien fundadas esperanzas
le dan amor alimento,
siendo triaca[1] prudente
contra el eficaz veneno,

CONTINUED ON 28R, SECOND COLUMN 28r
que estoy más que agradecida
a tus finezas confieso,
que no apreciar lo que valen
fuera ignorante desprecio.
No hay rigor, centella o rayo
que deje cenizas hecho
atrevimiento que es tuyo,
porque es cuerdo atrevimiento;
y, cuando en mi ofensa alguno
usaras, no ley del duelo,
mas la de mi estimación,
fraguara rayos sangrientos,

---

[1] Olivares and Boyce reads "tú acá."

I do not wish to be disdainful,
nor do I wish to reward you
with the favors that may cause
me to risk my reputation;
for, in order to respond to you,
accordingly, I do not have to,
from necessity, break
the requirements of modesty.
Perseverance in your love,
I hope for, not knowing if I am deceived;
and attentive to all that you oblige me,
I leave in full trust,
seeing you so unconvinced,
I suffer your same woes.
because I would like to be piteous
and give relief or remedy;
but I admire that you are so discreet
that in all sensible qualms,
as you say, you would not value
any favor you judged indecorous.
Well-founded hopes
nourish love,
being a prudent antidote
against deadly poison,

and I am more than grateful,
I confess, for your elegances,
for not valuing what they are worth
would be ignorant disdain.
There is no rigor, spark, or lightning bolt
that leaves ashes behind
equal to your boldness,
because it is wise daring;
and, when in my offense
you used, not the law of revenge,
but that of my estimation,
forged bloody rays,

cuantas Circes[1] te combaten,
que te contrasten no temo,
porque dudar tu verdad,
siento en mi agravio, no puedo,
paga mi satisfacción
con la tuya, no tan presto
te lamentes, que en tus dudas
mi crédito y gusto pierdo.

28v [Blank]

53. Romance que se cantó entre dos en la Concepción Real de Toledo, al Rvmo. P. Fray Baltasar Fernández, su Provincial de la provincia de Castilla, entrando a visitar el convento. 29r

FIRST COLUMN
1ª Publique mi voz el gozo
que hoy ocasiona a sus hijas
un padrenuestro del cielo
que su nombre santifica.
2ª Si en dulce y canoro metro
el gozo común publicas,
permite, pues, que la causa
alabe yo de esta dicha.
1ª Para lograr yo el deseo
que alabanzas solicita
de la causa, los efectos
son del acierto premisas.
2ª Ceder en mí el desempeño
es obligación precisa
pues, que son notorias cuantas
a procurarle me obligan.
1ª Sobre que el gran Baltasar
es blasón de la provincia
¿Qué dirás? Si en este solo
mil epítetos se cifran.

SECOND COLUMN
2ª Qué noblemente piadoso
con disposición divina
la libertad que Dios deja,

---

[1] In Homer's *Odyssey*, an enchantress who turned men into swine. Used to describe enchanting or astute women.

as many enchanting women as you may encounter
will be contrary to you, I do not doubt,
because doubting your truthfulness,
I cannot feel any offense,
and my satisfaction rewards
yours, not so quickly
as you would like, for in your doubts
I lose my trust and my pleasure.

53. **Ballad to be sung by two voices in the Royal Conception of Toledo for the most Reverend Father Balthazar Fernández, the Provincial of Castile[1] upon the occasion of his visit to the convent.**

1st Let my voice proclaim the joy
that today your daughters enjoy
and an "Our Father"
offer to praise your name.
2nd If in sweet and harmonious meter
you spread our common joy,
please permit that to the cause
of this good fortune, I may sing praise.
1st To achieve my desire
to solicit praises
for the cause, the effects
are certain premises.
2nd To grant me the privilege
is a distinct obligation
for the causes are obvious
and require the endeavor.
1st About the great Balthazar,
who is the honor of the province,
what can you say? To him alone
one can ascribe a thousand epithets.

2nd How nobly charitable
with divine disposition
the freedom that God gives,

---

[1] Religious authority over the convents of a province.

Baltasar la supedita.
1ª Dirás que es su descendencia
de prosa pía esclarecida,
y yo más, que a su nobleza
sus virtudes se anticipan.
2ª Diré que cultor de Cristo
en sus pensiles cultiva
maravillas que, a su ejemplo,
flores del sol se acreditan.
1ª Yo diré, pues, que reduce,
con atención erudita,
los ánimos femeniles
a su obediencia benigna.
2ª Pues, si a porfía le alabas,
vana será la porfía;
porque has de alabarle poco
cuando más pienses que explicas.

FIRST COLUMN
1ª Digo, pues, que a su obediencia
mi alma se sacrifica
porque para empleo tanto
es poco empeño la vida.

SECOND COLUMN
1ª 2ª Viva al Rvmo. Padre eternos días,
pues sus hijas consuela, piadoso
con su visita;
viva siempre feliz vida
en la voz de la fama que adquiere
y le eterniza.

54. A Santo Domingo. Villancico.

FIRST COLUMN
1º Esta luz que ilumina los cielos
con alma tan pura de bello esplendor,
miren la que del sol de justicia
es rayo de luz que la iglesia ilustró.
2º ¿Cómo fallece su luz
si nace de tanto sol?
1º Porque exhaló fervorosa
la que el sol le dispensó

Balthazar subdues.
1st You say that his legacy will be
his clear and pious prose,
and I, too, because of his nobility,
foresee his virtues.
2nd I say that he is a gardener of Christ
who cultivates in his beautiful gardens
marvels in the same way that
flowers give credit to the sun.
1st I will say that he brings under control,
with erudite attention,
feminine wills
to benign obedience.
2nd If you persist in praising him,
persistence will be vain;
because you will little praise him
for the more you try the less you explain.

1st I say that to his obedience
my soul renders itself
because such a vocation
is a life of little hardship.

1st 2nd Long life and eternal days for the most Reverend Father,
he charitably consoles his daughters
with his visit;
may he live a happy life
and may voices proclaim his fame
and eternalize his name.

54. Carol for Saint Dominic.

1st This light that illuminates the heavens
with a pure soul of beautiful splendor,
look at him who, as the sun of justice,
as a ray of light, enlightens the church.
2nd How could his light die
if it is born from such a sun?
1st For it fervently gave off
what the sun conferred on it

aquí, aquí del amor
que aunque rayo ha vencido,
Domingo esclarecido
que el mundo alumbra
tan bizarro ha quedado
estando más postrado,
que amor solo han juzgado
que rinde su valor;
pues, ven, que hoy la muerte
en vida trocó.
2º ¿Cómo el Guzmán valiente
rendido se vio?

SECOND COLUMN
1º Porque goce rendido
trofeos de amor.
2º ¿Cómo glorias de Jesucristo
llega a poseer?
1º Porque en fe de su gloria
defendió su fe.
2º ¿Cómo si muere el mundo
su luz no pierde?
1º Porque hereda reflejos
que la conserven.
2º ¿Cómo tantos reflejos
sol le acreditan?
1º Porque nieblas destierra
de la herejía.
2º ¿Cómo sola una estrella
cielo le aclama?
1º Porque es norte en el cielo
de estrellas tantas.

55. A la muy venerable Sra. Doña Beatriz de Silva, fundadora del Real de la Concepción de Toledo. 30r

FIRST COLUMN
La flor más brillante y pura
de la corte lusitana,
que nació prodigio hermoso
por naturaleza y gracia;

here, here that from love,
although his ray has been conquered,
bright-shining Dominic
who illuminates the world
so bravely has stood
by being the most prostrated,
they have judged that only love
surrenders to his valor;
see, then, that today death
has been turned into life.
2nd How did valiant Guzmán[1]
see himself conquered?

1st He rejoiced in surrender
as a triumph for love.
2nd How did he come to possess
the glories of Jesus Christ?
1st Because in testimony of his glory
he defended his faith.
2nd How, if he has died, the world
does not lose light?
1st Because it inherits reflections
that preserve it.
2nd How is so much gleaming
authorized by the sun?
1st Because it destroys the fog
of heresy.
2nd How as a singular star
does heaven acclaims him?
1st Because he is a guide in heaven
for so many stars.

55. **To the most venerable Lady Beatrice of Silva, founder of the Royal Convent of the Conception in Toledo.**

The most brilliant and pure flower
of the Lusitanian court,
who was born a beautiful prodigy
of nature and grace;

---

[1] Saint Dominic's family name.

la que es de monarcas prima
y fue Beatriz de las damas
prima que sonó entre todas
divinamente templada.
Ésta que de Portugal
es honorífica palma,
de Castilla lauro insigne,
del cielo, primor y gala.
Silva o Selva la apellidan
de maravillas tan raras
que dando asunto a mil plumas
ministran vuelo a su fama.
Pomposa gala del siglo
por un traje pobre cambia
y sólo luce en domingo
por humillarse en su casa.

SECOND COLUMN
Objeto puede el amor
de tantas rendidas almas
si caudillo de sancta fe
que alistó para Dios tantas.
Por el [sic] orden de Francisco
logra aciertos su esperanza,
pues, hijas, en él congrega
que de Dios el culto ensalzan.
De tu vida en el progreso[1]
vio milagrosas hazañas
el mundo que hoy acreditan
sus reliquias veneradas;
en los últimos deliquios
que ya su muerte amenazan
con orfandad de dos soles
belleza tanta desmaya.

---

[1] "Discurso" is written above "progreso" between the lines of the poem and seems to indicate that the poet was vacilitando between these two words to end this line.

she who is the cousin of kings
Beatrice was, of all the ladies,
the prime[1] who among all sounded
divinely tuned.
This one from Portugal
is an honored insignia of victory,
of Castile an illustrious glory,
of heaven, a treasure and a celebration.
Silva or Selva[2] is her last name
and her rare marvels
provide subjects for a thousand pens
that give flight to her fame.
The pompous festivities of the world
she exchanged for poor clothing
and she only wears finery on Sunday
humbly in her own house.

Love has such power
over surrendered souls
and such a leader of the holy faith
brings so many to the service of God.
In the order of Saint Francis
her hope achieves great things
because, daughters, into this order she gathers
us for the greater Glory of God.
In the course of your life
miraculous deeds were seen
in the world that now justify
the veneration of your relics;
in the last ecstasies
your death threatened
to orphan two suns
when so much beauty fades.

---

[1] Prime chord in music.
[2] A play on words since "silva" is a miscellany of musical compositions and "selva" is a forest or jungle.

Muere, y glorias comunica
de aquel que apenas miraban
rostro que cielo le admiran
de una estrella que en él campa

índice fue de sus glorias,
si no lucero de este alba
que amaneció al día eterno
del premio justo que alcanza.
Más en vano presume el que intenta
decir de Beatriz perfecciones y gracias
si de ingenio divino carece,
que vuelos merezca de angélicas alas.
Pensamiento atrevido para, para
que en un mar de prodigios ciego te embarcas.
Espera, espera, detente, aguarda
que a negarte podrás si navegas
el golfo supremo de sus alabanzas.

56. Romance melancólico.[1]

FIRST COLUMN

Pensamiento, si pensáis
en dar a mi mal remedio,
mal pensáis, porque es un mal
causado de pensamientos,
pienso con ajenos gustos
engañar propios deseos
y es engaño donde el alma,
pensando más, se halla menos.
Si en dormir buscar descanso
por ser el morir diseño,
más me canso porque lidio
con enemigos desvelos
siempre intento hallar alivio,
y siempre queda el intento
con el logro en esperanza
y con la esperanza a riesgo,
o apenas alivio hallo

---

[1] Partially transcribed in Serrano y Sanz (first 32 lines) and fully transcribed in Olivares and Boyce, 1st ed., 351–52.

She dies, and communicates glories,
although espied by very few
that face so admired by heaven
is a star that shines brightly there

as indicator of her glories,
she is a star at dawn
who awoke to the eternal day,
and earns her just reward.
But one tires in vain
to tell of Beatrice's perfections and graces
if one lacks divine wit
that can take flight on angelic wings.
A daring thought must stop, for
it embarks blindly upon a sea of wonders.
Wait, wait, stop, wait
for you will fail if you sail
the vast gulf of her praises.

56. Melancholic ballad.

Thought, if you plan
to provide a remedy for my pain,
you are not thinking clearly, because this is a grief
caused by thoughts,
I think with other delights
to deceive my own desires,
for there is deceit where the soul,
thinking more, finds less.
If I try to find rest in sleep
being so much like death,
I become more tired because I fight
with enemy wakefulness
and I always try to find relief,
and the intent always remains,
in hopes of achieving it,
and with hope itself at risk,
hardly[1] any relief do I find

---

[1] "Apenas" meaning "hardly," is a play on words with the phrase "a penas" (to pains) in the following verse.

cuando a penas ya le pierdo,
el intento examinando
convertido en escarmiento.
En mi dolor no hay templanza,
y si a la memoria apelo,

SECOND COLUMN
para el que tengo presente
me da pasados remedios.
En fin, peno, siento y callo,
por no decir lo que siento,
que sólo puedo quejarme
de qué quejarme no puedo.
Nacer amable es estrella,
suerte nacer con ingenio;
pero si falta ventura,
nada es gloria y todo infierno.
Nuestra derrota sigamos,
triste corazón, sin miedo
por el golfo de desdichas,
rumbo más seguro y cierto.
¡Ay de mí triste!
¡Socorro, cielos!,
¡Que me anego sin agua
en sentimientos!
¡Socorro, cielos, socorro os pido![1]
¡Dad en llanto a mis penas,
algún alivio!

57. Romance burlesco.[2] 31v

FIRST COLUMN
¡Oh, cómo intenta Leonida,
ya más que amorosa, cruel,
vengar previstos olvidos
de un ausente descortés!
Auséntase, pues, Lisardo,
y aunque asegura el volver,

---

[1] "Os pido" is missing in the Olivares and Boyce transcription (1st ed., 352). .

[2] Partially transcribed in Serrano y Sanz, 367–68 and fully transcribed in Olivares and Boyce, 1st ed., 361–62; Olivares and Boyce, 2nd ed., 257–59. Olivares and Boyce identify the folio as 31. This ballad is found on folios 31v and 32r of the manuscript.

when I lose my pains,
and examining my intention,
it is turned into a punishment.
In my grief there is no temperance,
and if I appeal to memory,

what I have at present
only serves up past remedies.
In all, I suffer, I hurt, and I keep quiet,
not saying what I truly feel,
because I can only complain
about what I cannot complain.
To be born lovable is good fortune,
to be born witty is lucky;
but if luck is lacking,
nothing is glorious and all is hell.
Let us follow our defeat,
sad heart, without fear
through the gulf of misfortunes,
the most certain and sure path.
Ay, sad me!
Help me heavens!
Since I am drowning without water
in my feelings!
Help, heavens, help I beg!
Let weeping give my pains
some relief!

57. Burlesque ballad.

Oh, how Leonida tries,
now more cruel than loving,
to revenge the predictable neglect
of an absent and discourteous lover!
Lisardo took his leave,
and even though he promised to return,

sabe Leonida que parte
al todo de su interés.
Prendas que estimaba el alma,
o ya de esmalte o pincel,
arroja y borra, ultrajando
al que dueño suyo fue.
Papeles al fuego entrega;
¿quién ha visto que se den
castigos de inquisición
a sobras tantas de fe?
Mas no es mucho que parezca
bárbara con el que, infiel,
la ley que le debe rompe,
porque se muda a otra ley.
Viéndola entre sentimientos
vendida al fiero tropel,
Anarda el motivo injusto
intenta desvanecer.

SECOND COLUMN
Vuelve in ti, Leonida, dice;
deja el morir esta vez
de sentimientos de amante
para aquéllos de Teruel.
Tú piensas que esto de amar
censo de por vida es,
y de su amor cada uno
un ensayo puede hacer.
Todo galán considera
que es hombre, sí, no mujer;
y cual más, cual menos, toda
lana pelos viene a ser.
Si es necio no hay quien le escuche;
si es discreto y habla bien,
satiriza, ensarta y parla,

Leonida knows that he is leaving behind
all his interest in her.
Finery that the soul esteemed,
of enamel or of brush,
she throws out and erases, despising
the one to whom they belonged.
She throws paper into the fire;
who has seen imposed
such inquisitional punishments
for an abundance of faith?
But it does not seem
barbarous for he who, unfaithful,
breaks the law that he owes allegiance to
because he changes to another's law.
Seeing her with such feelings
all in a jumble,
Anarda tries to undo
the injustice.

Come to your senses, Leonida she says;
do not die this time
from lovers' distress
like those of Teruel.[1]
You think that this loving
is a life-long sentence,
but everyone in love
can have a rehearsal.
Every young man considers
that he is a man, certainly, and not a woman;
and a little more or a little less, all
wool becomes thread.[2]
If he is an idiot, no one listens to him;
if he is discreet and speaks well
he satirizes, spins yarns, and chatters away,

---

[1] Refers to the legend of the star-crossed lovers from Teruel, similar to the story of Romeo and Juliet. The story is told by several authors, and Belisarda probably knew the version by Juan Pérez de Montalbán (1602–1638), *Los amantes de Teruel*. Perhaps the best known version today is Juan Eugenio Hartzenbusch's romantic drama of the same name, published in 1837.

[2] A saying meaning that there is little difference between things of little worth or importance.

dicho, hecho y por hacer.
En ninguno hallarás medio,
y si le llega a tener,
ya esa cuenta le dan mano,
quiere tomarse hasta el pie.
Muy bien me parecen todos
y a todos pienso querer;
pero, ¿sujetarme a uno?,
Libera nos Domine.

FIRST COLUMN
Bendita mi libertad,
Dios la conserve, porque
viva libre, libre viva
por siempre jamás, amén.
Aprende de mí, Leonida,
rígete por mi arancel:
quiere a todos y a ninguno,
sin querer a dos por tres,

SECOND COLUMN
y encomienda ese tu ausente
al apóstol calabrés
con intención de olvidarte,
y yo en tanto cantaré:
Alalalalelá,
vaya y nunca vuelva;
alalalalelá, que si fuera a Argel,
vaya Dios con él.

58. Otra a petición de un músico.

FIRST COLUMN
Antes Belisa que el sol
al campo sale tan bella
que aves, flores, fuentes, ramas
que es el sol Belisa piensan.

32r

all said, done, and yet to do.
In no one will you find a happy medium,
and if you do,
if you give him a hand
he will also want to take a foot.
All men seem fine to me
and I propose to love them all;
but, subject myself to one?
May God liberate me.

Blessed be my liberty,
may God preserve it, so that
I may live freely, freely I may live
forever and ever, amen.
Learn from me, Leonida,
be guided by my rules:
love all and none,
without loving very often,

and give the safekeeping of your absent one
to the Calabrian apostle[1]
with the intention of forgetting,
and meanwhile I will sing:
Alalalalela,
may he go and never return;
Alalalalela, if he went to Algiers,[2]
may God be with him.

58. Another at the request of a musician.

Belisa, like the sun,
shines so beautifully on the countryside
that birds, flowers, springs, and trees bow down
thinking that Belisa is the sun.

---

[1] According to Acts 28:13, St. Paul was in Reggio Calabria and laid the foundations for Christianity in this region of southern Italy. Olivares and Boyce associate this Calabrian apostle with the devil since the region of Calabria is famous for witches and satanic rites (2nd ed., 259).

[2] Capital and major city of Algeria.

Para verse más lucidas
de tanto rayo en la esfera,
el ave a ser flor se inclina,
la flor a ser ave anhela.
A su vista, porque sirva
de soborno a su asistencia
ramas y flores la adulan
con esmeraldas y perlas
que ufanamente orgullosas
briosamente pelean.

SECOND COLUMN
Todas juntas por lograrla
cada cual por merecerla,
y haciendo la reseña
incitan la batalla,
clarines de pluma,
trompetas de nácar:
al arma, al arma, al arma,
al arma, guerra, guerra.
Las flores se embisten,
las aves se encuentran:
al arma, guerra, guerra,
al arma, al arma.
Las fuentes se despeñan
y esgrimen las ramas

   y aves, flores, ramas y fuentes,
  ay, rosas lidiando, bizarras se muestran,
   más si atenta Belissa las mira
 de amores rendidas suspenden la guerra.

FIRST COLUMN
Si no sol, era deidad;
si no deidad, primavera
que entre las flores madruga
compitiendo con las selvas.
Querer reducir la pluma
a números su belleza
es en un mar embarcarse
donde la vista se anega.
Airosa desnuda el guante,

Seeing themselves shining more brightly
from so much brightness in the firmament,
the bird inclines toward the flower,
the flower desires to be a bird.
At the sight of her, serving
as a bribe for her presence,
the boughs and flowers flatter her
with emeralds and pearls,
and, boastfully proud,
vigorously fight among themselves.

All want to possess her,
each one to deserve her,
and making a muster
incite the battle,
plumed bugles,
pearl-colored trumpets:
to arms, to arms, to arms,
to arms, war, war.
The flowers charge,
the birds come out to meet them:
to arms, war, war,
to arms, to arms.
The springs flow over the cliffs
and tree limbs wield swords

  and birds, flowers, tree limbs, and springs,
   ay, roses fighting, show themselves brave,
  but if attentive, Belisa looks towards them,
  they surrender for love and suspend the fight.

If not a sun, she was a deity;
if not a deity, springtime
who arises at dawn among the flowers
competing with the forest.
The pen wants to reduce
her beauties to numbers
but this is to embark on a sea
where your sight will be drowned.
Gracefully she removes the glove,
or quiver for five arrows,

o carcaj de cinco flechas,
la mano o nieve jurando
de cristal en competencia.
Con ella tocando anima
cuanto bordando maneja,
enriqueciendo a glorias
aun cuando lo mira apenas.

SECOND COLUMN
De un racional sentimiento
y a presumidas se alientan
aves, flores, fuentes, ramas
a la conquista primera
vuelven, pues, a la batalla
en lúcida competencias;
y a un tiempo dos elementos
vistosa sirven palestra
y haciendo la reseña
incitan la batalla,
[clarines de pluma,
trompetas de nácar:
al arma, al arma, al arma,
al arma, guerra, guerra.]

59. Un estribillo de un tono decía.[1]   33r

        Corazón, pues venís a morir
        por lo mismo que os han de matar:
        dejadme llorar de vuestro reír,
        dejadme reír de vuestro llorar.
        Corazón, pues me halláis al vivir
        en lo mismo que os puede matar:
        dejadme llorar de vuestro reír,
        dejadme reír de vuestro llorar.

FIRST COLUMN
Tan sufrido y tan constante
os mostráis en la dolencia,
que del rigor la experiencia
os examina diamante;

---

[1] Olivares and Boyce, 1st ed., 367–68.

her hand like snow,
competing with crystal.
With her hand, she animates
everything she touches,
enriching all with glories
with even her slightest glance.

With rational feelings
are vainly encouraged
birds, flowers, springs, tree limbs
to the first campaign
return to the battle
in bright-shining competition;
and, at one time, two elements
serve the beautiful arena
and making a muster
are incited to battle
[plumed bugles,
pearl-colored trumpets:
to arms, to arms, to arms,
to arms, war, war.]

59. A refrain said in one tone.

Heart, you come to die
for the same reason that they kill you:
let me cry for your laughing,
let me laugh for your crying.
Heart, you find me living
in the same way that can kill you:
let me cry for your laughing,
let me laugh for your crying.

So long-suffering and so constant
you show yourself in your suffering,
so that the harshness of the experience
finds you like a diamond;

y pues sufrido el pesar,
gloria intentáis adquirir:
dejadme llorar de vuestro reír,
dejadme reír de vuestro llorar.
Sin quejaros del rigor,
hacéis gala del penar,
que quien se llega a quejar
alivio busca el dolor;
y pues sabéis ostentar
bizarría en el sentir:
dejadme llorar de vuestro reír,
dejadme [reír de vuestro llorar.]

SECOND COLUMN
Declarar en el deseo
una pasión advertida
es desaire de la vida
y del amor no es trofeo;
y si en su ley es callar,
más mérito que decía:
dejadme llorar [de vuestro reír,
dejadme reír de vuestro llorar.][1]
Hallado en el padecer
gozar aún no deseáis,
que a la tibieza os negáis
que si sigue al poseer,
porque el gusto de gozar
finezas suele mentir:
dejadme llorar [de vuestro reír,
dejadme reír de vuestro llorar.][2]

60. A una gran señora casada a quien aborrecía su marido.[3]   33v

FIRST COLUMN
Divino hechizo de amor,
en quien se admiran a un tiempo
la discreción y hermosura
en iguales paralelos,

---

[1] After "dejadme llorar," the manuscript reads "etc."
[2] After "dejadme llorar," the manuscript again reads "etc."
[3] Serrano y Sanz, 368; Olivares and Boyce, 1st ed., 358; Olivares and Boyce, 2nd ed., 255–56. Olivares and Boyce identify the folio as 33r when, in fact, this poem is found on 33v.

and bearing the suffering,
you intend to find glory:
let me cry for your laughing,
let me laugh for your crying.
Without complaining about the rigors,
you make a celebration of pain,
for one who begins to complain
is looking for relief from suffering;
but you know how to show yourself
brave in your sorrow:
let me cry for your laughing,
let me [laugh for your crying.]

The desire to declare
a daring passion
is to disdain life
and not a trophy of love;
and by its [love's] rules, not speaking
has more merit, then:
let me cry [for your laughing,
let me laugh for your crying.]
In suffering
you do not find joy,
and you deny any timidity
that may accompany it,
because the enjoyment of pleasure
usually belies elegance:
let me cry [for your laughing,
let me laugh for your crying.]

60. To a great lady married to a man who detested her.

Divine spell of love,
in whom one admires at once
discretion and beauty,
both in equal parts,

a todo sentir del alma,
todo penar del deseo,
justamente querellosa
vives de tu injusto dueño;
que, como siempre el amor
sólo del alma hace empleo,
no se opusieron al tuyo
imperfecciones del cuerpo.
Alma irracional sin duda
tiene, pues no aspira a un cielo
que tantas lleva en sus ojos,
cuantos hacen movimientos.
Tantos dotes nobles, ricos
engrandecen tu sujeto,[1]
que el más discreto en amarle
logra felices aciertos.

SECOND COLUMN
Que te adoran no lo dudas,
que a tu dueño envidian menos
los que no alcanzan su dicha
con mejor conocimiento.
Vive, pues, siempre gozosa
de que los cielos te hicieron
deidad que sólo merecen
gozarla los cielos mesmos [sic].

---

[1] Serrano y Sanz reads "secreto" for "sujeto," but this word is corrected in Olivares and Boyce's transcription and is confirmed by my reading of the manuscript.

to all feelings of the soul,
all longings of desire,
justly complaining
you live with an unjust master;
since, as always, love
only takes notice of the soul,
your [love] did not, therefore, presume
imperfections of the body.
Without doubt, he has an irrational soul
since he does not aspire to a heaven
whose eyes carry off so many souls
by merely looking at them.
So many noble and rich attributes
make you a great person,
and the most discreet in loving you
attains certain happiness.

That they adore you do not doubt,
they are less jealous of your master
those who do not realize his good fortune
with better understanding.
Live, then, ever joyful
that the heavens made you
a deity who only deserves to be enjoyed
by the heavens themselves.

61. Romance en el certamen del Evangelista San Juan que se 34r
inventó en el convento de San Pablo para su fiesta de mayo
de 1642 años. El asunto que dieron fue que el relámpago es
vapor sutil inflamado, que brevemente se desvanece en el aire,
que al que mejor relampague [sic] hace chistes introduciendo
el Cerro del Búho y la Peña del Rey Moro[1] que iban a dar la
norbuena a las religiosas de la fiesta se le daría premio y yo, sin
esa golosina, dije por obedecer a las religiosas.

FIRST COLUMN
De ocho asuntos del certamen
en el último se empeña
mi musa, que aun en las burlas
se examinan obediencias.
Al relámpago me aplico,
prenuncio de la tronera,
que en fiesta de rayo tanto
la que no truena, no suena.
Por vapor desvanecido
hoy a su costa chistean
con los versos que lo mismo
son en chollas de poetas.
Con extremo está enfadado
de la que de él hacen brega
y así tope ado[2] topare
ordenando va pendencias.

SECOND COLUMN
Encontró el Cerro de Búho
y la venerable Peña
Del Rey Moro a quienes jura(n)
ha de estrellar las cabezas.
Temblad, deberme les dije
con resabios de culebra
besando luego el azote
si no de grado, por fuerza.
Respondió el Cerro atufado:

---

[1] Two mountains near Toledo. The latter is believed to show on its surface the face of a Moorish king.
[2] adonde

61. Ballad for the contest of the Evangelist Saint John, invented in the Convent of Saint Paul for his festival in May of 1642. The subject they gave was a lightning bolt that is subtle, inflamed vapor that quickly disappears in the air and makes a flash, by making jokes introducing the Owl's Hill and the Rock of the Moorish King. To congratulate the nuns in the festival and to win a prize and I, without that incentive, said in order to obey the nuns.

Of the eight topics of the contest
in the last one my muse
puts her efforts, and even in the jokes
proves herself obedient.
I will first address the lightning bolt,
I will speak of the thunder
that in the festival of so many rays
she who thunders forth, makes no sounds.
About disappearing vapor
they come here to make jokes
with verses that are always rolling about
in the skulls of poets.
He is extremely angry
with whom he quarrels
and thus stumbles along
ordering fights.

He found the hill of the owl
and the venerable rock
of the Moorish king against which they swear
to burst open their skulls.
Tremble, I should have told them
from the bad aftertaste of the snake
later kissing the whip
by force if not willingly.
The angry hill responded:

¿posible es que a mí te atrevas
espanta niños y monjas
duende de luz en tinieblas?
Viendo el pleito mal parado,
la Peña dijo muy sesga:
haya paz entre dos ruines [sic]
ya que soy mujer se atienda.

El relámpago responde:
si vuestra merced por hermosa piensa
hacer paces, ningún ojo
le hará mal en mi conciencia,
no extraño la grosería.
Antes respondió muy cuerda:
bien puede ser que me aojen
que soy de sangre ligera.
y alzando la voz el Cerro,
dijo: Qué maldita bestia,
al fin mujer sin discurso
y sobre pesada necia.
Ella, pues, sin alterarse,
estiró un poco las cejas
a alzando al cielo las manos
responde: *Omnes homo mendax*.
Relámpago y Cerro a un tiempo
pronunciaron: puta vieja,
¿latín sabéis? A ser monja
id, pues, sois tan bachillera.
Paso, paso, ella les dije:
las mujeres no son bestias
que hay para necios algunas
que en ocasiones penetran
sin obra de ingenio macho.
El de la mujer engendra

vivos conceptos que ilustran
y que no relampaguean.
Temiendo el contrario juicio
no escribe alguna esta fiesta
porque royeran sus versos
fuera con dolor de muelas.

is it possible that you dare
to frighten children and nuns,
a ghost of light in the darkness?
Seeing the case come to a bad end,
the rock very serenely said:
let us make peace between two ruins
since one should listen to me, a woman.

The lightning bolt responds:
if your ladyship thinks for the sake of beauty
to make peace, no eye
will see evil in my conscience,
nor will I miss the insult.
Then she responded very wisely:
well it may be that they bewitch me
since I am not made of strong stuff.
And the hill, raising its voice,
said: What an evil beast,
is a woman without reason,
and a boring ignoramus.
She, without any reaction,
wrinkled her brow
and raising her hands on high
responds: all men are liars.
Lightning and hill at the same time
shouted: old whore,
do you know Latin? Since you are a nun
go on, if you are so well educated.
Go on, go on, she tells them,
women are not beasts,
stupid men, there are some [women]
who on occasion hit the mark
without the ability of ingenious men.
The genius of women engenders

lively ideas that illustrate
but do not cause sparks to fly.
Fearing a contrary judgment
no woman writes for this festival
because they would gnaw on her verses
like one with a toothache.

Es muy del evangelista
y en paz a ponernos llega
porque a sus devotas vamos
a darles la enhorabuena.
En un instante nos puso
en San Pablo, es hechicera
que mueve[1] peñas y cerros
fuego de San Juan en ella.
Señoras evangelistas,
Dios guarde a sus excelencias
que así en la voz de su fama
generosas las granjean.
Si el asunto no he seguido
no me vendo por poeta
y si alguno lo notare,
hoy callo como piedra.

62. **Glosa que dieron en el mismo certamen.** 35r

    Cristo con sed de amor cierto
    a Juan a pechos se echó
    y aunque está dormido, no
    se ha visto amor tan despierto.

FIRST COLUMN
Busca Cristo amor perfecto
que satisfaga su amor
y de Juan en el sujeto
solo le halla, con efecto,
igualmente a su valor,
porque a pecho descubierto
se examina amante experto
donde tales actos hace
Juan, que de él se satisface
Cristo con sed de amor cierto.
Con tan bizarra osadía
beber dijo el cáliz puede,
que cuando Dios le temía
en Juan el beber le fía
porque en aliento le excede.

---

[1] "Vuela" is written above "mueve" between lines as an alternative reading, perhaps.

It is well for the evangelist
that we come to a truce
because to his devotees we are going
to give congratulations.
In an instant we found ourselves
in Saint Paul's, by a magic spell
that makes rocks and hills move
with the fire of Saint John.
Lady evangelists,
may God keep your excellencies
that in voicing his fame
you earn generous rewards.
If I have not followed the charge,
I will not claim to be a poet
and if anyone should notice it,
I will stay as quiet as a stone.

62. **Gloss that they gave in the same contest.**

> With the thirst of steadfast love
> John reclined on Christ's breast
> and even though he is sleeping, no one
> has seen such a wide-awake love.

Christ looks for perfect love
that will satisfy his love
and John is the person
in whom He truly finds it,
equal to his valor,
because an open heart,
examined by an expert lover,
finds that John acts in a way
that satisfies
Christ's thirst for steadfast love.
With such brazen daring
he can drink of the chalice,
for when God fears
to drink, He can trust John
because in willingness he exceeds Him.

Con su pecho le estrechó
cuyo valor[1] pertrechó
Juan y en la acción más notoria
por salir Dios con victoria
a Juan a pechos se echó.

SECOND COLUMN
Empeño de Cristo ha sido
que opinión adquiera Juan
si en su amor le ha preferido
de que alcanza más dormido
que los que velando están.
Al pecho, pues, le inclinó
donde Juan determinó misterios
los rayos que el sol oculta
que despierto dificulta
Juan que está dormido, no.
No halla el reposo lugar
en quien es perfecto amante
mas tanto sabe de amar
Juan que aún puede reposar
teniendo la luz delante.
Dormido en el centro abierto
logra de amante el acierto
con primor tan advertido
que solo en este dormido
se ha visto amor tan despierto.

63. **Soneto del mismo certamen. El asunto dar la razón de no morir el evangelista ni con el fuego de la tina ni con el veneno del vaso.**

No el fuego material a Juan ofende
salamandra que en el divino posa
de la esfera de Cristo luminosa
donde éste de aquel fuego le defiende.
Preservativo antídoto suspende
del vaso la potencia venenosa,
el corazón de Dios que en Juan reposa
como en tesoro que su ser comprende;
Juan es rayo del sol, centella ardiente

---

[1] "Esfuerzo" is written under "valor" perhaps as an alternative reading.

He held him to His breast
and John was endowed with valor
in the most noteworthy act
so that God might be victorious,
He held John tightly to His breast.

He has been a pledge for Christ
and John wins such recognition
since, for his love, God preferred
that he attain more, sleeping,
than those who stay awake.
John reclines on Christ's breast
where mysteries manifest themselves
with rays that block out the sun,
for it is not difficult to wake
John who is not sleeping.
Repose cannot find a place
in him who is a perfect lover
and John knows so much about love
that he cannot sleep
having the light before him.
Sleeping in the open center,
the lover hits the mark
with such sharp skill
that only in this sleeping one
has one seen such wide-awake love.

63. **Sonnet in the same contest. My topic is to testify that the Evangelist does not die even from the flames of the vat nor from poison in the cup.**

Fire does not offend John's flesh
divinely poised on the stove,
illuminated from Christ's sphere
from whence He protects him from the fire.
Suspending a saving antidote
for the cup of potent poison,
the heart of God where John reposed,
recognizes him as a treasure;
John is a ray of the sun, a burning star

del incendio de amor, y el amor mismo
a cuya vista fuego y muerte calma,
y si el ser de Dios alma es evidente,
pues, de misterios le fió el abismo,
Juan no puede morir que es de Dios alma.

64. Al evangelista en la isla de Padmos. Romance.

Juan de excelencias, milagro
del amor, raro prodigio
que a todo riesgo fue amante
y a toda experiencia, fino.
El que fue lisonja al sol
si de sus rayos registró
cuando en tan divina esfera
de amor, querub encendido,
en la soledad de Padmos,
para el alma buen retiro,
dulcísima ambrosia bebe
amante contemplativo.
Mira el objeto que ama
semejante a su amor mismo
cual piedra jaspe cambiando
en Juan misteriosos visos,
tal vez fulminando rayos,
airado mira al sol Cristo.
Y tal libro donde estudia
de Dios, el ser infinito,
en éxtasis relevado
siempre engolfado el sentido,
del Padre en la omnipotencia
mira la esencia del hijo
y en tanto que contempla
de Dios su fiel archivo;
voces suenan acordes de regocijo,
canta el cielo, diciendo
que Juan mereció
sin celajes de fe ver la esencia
del mismo Dios.

afire with love, and love itself
at whose sight calms fire and death,
and if it is evident that his soul is God's
and that miracles saved him from the abyss,
John cannot die since his soul belongs to God.[1]

64. Ballad to the Evangelist on the Isle of Patmos.[2]

John is a miracle of excellence,
of love, a rare prodigy
who was a true lover in the face of all risk
and gallant in all his experiences.
He who flatters the sun
if it sees his rays
when in such divine sphere
of love is a cherub inflamed,
on the lonely isle of Patmos,
a goodly retreat for the soul,
where of sweet ambrosia
the contemplative lover drinks.
He looks at the object that he loves
so similar to love itself
like a stone turned into jasper
in John sparkling mysteries
perhaps radiating rays,
he fixes his gaze on the sun, Christ.
He studies a book
about God, the infinite being,
exalted in ecstasy
his senses always engaged,
he sees in the omnipotence of the Father
the eminence of the Son,
as he contemplates
this faithful archive of God;
voices, rejoicing in harmonious accord,
sing in heaven, saying
that John deserved
to see, without anything clouding his faith, the essence
of God himself.

---

[1] See John 21:23.
[2] See Revelation 1:9.

65. Romance.

FIRST COLUMN

Antes del mayo florido
sale al campo Anarda hermosa
primavera cuya vista
le ilustra, enriquece, adorna.
Emuló el sol a sus ojos
si de rendido, blasona
cuando a rayos los compite
mas alienta, anima, y dora.
Ríe un arroyuelo alegre
de repetir bellas copias
en el cristal, que corriendo
galantea, argenta y borda.
Parias las plantas tributan
a tanta florida pompa
de Anarda en cuya presencia
abundan, producen, brotan.
Que mucho las almas rinda
hermosamente imperiosa
si a lo que faltan potencias
rinde, obliga y enamora.

SECOND COLUMN

Con discreta gallardía
que beldad suma acrisola
del alma dulce lisonja
al más perezoso gusto
brinda, estimula y exhorta.
Oh, ¡qué ufanas alegres y vistosas
vuelan por el aire las aves sonoras
y, en parando su vuelo,
cantando alternan
panegíricos dulces
a Anarda bella!

65. Ballad.

Before flowery May
beautiful Anarda goes out into the country;
she is a vision of springtime,
manifesting, enriching, and adorning it.
The sun emulates her eyes,
and in defeat, boasts that,
when it competes with her rays
hers are more lively, animated, and golden.
A little creek laughs happily
and reflects beautiful images [of her]
on its crystal surface, flowing,
woos, silver-plates, and embroiders.
Plants pay her tribute
with florid pomp
and in the presence of Anarda,
abundantly flower and sprout.
Let souls surrender themselves to such
imperious beauty
for they have no power and must
surrender, oblige, and fall in love.

Discreet gallantry
that crystallizes consummate beauty
is such sweet flattery to the soul
that even the laziest pleasure
cheers, stimulates, and exhorts.
Oh, how proud, happy, and colorful
the sonorous birds fly through the air
and, stopping in their flight,
singing harmonies of
sweet praises
to the beautiful Anarda!

66. Terceto o redondilla que me dieron a glosar.[1]

FIRST COLUMN
Pues por tu dicha se nace
lengua al amor divino
alma sigue su camino.
Dios, su amor en fuego envía
alma, en él, fénix renace
pues por tu dicha se hace.
Hacerse para enseñarte,
guiando tu fiel destino
lenguas el amor divino.
Para llegar a este amor,
que es el más perfecto y fino,
alma sigue su camino.

67. Otra glosada.[2]

SECOND COLUMN
Pues, es tan corta esta vida,
huye sus vanos placeres
si vida eterna quieres.
Bien no busques ni descanso
que es diligencia perdida
pues, es tan corta esta vida.
El bien de esta vida es mal,
oh alma, y por él te mueres,
huye sus vanos placeres.
Solo en la vida te goza
cuando padecer te vieres
si la vida eterna quieres.

---

[1] This poem does not appear in Serrano y Sanz's inventory.
[2] This poem does not appear in Serrano y Sanz's inventory.

66. **Tercet[1] or quatrain[2] that they gave me to gloss.**

For your good fortune, your tongue
was born to divine love
and the soul follows its path.
God, who sent forth His love in fire,
Gives rebirth to the soul like a phoenix
to insure your happiness.
It was done to teach you,
guiding you to a faithful destination,
with tongues of divine love.
To attain this love,
that is love most perfect and fine,
the soul follows its path.

67. **Another glossed.**

Since this life is so short,
flee from its vain pleasures
if you desire eternal life.
Do not look for repose
that is diligence lost
since this life is so short.
The goodness of this life is evil,
oh soul, and since of it you may die,
flee from vain pleasures.
Only take pleasure in life
when you see yourself suffering
if you desire eternal life.

---

[1] A strophe of three lines, usually of eleven syllables each.
[2] A strophe of four, eight-syllable lines that may have assonant or consonant rhyme scheme.

68. **Al Santísimo Sacramento en metáfora de la jornada que hace el Rey este año de 1642 para cobrar a Portugal y quietar a Cataluña.**[1]

No quede alma, no quede alma
que al ver el Rey, no salga
que entre los de su corte celestial.
¡O qué galán, qué galán!
Hoy sale a la jornada su Majestad.
Vengan todos, vengan, a priesa, a priesa,
que vestidos de luz los cortesanos
adornados de plumas vuelan,
que bizarros volando, volando, van
haciendo escolta a la persona real;
y entre escuadrones lúcidos parece,
sol bello que a rayos de amor los enciende

CONTINUED IN TWO COLUMNS
FIRST COLUMN
a quietar guerras civiles
que la paz dulce contrastan
del mundo adonde consiste
toda la quietud del alma.

SECOND COLUMN
Sale, pues, el rey supremo
de paz con divisa blanca,
porque el que su error confiese,
seguro vuelva a su gracia.

En las rebeldes potencias,
de duro engaño muradas,
de blandura armado intenta
su amor hacer puerta franca.

---

[1] This is an historical event: Felipe IV with the Conde Duque de Olivares made an expedition to the Aragonese front in April 1642 to try to bring peace to Cataluña that had fallen into anarchy (Vinotea Recoba, *María Fernández López*, 296).

68. To the Most Holy Sacrament as a metaphor for the effort that the King made in 1642 to recover Portugal and pacify Cataluña.[1]

No soul remains, no soul remains
who does not come out to see the King
who enters with his celestial court.
Oh, how gallant, oh, how grand!
Today his majesty goes on a military expedition.
Come all, come, quickly, quickly,
for the courtiers are dressed in lights
and adorned with feathers that blowing,
dashingly flying, flying, they go out
escorting his royal majesty;
and he appears amidst bright squadrons,
a beautiful sun set afire by rays of love

to quieten civil wars
that threaten the sweet peace
of the world which brings
all quiet to the soul.

The supreme King sallies forth
in peace with a white flag,
and whoever confesses his error,
will surely be returned to his good graces.

Against the rebellious powers,
walled in by their hardened mistake,
with leniency he intends
with his love to offer them clemency.

---

[1] Two years earlier, on the first of Corpus Christi (7 June 1640), previous opposition in Cataluña to the Conde Duque de Olivares's winter quartering of his army fighting the French led to riots in Barcelona, which, resulted in the death of the Spanish viceroy. Felipe IV and Olivares went personally to fight against the Catalans in April 1642. This title may also refer to events that forced Castile to military and economic action in 1642: France attacking Spain, revolts in Cataluña and Portugal, and the wars in Flanders. Olivares was ready to enter into a treaty with Cataluña in 1642, and, by then, Portugal was *de facto* independent. I am grateful to David C. McDaniel for this information.

Mas, ay de él, reino obstinado
que no rindiere las armas
de gusto ofensible [sic] luego
que cruel rigor le amenaza,
que de enojos, que de iras,
que a fuego el mundo deshagan.
El que ven manso cordero
fulminará en la campaña
Luzbel, sedicioso altivo,
que al alma asciendes con alas
de soberbia cera, advierte
que aqueste sol las abrasa.
Si tanto reino conquistas
desiste de empresa tanta
que le adquirió a sangre pura
este divino monarca;
y tu alma que del mundo
un mar de engaños naufragas,
vuelve a tu rey, perdón pide
que ya a su mesa te aguarda.

69. **Al Santísimo Sacramento.**

Qué galán estáis, Señor,
mi Rey y mi amante tierno,
a la vida dando alma
cuando del alma sois cielo.
En esa forma que os miro
en que transformarme intento,
no quiero desear más
ni deseo querer menos.
Toda la gala de fineza
tan reducida en vos veo,
que no amaros a vos solo
que es no amarme a mi confieso.
Todo el gusto de mi amor
sois en grado tan perfecto
que en vos sosiega y descansa
como en dulce propio centro.
Dueño y bien que el alma adora
gozarme con vos espero,
excediendo a la esperanza
la grandeza del deseo.

But, woe to the obstinate kingdom
that does not put down its arms
of offensive intent,
that cruel rigor threatens,
with anger and ire,
to destroy the whole world with fire.
He who they see as a meek lamb
will burst forth in the campaign
as Lucifer, seditious and haughty,
for the soul that ascends with wings
of proud wax, be warned
that this sun will melt them.
If you would conquer territory,
give up this enterprise
for it was acquired with the pure blood
of this divine monarch;
and your soul, that in this world
founders in a sea of deceits,
return to your King, ask pardon
for he is waiting for you at his table.

69. To the Most Holy Sacrament.

How gallant you are, my Lord,
my King and my tender lover,
giving life to the soul
since You are the heaven of the soul.
In that form in which I see You
and in which I try to transform myself,
I do not want to desire more
nor do I desire to want less.
All the celebration of elegance
I see reduced in You,
that not loving You alone
I confess is not to love myself.
All the pleasure of my love
You are in measure so perfect
that in You reposes and rests
as in its own sweet center.
The soul adores its Lord and its joy
and I hope to enjoy with You,
exceeding all hope
is the magnitude of my desire.

No os ausentéis de mis ojos
que aunque no estáis manifiesto,
vive el corazón que os ama
con la fe que tiene en veros.
Cuando el alma, se goza, mi dulce dueño,
de miraros tan lindo,
galán en cuerpo, Jesús, que digo,
Jesús, que siento
que con flechas de gracia,
de amores muero.

70. Otra.

Hoy la que es de gracia llena
visita a Isabel porque hoy
logre el tesoro que observa
creces de inmenso valor.
En culto, si humano, claustro
visitado Juan se vio
de una reina por los menos
cuando por lo más, de un Dios.
En la gracia le acrisolan
con puro fuego de amor
porque en gracia y amor sea
prodigio de admiración.
De santo antes que nacido
privilegio concedió
Dios a Juan porque, en lo humano,
haga divina excepción.
No sólo Dios le hace santo
mas de todos, el mayor
le apellida, como a digno
de tan supremo blasón.
Dios con Juan hoy se carea
porque se vea en los dos
todo el poder en su lustre
y la gracia en su esplendor.
Apriesa, apriesa, zagales,
corred con paso veloz
a ver cifrada la gloria
en casa de Isabel hoy.

Do not absent Yourself from my sight
for even when You are not present,
the heart that loves You lives
with the faith that it has upon seeing You.
The soul remains, it takes pleasure, my sweet Lord,
in seeing You so beautiful.
gallant in body, Jesus, I repeat,
Jesus, and I feel that
from love's arrows of grace,
I am dying.

70. **Another.**
Today she who is full of grace
visits Elizabeth because today
she gains the treasure that
exceeds immense value.
In blessed, although human, cloister[1]
John is visited
by no less than a queen,
and, moreover, by God himself.
In grace He purifies her
with the pure fire of love
so that in grace and love she may be
a prodigy to be admired.
To be a saint before birth
this privilege was conceded
by God to John so that in his human form,
he might be a divine exception.
Not only did God make him a saint
but of all the saints, the greatest
he is called as one worthy
of the supreme glory of sainthood.
Today John and God come face to face
so that one sees in the two
all power in their luster
and grace in their splendor.
Hurry, hurry, boys and girls,
run quickly
to see all glory manifest
in Elizabeth's house today.

---

[1] A reference to Mary's pregnancy, i.e., Christ inside a human mother's womb (cloister).

71. A nuestro patrón San [sic] Santiago. Villancico entre dos.

1º Atención, señores, pido
que cantar quiero esta vez
excelencias de aquel bravo
terror del protervo infiel.
2º Todos a mi voz atiendan,
señores, que yo soy quien
diré, cuanto por amante
ha llegado a merecer.
1º Que puedes decir que exceda
a decir que Diego es
el que apoyó la grandeza
de Dios plantando su fe.
2º Que es Diego, del sol divino
un rayo amante diré,
y que de su ardor sediento
sus luces llega a beber.
1º Oh, qué bien, oh qué bien;
y qué poco dices
cuando más decir podré.
2º Oh, qué bien, oh qué bien;
que a decir las grandezas de Diego
sólo un querub se puede atrever.
1º2º Oh, qué bien, oh qué bien;
que los cielos le cantan
por timbre de sus glorias
al sol de España.
Oh, qué bien, oh, qué bien;
los angélicos coros
repiten sonoros
una y otra vez,
que el primero ha ganado
corona y laurel.
1º Diré que este sol de amor,
aunque eclipsado le ven,
fénix ya en su ardor activo
fulgente ha de renacer, ¡oh, qué bien, oh, qué bien!
2º Yo diré que en el imperio
sol de mártires se ve,
estrenando a rayos puros
su flamante rosicler, ¡oh, qué bien, oh, qué bien!
1º Y, oh, qué el privado más fino

71. To our Patron, Saint James. Carol in two parts.

1st I ask for your attention, ladies and gentlemen
for this time I want to sing of
the excellency of him who was the fierce
terror of the obstinate infidel.
2nd All attend to my voice,
ladies and gentlemen, for I am the one
who will tell you as a lover
how much he was worthy.
1st You may say that I go too far
in saying that James is
the one who upheld the greatness
of God, sowing the faith.
2nd For I will say that James from the divine sun
is a loving ray,
and that with ardor he thirstily
drinks from [God's] light.
1st Oh, how fine, oh, how fine;
and how little you say
when I will be able to say more.
2nd Oh, how fine, oh, how fine;
for to tell of the greatness of James
only a cherub would dare.
1st 2nd Oh, how fine, oh, how fine;
the heavens sing of him
for the timbre of his glories
to the sun of Spain.
Oh, how fine, oh, how fine;
angelic choruses
harmoniously repeat
time and again,
as the first, he has gained
crown and laurel.
1st I will say that this sun of love,
even though they may see him eclipsed,
will be a phoenix in his active ardor
brilliantly reborn, oh, how fine, oh, how fine!
2nd I will declare that in the kingdom
he is the sun of martyrs,
emanating pure rays
of flaming rose color, oh, how fine, oh, how fine!
1st And, oh, the most elegant minister

es Diego invencible, pues,
dio de sus venas la sangre
por su rey y por su ley; ¡oh, qué bien, oh, qué bien!
2º Si el ser está en la opinión,
yo a decir me atreveré,
pues, Diego a Dios acredita
que le debe Dios su ser; ¡Oh, qué bien, oh, qué bien!

72. **Burlesco soneto. Alabáronme un soneto tanto que le pedí con instancia aunque después de leído, no entendí nada y respondí el siguiente confesando mi poco saber.**

Vuelvo a enviar el que pedí, Soneto,
confesando, señora y reina mía,
que de tenerle poco más de un día
mi juicio siento con algún defecto.
Cuando más le adjetivo e interpreto,
curiosa mi ambición en su porfía,
más de mi entendimiento se desvía
su delicado altísimo concepto.
Alguna soberana inteligencia
escribió para sí tan ardua suma
que no alcanzo aunque más y más discurro,
y, hablando como debo, en mi conciencia,
otra intención de mí no se presuma,
digo que no es la miel para este burro.

73. **A la venerable señora Doña Beatriz de Silva, fundadora de la Concepción de Toledo, entre dos y en fiesta de Nuestra Señora.**

42r

Pregunta. 1º ¿Quién será esta luz que miro
de incomparable belleza,
ostentar candores tantos
entre tantas luces bellas?
Respuesta. 2º Es el alba lusitana
que del sol, amante tierna,
madrugó para lograrle
en su hermosa primavera.
Pregunta. 1º ¿Quién es que selvas[1] de pluma
bizarras la galantean,
cuando el orbe clarifica

---

[1] Note the word play with Beatrice's last name, Silva.

is invincible Diego
who gave the blood of his veins
for his king, for his law; oh, how fine, oh, how fine!
2nd If his life deserves an opinion,
then I will dare to say
that James gives credit to God,
for God gave him his essence, oh, how fine, oh, how fine!

72. **Burlesque sonnet. I heard of such an admired sonnet that I asked to read it and when I did, I did not understand a word of it and I responded, confessing my ignorance.**

I am returning the sonnet that I asked for,
confessing, my lady and my queen,
that having had it a little more than a day
I think that my judgment has some defect.
When the more I try to unravel and interpret it,
persistent in my curious ambition,
the more my understanding fails to grasp
its delicate and grand idea.
Some sovereign intellect
wrote such an arduous piece
but I do not understand it no matter how much I try,
and, speaking, as I should, in good conscience,
it would presumptuous to keep on trying,
for I tell you that it is not honey for this donkey.

73. **To the venerable Lady Doña Beatrice of Silva, founder of the Conception of Toledo, for two voices for the festival of Our Lady.**

Question. 1st Whose is that light I see
of incomparable beauty,
boasting such whiteness
among so many beautiful lights?
Answer. 2nd She is the Lusitanian dawn
who was the tender lover of the sun,
who dawned so that springtime
might be born of her beauty.
Question. 1st Who is she who forests of plumes
so gallantly court
when she illuminates the world

enriqueciendo las selvas?
Respuesta. 2º Es de la humildad el lustre
símbolo de la pureza,
el resumen de virtudes,
y ya del imperio, estrella.
1º Válgame Dios qué corre, qué vuela,
qué alumbra, qué brilla,
qué admira y alegra.
2º Ay, qué bien suenan
clarines y trompetas
entre angélicas voces sonoras
que su triunfo dichoso celebran.
2º[1] Ésta es Beatriz que a su esposo,
del mundo hollando riquezas,
se la da por pobre, rica
si al mundo, pobre se niega.
1º Feliz mil veces la aclaman,
pues, los cielos la festejan
de Dios como a esposa amada,
si de este Rey como a Reina.
2º Hoy en fiesta de María
se solemniza la fiesta
de Beatriz, que por amante
de Dios, su madre la premia.
1º Pues ilustró su real sangre
Beatriz con obras perfectas;
es bien que la Reina pura
a la que es pura, engrandezca.

74. A la Magdalena.

La que de naturaleza
fue bizarro desempeño,
hermoso imán de las almas,
y blanco de los deseos;
la que al son de aplausos tantos
dormía engañoso sueño
y, con luz del sol divino,
despertó al conocimiento.
Magdalena, en fin, gallarda,
hermosa y discreta a un tiempo,

---

[1] This is not an error; "2º," repeats in the manuscript.

and enriches the forests?
Answer. 2nd She is of humility the lustrous
symbol of purity,
the sum of all virtues
and a star of the empire.
1st God bless me, how she runs, how she flies,
how she illuminates, how she shines,
how she amazes and gladdens.
2nd Oh, how sweetly sound
bugles and trumpets
among harmonious angelic voices
who happily celebrate her triumph.
2nd This is Beatrice that, for her spouse,
rejecting the riches of the world,
although wealthy, assumes a life of poverty
and, in her poverty, denies the world.
1st A thousand times they happily acclaim her
and the heavens fête her
as a beloved bride of God
like a Queen for her King.
2nd Today is the festival of Mary,
A holy day
for Beatrice, who is a lover
of God, is rewarded by His Mother.
1st Beatrice enriched her royal blood
with good works;
it is well that such a pure Queen
should acclaim one so like her in purity.

74. To the Magdalene.

She that by nature
was generously redeemed,
a beautiful magnet for souls,
and the target of desires;
she who to the sound of applause
was dreaming a deceitful dream
but, with the light of the divine sun,
her consciousness awoke.
The Magdalene, intelligent,
beautiful, and discreet at once,

de perfección tan amable
cuando atractiva despejó,
hoy yace rendida, no
de la muerte al golpe acerbo,
sí de su Dios a las flechas
dulces que de amor la hirieron.
Ama a Cristo, luego, adquiere
nueva luz su entendimiento,
y elocuente enseña y sabe
amar en grado perfecto.
Contempla este bello esposo, 43v
fénix de amor renaciendo,
si aroma exhalada en llanto
se sacrifica en su fuego.
Pena entre el fuego y el llanto
y al agua el fuego excediendo
por donde templarle intenta
más llama introduce al pecho.
A morir, pues, se retira,
huérfana ya de su dueño,
que el que vive sin quien ama,
vive sin duda muriendo.
A esta esposa, amante,
del Rey supremo,
hoy con voces suaves
cantan los cielos:
llegue en buena hora
a recibir de amante,
palma y corona.

75. **Otro a San Bernardo.** 44r

Aquel Padre de la iglesia
que en ella congrega sabio
hijos suyos que la ilustran
siendo del cielo milagros;
aquél como piadoso,
docto y ejemplar prelado,
que gobernando prudente
dio a su fama timbres tantos;
y, para decirlo todo,
el prodigioso Bernardo
a quien María engrandece

attained such delightful perfection
when she put away her attractions,
today lies surrendered, not
to death's bitter blow,
but rather to the arrows of her God
that wound her with sweet love.
She loves Christ and, thus, she gains
new insight for her understanding,
and eloquently she teaches and knows how
to love perfectly.
The beautiful bridegroom contemplates
a phoenix reborn by love,
like perfume exhaled in weeping
she sacrifices herself in His fire.
She suffers, weeping in the fire,
and water, exceeding fire,
tries to dampen the blaze
but only inspires more flame in her breast.
To die, then, she withdraws,
an orphan now of her Lord
for one who lives without whom one loves
lives without doubt dying.
To this bride, lover,
of the supreme King,
today with sweet voices
the heavens sing:
may she arrive in good time
to receive as a lover
palm and crown.

75. Another for Saint Bernard.

That father of the church
who in her wisely assembles
his sons that glorify her
as miracles from heaven;
as a pious,
learned and exemplary prelate,
whose wise governance
brought such renown to his fame;
and, to tell all,
the prodigious Bernard
was blessed by Mary

con favores soberanos,
cristal de sus pechos cede
a este cristalino vaso
para verle en su pureza
dignamente atesorado;
y, entre sonoras tropas
de espíritus alados
que al cielo le conducen
con júbilos y aplausos.
Llega el virgen insigne,
amante sabio,
a gozar en la gloria
eternos lauros.
Afuera, afuera, afuera,
retírense los astros,
que Bernardo con luces más puras
ilumina once cielos a rayos.
Éste, cual Joseph hermoso,
para conservarse casto
impúdicos desvaríos
venció de modestia armado.
Hijo es de Cristo y María
puesto que le dieron ambos,
María sus dulces pechos,
Jesucristo sus pechos y brazos.
Goce en Dios eternas glorias
pues, de Dios alcanzó tanto
que le ve nacer divino
cuando le contempla humano.
Y, entre sonoras tropas
[de espíritus alados
que al cielo le conducen
con júbilos y aplausos.]

76. Otro.

Por festejar a Bernardo,
oh, qué lisonjeros corren
las aves entre los aires
los aires entre las flores.
El prudente como sabio,
que humilde fue como noble,
a su patria y sangre dando

with sovereign favors,
the crystal of his breast is transferred
to this crystalline vessel
and seeing him so pure
she rewards him with dignity;
and, harmonious throngs
of winged spirits
carry him up to heaven
with jubilations and applause.
The pure virgin [man] arrives,
a wise lover
who enjoys in glory
eternal rewards.
Away, away, away,
let the stars fly away,
for Bernard with purer lights
illuminates eleven heavens with rays.
He, like a beautiful Joseph,
in order to preserve chastity
conquered imprudent desires
armed with modesty.
He is a son of Christ and of Mary
since each one gave him,
Mary her sweet breasts,
Jesus Christ his breasts and arms.
May he enjoy eternal glories in God,
for he achieved so much through God
that he was born divine
even though we see him as human.
And harmonious throngs
[of winged spirits
carry him up to heaven
with jubilations and applause.]

76. **Another.**

To celebrate Bernard,
oh, how pleasingly the birds
fly through the air
and the wind through the flowers.
He who was both prudent and wise,
who was as humble as he was noble,
giving to his homeland his blood

gloriosa fama y renombre.
Los cielos se ven gozosos
que con armónicas voces
publican de sus virtudes
las excelencias más nobles.
El querub ardiente y puro,
emulando sus candores,
hoy a Bernardo contempla,
un querub en forma de hombre.
Por hijo, en fin, de María
ya todos le reconocen
porque, a sus pechos criado,
imitó sus perfecciones.
Bien es que Bernardo ilustre
tan alto título goce
pues, en lo amante y lo puro
logró tantas atenciones.
Aquel jazmín que del alba,
néctar dulce en perlas coge,
dando hermosa luz al día,
hoy, a la del sol, se opone.

45v

77. Otro.

¡Qué bizarros serafines
de los cielos se descuelgan
para subir con Bernardo
hoy a la región excelsa!
Ya pendientes de los aires
vistosamente se ostentan,
ramilletes de la gloria
que a flores lóbrego[1] pueblan,
y, a la distancia, girando
del globo inferior se alejan.
Ya el superior, ya vecinos
rompen azules troneras;
llega Bernardo al imperio,
el asombro de pureza,
a cuyo dichoso triunfo
dulces elogios alternan.
Aquel galán de María

46r

---

[1] There is an apparent error here, as the manuscript reads "lobrago."

and glorious fame and renown.
The heavens are joyful
and with harmonious voices
they publicize his virtues
and his most noble excellences.
The cherub, ardent and pure,
emulating his innocence,
today looks on Bernard,
a cherub in the form of a man.
He is a true son of Mary
who all recognize
because, raised at her breasts,
he imitated her perfections.
It is well that illustrious Bernard
enjoys such an exalted title
since in love and in purity
he gained such renown.
That jasmine of the dawn
catches sweet nectar in pearls
giving beautiful light to the day,
and today outshines the light of the sun.

77. Another.

What gallant seraphim
come down from heaven
to rise with Bernard
to the lofty region!
Hanging in the air
they brightly show off
bouquets of glory
that populate the darkness with flowers,
and, in the distance turning
they fly away from the inferior world.
Now above, now to the side, they
break though blue portals;
Bernard arrives to the kingdom,
a wonder of purity,
for his fortunate triumph
sweet praises are sung.
That gallant of Mary

a quien dio de amor en prendas
del tesoro de su pecho
cristal aljófar y perlas;
aquél que al sol increado[1]
cuando nace, ver desea
y, entre el rosicler más bello,
de vio nacer de una estrella.
Resuenen chirimías, clarines y trompetas,
que publiquen victoria, victoria, victoria,
pues Bernardo a la gloria triunfante llega.[2]

78. Otra divina. 46v

    Qué alegre llega María
    a engrandecer hoy a Juan,
    que el divino sol que oculta
    con sus rayos, le quiere ilustrar.

FIRST COLUMN
Que ha de ser el lucero divino,
que le ha de anunciar
hace Dios a Juan favores
con tan divinos primores;
que el mayor de los mayores,
como Dios, le aclamaran.
Que ha de ser el lucero
[que le ha de anunciar
hace Dios a Juan favores
con tan divinos primores.]
De Isabel en las entrañas
obra Juan tantas hazañas
por Dios, que en glorias tamañas,
aun Dios se llega a gloriar.
Y ha de ser el lucero
[que le ha de anunciar
hace Dios a Juan favores
con tan divinos primores.]

---

[1] "Not created," therefore, divine.
[2] These last two verses are found at the bottom of folio 46r after one-third of the page is left blank.

to whom she gave gifts
from the treasury of her bosom
crystal dewdrops and pearls;
He who was not created [i.e., divine)]
when He was born wants to see the sun,
and in the most beautiful pink dawn,
He saw him born from a star.
Let the horns, bugles and trumpets sound,
to call out victory, victory, victory,
for Bernard arrives triumphantly to glory.

78. Another divine.

How happy Mary arrives
today to exalt John,
for the divine sun that conceals
with its rays, wants to enlighten him.

It must be a divine, bright star
that announces that
God gives great favors to John
with divine delicacies;
for the greatest among greats,
like God, they proclaim him.
It must be a bright star
[that announces that
God gives great favors to John
with divine delicacies.]
From within Elizabeth's womb
John performed so many deeds
for God in such measure
that God is greatly glorified.
It must be a bright star.
[that announces that
God gives great favors to John
with divine delicacies.]

Visita el verbo humanado
hoy a Juan, y, como en grado
supremo le ha levantado,
por Dios le reputaran.
Y ha de ser el lucero
[que le ha de anunciar
hace Dios a Juan favores
con tan divinos primores.]

SECOND COLUMN
De Dios la voz ha de ser
Juan, con que ha de establecer
su magnífico poder
y su crédito asentar.
Y ha de ser el lucero
[que le ha de anunciar
hace Dios a Juan favores
con tan divinos primores.]
Como es Juan el que ha de dar
luz de la luz infalible,
vio de Dios la inaccesible
en su centro virginal.
Y ha de ser el lucero divino
que le ha de anunciar.

79. Otra humana. Para cantada.   47r

Ay, qué me abraso de amor;
ay, qué fénix de su incendio;
muriendo de lo que vivo,
viviré de lo que muero.
El sentimiento del alma
se remite ya al silencio,
que o no es grande el que se explica
o le siente sólo el cuerpo;
y, si en fiarse a la lengua,
desluce el merecimiento,
calle, pues, y sólo diga,
en tantos desasosiegos,
las campanas que hacen la salva
sonoras al alba;
toquen a fuego,
que de amor me abraso y me muero.

The Word made flesh visits
John today, and to such a great
height he has been raised
that they deem him to be God.
It must be a bright star
[that announces that
God gives great favors to John
with divine delicacies.]

It must be God's voice
that grants to John
his magnificent power
and affirms his worth.
It must be a bright star.
[that announces that
God gives great favors to John
with divine delicacies.]
Since it must be John who gives
light to the infallible light,
he saw God's inaccessible [light]
in the virginal womb.
It must be a bright, divine star
that announces him.

79. **Another secular, to be sung.**

Oh, I am burning from love;
oh, what a phoenix from the fire;
dying from what I live for,
I will live from what makes me die.
The sentiment of the soul
submits now to silence,
for either what it explains is not great
or only the body feels it;
and, if entrusting it to the tongue,
tarnishes its merits,
stay quiet, then, and only say
with so much unease,
bells sound the salute
harmoniously to the dawn;
let then ring out the fire
that is burning me up with love and I die.

Toquen a fuego,
no a mi reposo,
no a mi sosiego
que ya es perdido,
como yo me pierdo,
pero confieso
que en mí sólo sea vista
ganar perdiendo.
Miro el riesgo en lo imposible,
firme adoro, por fe creo
que aquél tiene amor más firme
que la afianza en el riesgo.
Amando muero, ¡qué dicha!
No quiero vida, ¿qué acierto?
Que quien de amor noble muere
gana vida y logra premio,
entre efectos diferentes,
pena y gloria hallando a un tiempo.
El alma busca delicias,
y el amor dulces recreos.
Las campanas hacen la salva
sonoras al alba:
[toquen a fuego,
que de amor me abraso y me muero.]

80. **Otra a una religiosa que lloraba sin medida la muerte de otra que la había criado.**

FIRST COLUMN
No llores del mal que sientes,
discreta Virena, pues,
cuando te obligo a sentirle
quedó convertido en bien.
Dos veces la causa envidio
que, si llega a merecer
con la de tu amor dos glorias,
dos veces dichosa es.
Tiempla [sic] el fuego a los suspiros,
basta que en lágrimas des
tanto entre rayos al aire
que un Etna ardiente se ve.
Modera el llanto, así vivas,
pero mal dije, pues, sé

Let them ring out fire,
not for my repose,
not for my rest
that is now lost
just as I am losing myself,
but I confess
that only in me may be seen
winning while losing.
I see risk in the impossible,
I adore firmly and, by faith, I believe
that one who has the most steadfast love
will vouch for the risk.
Loving I die, how fortunate!
I do not want life, am I right?
For one who dies for noble love
wins life and gains a reward,
among different effects,
finding pain and glory at the same time.
The soul looks for delights
and love for sweet amusements:
bells sound the salute
harmonious to the dawn;
[let then ring out the fire
that is burning me up with love and I die.]

80. **Another for a nun who grievously mourned the death of the one who had raised her.**

Do not cry for the grief that you feel,
discreet Virena,
for I want to help you
to convert it into good.
I envy twice the cause
for she who deserves
from your love two glories,
is blessed two times.
Temper the fire of your sighs,
for you have shed so many tears
that they are like lightning in the sky
and it appears as if Etna is erupting.
Moderate your wailing, so that you may live,
but I said it badly, I know

que maltratando dos vidas
te negocias muerte cruel.
Tus soles que a rayos matan
visten de luto, porque
llorando una muerte sola
hacen mil muertes tal vez.

SECOND COLUMN
No de tus años marchites
el verdor bizarro que es
frustrar las lúcidas flores
de ese ingenioso vergel.
Si al cielo penas no llegan
como tanto siente quien,
con discreción tan divina,
desmiente el humano ser.
No llores, cántete [sic] endechas
tu dulce voz que, a mi ver,
si en ella atenta te miras,
Narciso serás después.
Canta, basta que llore
quien te quiere bien,
pues, de entre ambos [sic] la pena
viene a ser.
Canta, canta,
darás gloria a la pena
como a la causa.

81. **A la Natividad vuelto del humano que queda en la plana**[1]   48v
por lograr el estribillo de batalla.

FIRST COLUMN
Hoy que nace el sol divino
del alba cándida y bella,
si no el más hermosos infante
de la más divina Reina.
Todo brotando alegría,
el diciembre, abril se ostenta;
Febo, bañando los valles,
Flora, vistiendo las selvas,

---

[1] The meaning of "plana" here is "page" or "sheet of paper."

that mistreating two lives
you are negotiating with cruel death.
Two suns that kill with rays
are dressed in mourning, because
crying for one death alone
perhaps causes a thousand deaths.

Do not let your years fade
from the gallant green they are now
or frustrate the bright flowers
of that lush garden.
Grief does not have a place in heaven
as believe those who,
with divine discretion,
belie human existence.
Do not cry, sing songs
with your sweet voice
so that when you look at yourself,
you will become like Narcissus.
Sing, for it is enough that one cries
who loves you well
and between the two, the pain
will be shared.
Sing, sing,
you will give glory to grief
as well as to its cause.

81. **To the Nativity, based on a secular poem, written so as to maintain its refrain about a battle.**

Today the divine sun is born
from a dazzling and beautiful dawn,
the most beautiful infant
of the most divine Queen.
Everything blooms with happiness,
December is showing off as if she were April;
Phoebus,[1] bathing the valleys,
Flora,[2] dressing the forests,

---

[1] The sun.
[2] The goddess of plants, flowers, and fertility in Roman mythology.

imitando a los pastores
que el nacimiento celebran.
Aves, flores, fuentes, ramas
se concitan a la fiesta
que ufanamente orgullosas
briosamente pelean
todas juntas, por lograrse
cada cual, por ser primera;
y haciendo la reseña,
incitan la batalla
clarines de pluma,
trompetas de nácar:
al arma, al arma, al arma,
al arma, guerra, guerra.
Las flores se embisten,
las aves se encuentran:

SECOND COLUMN
al arma, guerra, guerra,
al arma, al arma.
Las fuentes se despeñan
y esgrimen las ramas,
y aves, flores, ramas y fuentes
airosas lidiando bizarras se muestran.
Mas, si esparce el infante sus rayos
de amores, rendidas suspenden la guerra;
si el niño es sol, es deidad;
si deidad, es primavera;
si de nácar, concha hermosa
que produce ricas perlas.
Querer reducir la pluma
a números su belleza
es ignorarse la vista
en océano de estrellas.
Con los diamantes que mira
de amor lucientes[1] esferas
todo el orbe diviniza
cuando sus rayos dispensan.

---

[1] "Radiantes" is written under "lucientes," possibly as an alternate reading.

imitating the shepherds
who celebrate the birth.
Birds, flowers, springs, tree limbs
gather for the feast
and boastful and proud
fight with spirit,
striving among themselves
each one to be the first;
and passing in review
they initiate the battle,
plumed bugles,
pearl-colored trumpets:
to arms, to arms, to arms
to arms, war, war.
The flowers charge,
the birds square off:

to arms, war, war,
to arms, to arms.
The springs flow forth
and the tree limbs brandish swords,
and birds, flowers, tree limbs, and springs
prove themselves graceful and brave in battle.
But, when the Child spreads His rays
of love, all surrender and suspend the war;
the Child is the sun, a deity;
as a deity, He is springtime;
He is of mother-of-pearl, a beautiful shell
that produces valuable pearls.
For the pen to try to reduce
to numbers His beauty
is like trying to ignore sight among
an ocean of stars.
With the gaze from His diamonds [His eyes]
bright spheres of love,
He makes the whole world divine
when He spread his rays.

De un racional sentimiento
y a presumidas se alientan
aves, flores, fuentes, ramas
a la conquista primera.
Y haciendo la reseñan,
[incitan la batalla
clarines de pluma,
trompetas de nácar:
al arma, al arma, al arma,
al arma, guerra, guerra.]

82. Otra.

FIRST COLUMN
A divertir su tristeza
Jacinta al campo salió,
aquélla de cuyos ojos
mendiga rayos el sol.
Con simulada alegría
salud miente al corazón,
pero, qué mal que se miente
donde hay achaques de amor.
De tal tristeza sin duda
es ausencia la ocasión,
que amar sin ver es desdicha,
y si con celos, mayor.
Favorecido en su vista
se halla el campo feliz hoy,
que gozoso la divierte
con florida ostentación.
Y alegres las selvas,
ríen los valles,
brincan las fuentes,
cantan las aves
de contento de ver a Jacinta
que el sol enriquece con rayos brillantes
con dulces requiebros,
armónicos quiebros.

SECOND COLUMN
Por dulces amores
los ruiseñores
en medio las flores

From a rational feeling
vainly take heart
birds, flowers, springs, tree limbs
to the first conquest.
And passing in review,
[they initiate the battle,
plumed bugles,
pearl-colored trumpets:
to arms, to arms, to arms
to arms, war, war.]

82. **Another.**

To try to cheer herself up
Jacinta went out into the countryside,
she from whose eyes
the sun begs for rays.
With simulated joy
health lies to the heart,
but, how badly it lies
where there is love sickness.
Of such sadness without doubt
absence is the reason,
for loving without seeing is misery,
and if accompanied by jealousy, worse.
Favored by her sight
the countryside is happy today,
and joyfully amuses her
with a flowery show.
And the forests are happy,
the valleys are laughing,
the springs are leaping,
the birds are singing
so content are they to see Jacinta
who the sun enriches with bright rays
with sweet endearments,
harmonic trills.

From sweet love
nightingales
in the midst of the flowers

solfean amantes
del contento de ver a Jacinta,
que al sol enriquece
de rayos brillantes.
Ya en el discurso vencida
duda el linaje a dolor;
tan extraño al sentimiento,
cuanto imposible a la voz,
suspiros dando hacia el alma
al campo niega el rumor,
de penas que hasta en el campo
escándalo triste son.
No ajada belleza tanta
en Jacinta, pues, se vio
que aun lo vegetante rinde
a prisiones de afición.
Alegres las selvas,
ríen [los valles,
brincan las fuentes,
cantan las aves.]

83. **A instancia de una monja muy evangelista en Día de Todos Santos, se hizo esta letra introduciendo a San Juan por cifra de todos.** 49v

FIRST COLUMN
Por ser la fiesta de todos
los que santos la fe aclama;
sus cambiantes viste el cielo
y la tierra, nuevas galas.
La madre y Reina María
se goza de ver que cantan
todos la gloria a su hijo
que santo de santos llaman.
Es de Juan toda la fiesta,
aquel águila encumbrada,
pues, todos de él aprendieron
buenas obras y palabras.
De vista no pierde al sol,
que en transformaciones tantas,
nunca errante, siempre fijo,
le examina cara a cara.
Atención a la copia

sing like lovers
so content are they to see Jacinta,
who the sun enriches
with bright rays.
Now, conquered by their discourse
she doubts the cause of her grief;
so strange a feeling,
almost impossible for words,
the sighs giving to the soul
sounds denied to nature,
for pains in the countryside
are a sad scandal.
No withered beauty
is seen in Jacinta
and even the vegetation surrenders
to prisons of affection.
The forests are happy,
[the valleys are laughing,
the springs are leaping,
the birds are singing.]

83. **At the insistence of a nun very dedicated to the Evangelist on the Day of All Saints, in which I use Saint John as an emblem for all the saints.**

To be the feast of all
the saints the faith acclaims;
heaven is dressed in its iridescent garments
and the world, in its finest garb.
The mother, Queen Mary,
is happy to see that all sing
to the glory of her Son
who is called the holiest of the holy.
All the feast is for John,
that lofty eagle,
since from him they all learned
good works and good words.
He never lost sight of the sun
who in so many transformations,
never erring, always faithful,
he examines face-to-face.
Attentive to the reflection

de Juan excelso
en quien todos se miran
como en espejo.
Si apóstol, es virgen
y mártir supremo,
sabio evangelista,
de todos maestro,

SECOND COLUMN
y en quien todos se miran
como en espejo.
A ti, Juan, es de María
hermano del verbo
que hizo a Juan archivo
para sus misterios,
y en quien todos se miren [sic]
como en espejo.

84. A San Diego de Alcalá, logrando el estribillo. 50r

FIRST COLUMN
Diego de humildad prodigio
que de Francisco heredó,
en la virtud más perfecta,
el más lúcido blasón.
El que en remotas naciones,
con heroico fervor,
cual Diego en bárbaros pechos
la fe de Cristo plantó.
Aquél que en batallas tantas,
imitando este patrón,
salió con la cruz armado,
siempre de sí vencedor.
Al arma, al arma, al arma,
oh, celebre español,
que muchos son los riesgos
que a España cercanos
y diciendo al arma,
guerra, guerra.

of exalted John
in whom all see themselves
as in a mirror.
He is apostle, virgin,
and supreme martyr,
wise evangelist,
master of all,

in whom all see themselves
as in a mirror.
For you, John, are of Mary
brother of the Word
who made John an archive
for His mysteries,
and in whom all see themselves
as in a mirror.

84. To Saint Diego of Alcalá, repeating the refrain.

Diego of prodigious humility
who inherited from Francis,
in most perfect virtue,
the most shining glory.
In remote nations,
with heroic fervor,
in barbarous breasts
Diego planted the faith of Christ.[1]
He who in so many battles,
imitating this patron,
went out armed with the cross
always the conqueror.
To arms, to arms, to arms,
oh, celebrated Spaniard,
many are the risks
that besiege Spain
and saying, to arms
war, war.

---

[1] Saint Diego of Alcalá (1400–1463) served as a missionary in the Canary Islands.

Van rompiendo las nubes,
rasgando esferas
anime la caja,
aliente la tropa,

SECOND COLUMN
y España, en el nombre
de Diego, responda:
victoria, victoria,
que es muy corta la fama
para sus glorias.
Despreció riquezas Diego
con tan bizarra atención
que cambiar por ellas quiso
lo que sin ellas ganó.
No oscureció la ignorancia
el científico esplendor
de alma que fue iluminada
del espíritu de Dios.
Y, por resumirlo todo,
fue Diego en quien Dios cifró
las virtudes de Francisco
y de otro Diego el valor.
Al arma, al arma,
[oh, celebre español,
que muchos son los riesgos
que a España cercanos
y diciendo al arma,
guerra, guerra.]

85. **A la presentación de Nuestra Señora, logrando el estribillo.** 50v

FIRST COLUMN
Hoy Ana y Joaquín presentan
con afecto humilde a Dios
la prenda de más estima,
la joya de más valor,
tan perfectamente hermosa
todo el templo la admiró
que igual no hallaron ninguna;

Breaking through the clouds,
tearing the spheres
strike up the drum,
encourage the troops,

and may Spain, in the name
of Diego, respond:
victory, victory,
for fame is short
for his glories.
Diego disdained riches
with such gallant attention
that he wished to exchange them
for what he won without them.
Ignorance did not obscure
the eminent splendor
of a soul that was illuminated
by the spirit of God.
And, to sum it all up,
God imbues Diego with
the virtues of Francis
and the valor of another Diego.[1]
To arms, to arms,
[oh celebrated Spaniard,
many are the risks
that besiege Spain
and saying, to arms
war, war.]

85. To the presentation of Our Lady, repeating the refrain.

Today Ann and Joachim present
to God with humble love
the gift of great worth,
the most valuable gem,
so perfectly beautiful
all the temple admired her
for there was no one to be found there who was her equal;

---

[1] St. James, Patron of Spain.

si ella a todas superior
de gracia armada la niña.
desde el punto que nació,
capitana valerosa
rinde al infernal dragón.
Al arma, al arma, al arma,
celeste escuadrón,
que vuestra capitana
sale en campaña hoy.
Al arma, cierra, cierra
van rompiendo las nubes,
rasgando esferas.
Anime la caja
y aliente la tropa,
y el cielo, en tu nombre,
María, responda:
victoria, victoria.

SECOND COLUMN
Que a tu nombre y tu gracia
todos se postran.
Al primer lustro esta aurora
tan luciente amaneció,
como aquélla que escogida
es para madre del sol.
Sabiduría y belleza
el cielo en ella cifró,
que lograr quiso en su reina
las gracias de más primor.
Es tan divina aunque humana
que en sola su perfección
afianza el desempeño
todo el poder de su autor.
Al arma, al arma,
[celeste escuadrón,
que vuestra capitana
sale en campaña hoy.]

she was superior to all others
this child armed with grace.
Since the moment of her birth,
this victorious [female] captain
defeats the infernal dragon.
To arms, to arms, to arms,
celestial squadron,
for your captain
today sallies forth into battle.
To arms, close off, close off
breaking through the clouds,
tearing the spheres.
Strike up the drum,
encourage the troops,
and heaven, in your name,
Mary, responds:
victory, victory.

To your name and to your grace
all prostrate themselves.
At first light this dawn
was so brightly born,
as the one chosen
to be the mother of the sun.
Wisdom and beauty
heaven placed in her,
wanting to impart to this queen
the most delicate of graces.
She is as divine as she is human
for only her perfection
gives credit to the work
of her all powerful author.
To arms, to arms,
[celestial squadron,
for your captain
today sallies forth into battle.]

86. A una copia devotísima del Santísimo Cristo de Burgos. 51r

FIRST COLUMN
Si a la vista no feneces
de este cruento cadáver,
di: ¿para cuál sentimiento
corazón te reservaste?
Pero dirás que su muerte,
piadosa aunque formidable,
de gracia te restituye
la vida que profanaste;
que este Dios mal ofendido
siempre a tu bien propiciable [sic]
mas a padecer te alienta
cuando sin aliento yace.
Por tu amor murió, no hay duda,
que así lo afirman constantes
en todo su rostro y cuerpo
cinco mil y más señales.
De par en par el costado
puerta de perdón te abre,
que a la sed de gracia brinda
con dos licores suaves.

SECOND COLUMN
Tantas bocas como admiras,
brotar bermejos raudales,
fieles testigos te intiman
su amor con lenguas de sangre
bien que son, corazón mío,
de tu ingratitud fiscales
porque afectados deseos
sin obras no satisfacen.
La cabeza cuyas hebras
ensartan rojos granates,
que siendo de oro nativo
son dulce prisión del aire.

86. To a very exact copy of the Most Holy Christ of Burgos.[1]

If you do not die at the sight
of this bloody cadaver,
say, for what feeling
is your heart saving itself?
But you will say that His death,
pious although daunting,
restores grace to you
that you profaned in life;
this God, badly offended,
always attentive to your well-being,
encourages you to suffer
when He lies before you without breath.[2]
For love of you He died, there is no doubt,
and this is constantly affirmed
in all His face and body
by five thousand and more signs.
His side He opened wide
as a gate of pardon,
for the thirst for grace He offers
two sweet liquors.[3]

All the mouths as you see,
flowing with red torrents
are faithful witnesses that bring you close to
His love with tongues of blood
that are, my heart,
prosecutors of your ingratitude
for affected desires
without works do not satisfy.
The head whose hair
is threaded with red garnets,[4]
that, being of native gold,
are a sweet prison in the air.

---

[1] Refers to a statue of Christ.
[2] A play on words: "te alienta" from the verb "alentar" meaning "to encourage" and "aliento" meaning "breath."
[3] The blood and water that flowed from Christ's pierced side. See John 19:34.
[4] I.e., drops of blood.

Cuántas la hieren espinas;
cuántos la ofenden ultrajes;
son avisos que estimulan,
recuerdos son que combaten.
Huye la engañosa vida
que entre flores te distrae,
donde la muerte del alma
cual áspid suele ocultarse.

87. Villancico de Navidad.

FIRST COLUMN
Airosa cuando lúcida
la noche de negro sale,
bordada de resplandores
sobre argentados follajes.
El manto azul que la cubre
siembran lucientes diamantes
y de penachos vistosos
corona la ofrece el aire.
En esta felize [sic] noche,
que día el mundo la aplaude,
porque en ella el sol madruga,
desterrando oscuridades.
Nace, pues, Dios, niño hermoso
de quien da noticia el ángel
al hombre con quien se humana
Dios a hacer eternas paces.
Llega Bras al portalillo
a adorar al tierno infante
y, sin juicio de contento,
parte al llamar los zagales:
zagalejos, los de Belén,
venid a la fiesta;

SECOND COLUMN
veréis por milagro
el cielo en la tierra.
Volar por el aire
millares de estrellas;

So many thorns pierce it;
so many insults offend Him;
these are warnings that stimulate,
memories that fight with one another.
Flee from the deceits of life
where you distract yourself among flowers,
where the death of the soul
waits likes a hidden asp.

87. Christmas Carol.

Graceful and bright
the dark night vanishes,
embroidered with bright light
on silvery foliage.
The blue cape that covered the night
sows bright diamonds
and with colorful crests
offers a crown to the air.
On this happy night,
on this day the world applauds,
because on this day the sun dawns,
exiling all darkness.
He is born, God, as a beautiful babe
about whom the angel gives notice
to man for whom God has become human
to bring about eternal peace.
Bras[1] arrives at the doorway
to adore the tender infant,
and crazy with happiness
runs off to tell the shepherds:
Lads and lasses of Bethlehem,
come to the party;

you will see the miracle
of heaven on earth.
Flying through the air
thousands of stars;

---

[1] A name given to one of the shepherds who pay homage to the Christ Child.

qué lindas que corren,
qué hermosas que vuelan,
y toque Gil
el tamboril
y Llorente su bandurria;
danzaremos a toda furia,
sin que cese pie ni mano,
el canario y el villano
saltarén y la españoleta.
Vamos a ver
el cielo en la tierra;
veréis trepar por el aire,
cantando como unas ardeas,[1]
unos que según el habla
pienso que escolares eran.
Todos: vamos a ver el cielo en la tierra.

Veréis luego en el portal
rayos de tanta belleza
que los ojos que los miran,
despestañados se quedan.   Vamos a ver el cielo en la tierra.[2]
Veréis allí una zagala,
como una pura azucena,
más hermosa y repulida
que Antona la panadera.   Vamos a ver el cielo en la tierra.
Veréis un niño divino
como el sol, y en mi conciencia,
que es sin llamas, pues, abrasa
a los que a su luz se llegan. Vamos a ver [el cielo en la tierra.]
Veréis como salto y brinco,
más que diez novios de aldea,
y que si no me desmiembro
no soy Bras de noche buena.   Vamos a ver [el cielo en la tierra.]
Ea, zagales pastores,
bailes, ordenad y fiestas,
y no quede a quien me escucha

---

[1] Bittern, heron-like a wading bird with a booming cry.
[2] This is the configuration in the manuscript with the lines of the refrain written to the right of the poem itself.

how beautifully they cascade,
how lovely they fly.
Let Gil play
the tambourine
and Llorente his mandolin;
we will dance furiously
without foot or hand slowing down,
the canario and the villano[1]
a guitar tune and the españoleta.[2]
We are going to see
heaven on earth;
you will see climbing up through the air,
singing like birds
some who, from how they speak,
I think must be scholars.
Everyone: We are going to see heaven on earth.

You will see in the crib
rays of such beauty
that the eyes that behold them
become strained.[3]   We are going to see heaven on earth.
You will see there a young girl,
like a pure, white lily,
more beautiful and refined
than Antona, the baker.   We are going to see heaven on earth.
You will see a divine infant
like the sun, and to my way of thinking,
He is without flames but still burns
those who come to His light.   We are going to see [heaven on earth.]
You will see how I jump and skip
like more than ten bridegrooms of the village,
and if I do not fall down, exhausted,
I am not Bras of Christmas Eve.   We are going to see [heaven on earth.]
Ay, all you shepherds,
arrange dances and parties,
and let no one who hears me

---

[1] "Canario" and "villano" are two types of Spanish dances.
[2] Ancient Spanish dance.
[3] Literally, one loses one's eyelashes from looking on the bright rays emanating from the Christ Child.

en su ser, brazo ni pierna
zagalejos, los de Belén. [Vamos a ver el cielo en la tierra.]

88. **Para lograr la música de la primera copla y del estribillo (que no escribí yo) me pidieron hiciese a propósito las demás coplas para la Navidad de Cristo, cantóse en la Santa Iglesia, año 1642, en Toledo.**[1]

FIRST COLUMN
Del imperio se descuelgan
tropas de aladas escuadras
que del golfo de zafir [sic]
surcan las celestes playas.
En Belén el real asientan
donde, entre brutos y pajas,
traje humano y pobre viste
la deidad más soberana.
Contra la niebla y el cierzo,
que al hermoso infante asaltan,
con fuego de amor se oponen
de rayos de luz se arman.
Bizarramente pelean,
(siendo el viento la campaña,)
los rayos contra la niebla,
el fuego contra la escarcha.
Ya suenan los clarines
y hacen señal las cajas,
ya el escuadrón se acerca
y ya embisten sus mangas.
Y repiten los ecos
de las montañas:

SECOND COLUMN
los unos, guerra, guerra,
los otros, arma, arma.
Y, riéndose alegres,
corren las aguas,
porque un niño desnudo
triunfó de sus armas.
El infante a quien se atreven
que hoy a padecer se humana,

---

[1] This poem does not appear in Serrano y Sanz's inventory.

keep arms or feet still,
lads and lasses of Bethlehem.   [We are going to see heaven on earth.]

88. In keeping with the first couplet and refrain (that I did not write), I was asked to write these additional stanzas for the Nativity of Christ, and it was sung in the Holy Church in 1642 in Toledo.

From the empire fly down
troops of winged squadrons
who from the gulf of sapphire
plow the celestial beaches.
In royal Bethlehem they alight
where, among beasts and straw,
in poor human garb is dressed
the most sovereign deity.
The fog and north wind
assault the beautiful infant,
but they are opposed by the fire of love
armed with rays of light.
Gallantly they fight,
(being the wind the campaign,)
the rays against the fog,
the fire against the frost.
Now sound bugles
and the drums roll,
the squadron is approaching,
and attacks the lines of troops.
And the echoes repeat
in the mountains:

some, war, war;
others, to arms, to arms.
And happily laughing
the waters flow,
because a naked infant
was triumphant in arms.
The infant for whom they are so bold
today becomes human to suffer,

siente como quien no obliga
de amor con finezas tantas.
Gigante de amor si niño
llora tibiezas del alma
que el llorar es valentía
cuando es el rendirse hazaña.
La niebla, escarcha y el cierzo
que al sol de Belén contrastan
una y otra vez embisten,
combatiendo las murallas.
Ya suenan los clarines
y hacen señal [las cajas,
ya el escuadrón se acerca
y ya embisten sus mangas.]

89. Al bautismo de Cristo, año de 1643.

53r

Vengo del Jordán, zagales,
de contento tan fuera de mí
que no acierto a decir si entre flores
y entre plumas de varios colores,
la gloria del cielo en la tierra vi.
Ay, que no, mas, ay que sí,
porque ya advierto
que, para honrar al baptista,
hoy baja a la tierra el cielo.
Coplas: En el cristal del Jordán
miré de un sol y un lucero,
(en competencia de luces,)
equívocos los reflejos.
Vi, de uno y otro, los rayos
que en luciente golfo inmenso
corona son de la gracia
que se acrisola en su fuego.
Vi que el Verbo se bautiza,
 a Juan le gracia pidiendo,
que quiere que la autorice
en el primer sacramento.

FIRST COLUMN

53v

Vi de Cristo en la humildad,
y de Juan en lo supremo;
la disculpa de los hombres

and the love He feels
does not bind or oblige us.
This child is a giant of love
who gently cries,
for crying is valiant
when to surrender oneself is a heroic feat.
The fog, frost, and, the north wind
that contrast with the sun of Bethlehem
attack again and again
assaulting the walls.
Now sound the bugles
and the drums roll,
[the squadron is approaching,
and attacks the lines of troops.]

89. For the Baptism of Christ. 1643.

I come from the Jordan, lads and lasses,
so content that I am beside myself
for I do not know how to say, but among flowers
and among plumes of various colors,
I saw the glory of heaven on earth.
Ay, it cannot be, ay, but it is,
because now I assert
that, to honor the Baptist,
today heaven comes down to earth.
Stanzas: In the crystal water of the Jordan
I saw a sun and star,
in a competition of lights,
their reflections, ambiguous.
I saw, from one and the other, rays
that in a shining immense gulf
are a crown of grace
refined in their fire.
I saw the Word baptized,
asking this grace from John,
and thus wanting to authorize
this, the first sacrament.

I saw Christ in humility,
and John on high;
the pardoning of all men

que por Dios a Juan tuvieron.
Vengo del Jordán, [zagales,
de contento tan fuera de mí
que no acierto a decir si entre flores
y entre plumas de varios colores,
la gloria del cielo en la tierra vi.]
Aun en acto tan humilde
en Cristo y en Juan se vieron
de la grandeza, dos polos
y del poder, dos extremos.

SECOND COLUMN
Y como a Dios no acredita
allí Juan con voz ni dedo,
sólo el padre afirmar pudo
que el Baptista no era el Verbo.
No es mucho que por deidad
veneren a Juan los cielos
si a su dueño y Rey admiran
a sus pies con rendimiento.
Vengo del Jordán, [zagales,
de contento tan fuera de mí
que no acierto a decir si entre flores
y entre plumas de varios colores,
la gloria del cielo en la tierra vi.]

90. Décimas dándome el asunto.[1]

FIRST COLUMN
Enemigo pensamiento,
di, ¿qué pretendes que así
violentos llevas tras ti
la razón y entendimiento?
Advierte que el sufrimiento
tal vez se pierde al sufrir
lo que me das que sentir;
y pues importa callar,
o no me des que penar,
o exclúyame del vivir.

---

[1] Serrano y Sanz, 369–70; Olivares and Boyce, 1st ed., 336–37.

God accomplished through John.
I come from the Jordan, [lads and lasses,
so content that I am beside myself
for I do not know how to say, but among flowers
and among plumes of various colors,
I saw the glory of heaven on earth.]
Even in such a humble act
Christ and John appeared
as two poles of grandeur
and two extremes of power.

Since God did not authorize
John by word or by touch,
only the Father could affirm
that John was not the Word.
We should not be surprised that, as a deity,
John is venerated in the heavens
since they see their Lord and King
surrendered at his feet.
I come from the Jordan, [lads and lasses,
so content that I am beside myself
for I do not know how to say, but among flowers
and among plumes of various colors,
I saw the glory of heaven on earth.]

90. Décimas, charging me with a topic.

Enemy thought,
say, what are you trying to do
carrying off so violently
my reason and understanding?
It is said that by suffering
perhaps one ceases to suffer
what you are making me feel;
and it is important to keep quiet,
either do not give me grief,
or preclude me from living.

El deseo a sus antojos
propone remedios vanos
que aún no ejecutan las manos
cuando se ofenden mis ojos;
y aumentando estos enojos
pensamientos y deseos,
digo: Dejad devaneos,
crezca a la pena el rigor,
que si me niego al dolor,
no rindo al amor trofeos.

SECOND COLUMN
Si no pretendo romper
leyes de lo recatado,
¿para qué tanto cuidado
quiere el recato poner?
Viva espuela suele ser
del deseo y pensamiento
poner límite al intento
que amor sus alas prestó;
y si antes cortés nació,
vuela a ser atrevimiento.
No diga, no, que ama quien
tanto a la cordura atiende,
que el cariño se defiende
como si fuera desdén,
siendo preciso un vaivén
y forzosa una piedad
en quien tiene voluntad
efectos que aun Dios disculpa,
porque halla una noble culpa
perdón con facilidad.

91. Billete en verso de chanza, a una señora que me llamaba su galán. 54r

FIRST COLUMN
Señora, la nueva amiga
besa a usiría las manos,
y que excusa el escribiros
porque recela cansaros.
Que no gusta que queráis
a otra persona, está claro
que excluye de vuestro amor

Desire in the face of your whims
proposes vain remedies
that hands cannot execute
when the eyes are offended;
and augmenting this anger
are thoughts and desires,
I say: leave off, idle pursuits,
increase rigor in the face of pain,
for if I deny the suffering,
I do not render trophies to love.

If I do not intend to break
the laws of modesty,
why is so much care taken
to impose modesty?
It is usually a lively stimulus
of desire and thought
to put limits on one's intention
to which love gave wings;
if formerly, born courteous,
it boldly flies away.
Do not say, do not, that one who loves
pays attention to prudence,
and defends itself from affection
as if it were disdain,
being necessarily a risk
and obligatory pity
in who has the will
even these effects God forgives,
because He finds it a noble fault
to easily pardon.

91. **A joke in verse for a lady who called me her ladies' man.**

My lady, your new friend
kisses the hand of your ladyship,
please excuse me writing to you
because I fear I will bore you.
It is not pleasing that you love
another person, that is clear
and excluded from your love

así damas como damos.
Y aunque vuestra voluntad
la obediencia no la ha dado,
temo ya que sus preceptos
guarde vuestro modo hidalgo,
con que es preciso que pene
entre celos y cuidados
aqueste galán de anillo
como obispo Casamanio.
Favorecido se juzga
aunque le pongáis en grado
que le precedan amigas,
galanes, perros y gatos.

SECOND COLUMN
Si gloria a todos concede
el cielo de vuestro agrado,
vendrá a ser el capricornio,
signo al fin de armados cascos.
Advertid, pues, que los celos
dicen son hijos bastardos
de amor, y que si se enoja,
tendrá el galán dos trabajos.
Adiós, dama de mis ojos,
perdonad lo mal rimado
de estos versos que mi musa
por ahora está de paso.
Todas las de vuestra celda
os envían mil recaudos
amorosos, finos, firmes
y yo a Antandra diez abrazos.

92. Romance. Al niño perdido.

FIRST COLUMN
A celebrar del cordero
la alegre y festiva Pascua
en Jerusalén madruga
hoy la aurora soberana.

are both ladies and gentlemen.
And even though your will
has not given it obedience,
I fear its precepts
are hiding behind your gentlemanly manner,
and so he must pine away
between jealousy and cares
that gentlemen with a ring
like Bishop Casamanio's.[1]
One judges oneself favored
even though you find yourself in line with
girlfriends who precede you
along with young men, dogs, and cats.

If glory to all concedes
the paradise of your gratitude,
Capricorn will become
the sign of armed helmets.[2]
Take warning, for they say that jealousy
is the bastard son
of love, and that if he gets angry,
a lover will have two jobs.
Farewell, lady of my eyes,
pardon the bad rhymes
of these verses for my muse
has momentarily left me.
All those of your convent
send you a thousand greetings
loving, fine, and true,
and I, to Antandra, ten hugs.

92. Ballad for the lost Child.

To celebrate the lamb
a happy and festive Passover
dawns in Jerusalem
today the sovereign morning.

---

[1] Unidentified person.
[2] A reference to horns of a goat since the goat is the animal associated with the sign of Capricorn. "To wear horns" in Spanish means "to be cuckolded."

Síguela el sol y, vestidos
ambos de radiante gala,
el cielo a glorias inundan,
si la tierra a luces bañan.
Llegan al templo y advierten
de misteriosas palabras
en alegres profecías
las penas anticipadas.
Vuelve a Nazaret María,
(a quien Joseph acompaña,)
y, hallando menos el niño,
halla en sí menos el alma.
El camino retrocede,
impelida de sus ansias
donde nubes de tristeza
en lluvia hermosa desata.
(Si han visto, pregunta a todos,)
el hijo y Dios a quien ama
que es cifra de perfecciones,
de su pena hermosa causa.

SECOND COLUMN
No hay respuesta que aun dudoso
camino dé a la esperanza,
que quien triste busca alivio
tal vez en la duda, lo halla.
Entra al templo, ve a Jesús
y el gozo, entre penas tantas,
ya indeciso la detiene,
ya incrédulo la embaraza.
Reconoce al bello niño
luego a sus brazos se enlazan,
los de María gozosa
tanto como enamorada.
Fue igual a la pena el gusto
en quien a Jesús amaba
con el amor de justicia,
de naturaleza y gracia.
Y la madre en qué ha estado,
pregunta al hijo.
Y en negocios del Padre,
dice ha entendido.

The sun follows, and, dressed
both in radiant regalia,
heaven is flooded with glories
that bathe the earth with light.
They arrive at the temple and are advised
in mysterious words
about happy prophecies
and anticipated sufferings.
Mary returns to Nazareth,
Joseph accompanies her,
and, finding the child missing,
she feels as if she is missing her soul.
She retraces her steps,
propelled by her anguish
where clouds of sadness
release beautiful rain.
(She asks everyone if they have seen)
the Son and God whom she loves
who is a figure of perfections,
a beautiful cause for her pain.

There is no reply but even a doubtful
path can give hope,
for one who sadly seeks relief
perhaps will find it in doubt.
She enters the temple, she sees Jesus,
and the joy, amidst so much pain,
detains her, indecisive,
and disbelief restrains her.
She recognizes the beautiful child
who she then enfolds in a warm embrace,
Mary is as happy
as she is in love.
The joy was equal to the pain
in she who loved Jesus
with the love of justice,
naturally and gracefully.
The mother asks her son:
what were you doing.
Attending to the business of my Father,
He says in reply.

93. A la Purificación de Nuestra Señora. 55r

FIRST COLUMN
Hola, ao [sic], zagalejos,
que por el valle habitáis;
hola, ao, llegad,
que hoy la mayor fiesta
podéis celebrar,
pues Jesús y María
en el templo están.
Hola, ao, venid;
del globo celeste
veréis descendir [sic]
serafines bellos
aquí de mil en mil.
Hola, ao, llegad,
y veréis que en el templo
asientan el real
que compite en glorias
al orbe un mortal.
Hola, ao, venid:
mirad que la Reina,
más pura y feliz,
hoy al templo viene
la ley a cumplir.
Venid, venid:
que a la mayor fiesta
podéis asistir.
Llegad, llegad:
pues, se viene María
a purificar.

SECOND COLUMN
Zagalejos, yo confieso
que vi esta hermosa deidad
entre aladas jerarquías
de ese Olimpo celestial,
el sol, que en brazos conduce
con ostentosa beldad,
se retrata en los reflejos
de su virgíneo cristal.
Aunque la misma pureza,
en ella viéndose está,

93. To the Purification of Our Lady.

Hello, hello, lads and lasses,
who live in this valley;
hello, hello, come,
for today the greatest festival
you can celebrate,
for Jesus and Mary
are in the temple.
Hello, hello, come;
from the celestial globe
you will see descending
beautiful seraphim
here by the thousands.
Hello, hello, come;
and you will see that in the temple
seated royally, a mortal
who competes in glories
with the world.
Hello, hello, come;
see that the Queen,
so pure and so happy,
today comes to the temple
to comply with the law.
Come, come;
you can attend
the greatest festival.
Come, come;
Mary has come
to be purified.

Lads and lasses, I confess
that I saw this beautiful deity
among winged hierarchies
of that celestial Olympus,
the sun, that in its arms carries her,
with ostentatious beauty,
is portrayed in the reflections
of her virginal crystal.
Even though purity itself
is embodied in her,

humilde se purifica
con que se aquilata más.
El premio de su obediencia
llega María a lograr
en que hoy, obediente madre,
vuelve a Dios lo que la da.
Hola, ao, zagalejos que el valle habitáis;
hola, ao, llegad:
que hoy la mayor fiesta podéis celebrar,
pues María se viene
a purificar.

94. **A la traslación de una imagen de Nuestra Señora de una capilla a otra nueva en su fiesta de la Purificación, pidiéndome, se hiciese en la forma que el mismo villancico, dirá el que se sigue.**

FIRST COLUMN
Hoy que la fiesta celebran
en que la Reina divina
se purifica en el templo,
siéndola pureza misma.
Hoy, que ejemplo dando al mundo,
la cándida flor, María,
el que nos dio fruto hermoso
ofrece a Dios por primicia.
Con afecto reverente
la colocan a más rica
nueva mansión que en el templo
en vistosa maravilla.
De la antigua se despide
porque si es razón que obliga
mudarse por mejorarse
nunca más se verifica.
Dispensando inmensos rayos
de belleza peregrina
ya llega donde la cantan
las celestes jerarquías.

humbly she purifies herself
so that she might improve more.
The reward for her obedience
Mary attains
today, as obedient mother,
she returns to God that which He gave her.[1]
Hello, hello, lads and lasses who live in the valley;
Hello, hello, come:
for today is the greatest feast you can celebrate,
for Mary comes
to be purified.

94. **For the moving of an image of Our Lady from one chapel to another on the Feast of her Purification, I was asked to compose a carol and I did so, as follows.**

Today they celebrate the festival
when the divine Queen
purified herself in the temple,
being purity itself.
Today, giving an example to the world,
the white flower, Mary,
who gave us beautiful fruit,
offers her first fruits to God.
With reverent affections
they place her in a richer
new mansion in the temple
in spectacular marvel.
Of the old she takes leave
because reason dictates that
moving her to a better place
was never more justified.
Spilling out immense rays
of rare beauty
she now arrives where
celestial hierarchies sing to her.

---

[1] I.e., her purity.

SECOND COLUMN
Estribillo: Y alegres se imitan,
sonoros se compiten,
volando por el aire
los serafines,
dando con dulces voces
la bienvenida
a la Madre del sol que es aurora
de nuestro día.
Ya en su regio solio entra
y siguiendo a la capilla,
del cielo, la de la tierra
dicen en voces festivas:
Todos: sea bienvenida
la aurora soberana
de nuestro día.
Todo brilla en su presencia
y todo a su hermosa vista
impíreo [sic] cielo parece
que las almas glorifica.
Todos: sea bienvenida.

FIRST COLUMN
Los mayordomos insignes
de esta Reina esclarecida
que alcázar tan suntuoso
a su costa la fabrican
con espíritu bizarro,
con generosa hidalguía;
en el clarín de la fama
hoy sus nombres eternizan.

SECOND COLUMN
Todos la Reina festejen
y una y otra vez repitan:
sea bienvenida.
Todos: sea bienvenida,
la que es dulce instrumento
de nuestras dichas.
Estribillo: Y alegres se imitan
sonoras se compiten,
[volando por el aire
los serafines,

56r

Refrain: And happy they imitate,
harmonies compete,
flying through the air
the seraphim,
giving with sweet voices
welcome
to the Mother of the sun that is the dawn
of our day.
Now on her canopied throne she enters
her own chapel,
from heaven and from earth
they say in festive voices:
All: welcome
the sovereign dawn
of our day.
All shines in her presence
and everything in her beautiful view
seems an imperial heaven
that glorifies souls.
All: welcome.

The illustrious stewards
of this noble Queen
whose sumptuous castle
was built at their cost
with liberal spirit,
and generous nobility;
in the bugling of fame
today their names are eternalized.

All celebrate the Queen
and over and over repeat:
welcome.
All: Welcome
she who is a sweet instrument
of our good fortune.
Refrain: And happy they imitate,
harmonies compete,
[flying through the air
the seraphim,

dando con dulces voces
la bienvenida
a la Madre del sol que es aurora
de nuestro día.]

95. Romance burlesco para un billete.[1]

FIRST COLUMN
Dícenme que deseáis,
ilustrísima Señora,
saber de mi cara y talle
la disposición y forma.
Y porque quien me pintare
ni me quite ni me ponga,
quiero haceros de mi mano
una verdadera copia.
La cara, en buen pie lo diga,
ni bien es ancha ni angosta,

SECOND COLUMN
ni espantable por lo fea,
ni matante por lo hermosa;
y aunque cruda y aunque opaca
tan apacible se porta
que más de dos el verano
pueden pasarlo a su sombra.
Los dos troneras que llaman
son, (según dice el espejo,)
naturales de Etiopía.

FIRST COLUMN
A todos ven cuantos miran,
y cuando alguno aprisionan,
mandamiento de soltura
le dan a muy poca costa.
Las negras cejas en arco
preciadas siempre de ociosas
por no pagar, nunca tiran,
que adonde las dan, las toman.

---

[1] Serrano y Sanz, 370–71.

giving with sweet voices
welcome
to the Mother of the sun that is the dawn
of our day.]

95. **Note for a burlesque ballad.**
They tell me that you desire,
illustrious lady,
to know of my face and appearance
its disposition and form.
So that whoever paints me
may not take away anything or add anything
I want to make, with my own hand,
a true image.
My face, if all truth be told,
is not very wide nor very narrow,
not frighteningly ugly,

nor a killer beauty;
and although crude and opaque
it so gently carries itself
in the summer more than two
can shelter beneath its shadow.
The two openings, as they are called
windows of the soul,
are, according to the mirror
naturals of Ethiopia.

They see all they look at
and when they imprison someone
the order for release
they give at little cost.
The black eyebrows in an arch
valued as idlers
for they do not pay but neither do they take
and they always go where they are taken.

La nariz, que Dios mantenga,
algunos dicen, es roma,
mas no dirán que concede
el Papa gracias ni glorias.
Ya cuando menos me cato
hemos llegado a la boca
y es cual dicen que la casa
la buena portada honra.
Grande es por su majestad
de quien privilegio goza
de limpia y noble en aliento,
calidad de que blasona.

SECOND COLUMN
Las manos en el invierno
repiten a zanahorias,
moradas porque y por cuando
son ellas muy amorosas.
En el verano se mudan,
mas de una parte a otra,
que no es poco siendo mías,
pero de color mejoran.
El talle, aunque no es de los
de a mil ducados la onza,
por lo menos no me han visto
en las espalda corcova.
En fin, soy mujer cabal,
y esta verdad es notoria,
porque miembros, muelas, dientes,
ni mi faltan ni me sobran.
Aquesto, señora mía,
es cuanto a mi cuerpo toca;
cuanto al alma a Dios se quede,
no quiero apurar historias.
Tal cual soy me tendréis siempre
a vuestro servicio prompta,[1]
y si un tal para cual fuese
sería cosa de cosas.

---

[1] Although "pronto" is the modern form, here the poet uses the learned variation, "prompta."

The nose, may God preserve it,
some say, is Roman,
but they will not maintain that
the Pope concedes it graces or glories.
Now, looking at myself,
we have arrived at the mouth
and they say that a house
is honored by a good doorway.
It is grand in its majesty
and it enjoys the privilege of
being clean and of sweet breath,
a quality to be praised.

The hands in winter
look like carrots,
reddened because and when
they become amorous.
In the summer they move,
not from one place to another,
that would be strange since they are mine,
but they take on a better color.
My figure, although not one of those
that goes for a thousand ducats an ounce,
at least I do not have
a crooked back.
All in all, I am a complete woman,
and the truth is obvious,
because of limbs, molars, and teeth,
I do not have too many or too little.
That, my lady,
is all there is to my body;
as regards my soul, it is for God to say
and I do not want to hurry its story.
As I am, I will always be yours
and prompt to your service,
whether this, that, or the other
it will be my pleasure.

96. Romance burlesco a instancia de una amiga, cuyo galán 57r
pretendía picarla con otra dama, haciendo pruebas en su
voluntad.[1]

FIRST COLUMN
Que me quiera o no me quiera
importa poco, rey mío,
que soy de casta del huevo,
que a cualquier humor me aplico.
A quien me quisiere, quiero;
y a quien me olvida, le olvido;
quiérame, pues, y querránle [sic][2];
y si no loado sea Cristo.
Si piensa que con los celos,
como otras daifas, me pico,
para despicarme piense[3]
que son remedio efectivo;
que ésas viendo el cuerno al ojo
piensan que la muerte han visto,
y yo, que en sueño de toros,
amores nuevos concibo.
Confieso, pues, que los celos
son de amor claros indicios,
mas por no tener los celos,
tengo al amor en un hilo.

SECOND COLUMN
Gaste vsced[4] de esos cornados
con mujeres de poquito,
mas para mí que las vendo,
busque otra moneda, amigo.
Sepa que es mi pensamiento
por lo singular y activo,
si cuidando del bosque,
de las estrellas vecino.

---

[1] Olivares and Boyce, 1st ed., 364–65; Olivares and Boyce, 2nd ed., 259–61.

[2] Olivares and Boyce, 1st ed., reads "querréle." Their correction to the first-person singular is the most logical reading.

[3] Note the play on words of "picar" ("to sting") and "despicar" (literally, "to unsting").

[4] Abbreviation for "vuestra merced."

96. Burlesque ballad written at the insistence of a friend, whose lover tried to make her jealous with another woman to prove her loyalty.

That he loves me or does not love me
is of little importance, my king,
for I am can adapt to anything[1]
and I apply myself to whatever humor.
Whoever might love me, I love;
and he who forgets me, I forget him;
love me then, and I will love you;
and if not, may Christ be praised.
If he thinks that with jealousy,
like other ladies, he can sting me,
just repelling the sting I think
is the most effective remedy;
and women who see their lovers with other women[2]
think they have seen death,
and I, in dreams of bulls,[3]
new loves conceive.
I confess that jealousy
is a clear indicator of love,
but by not being jealous,
I have love by a string.

Wear yourself out with worthless ones,
with women of little worth,
but for me, I would sell them
for another coin, friend.
Well know that my thoughts
although singular and haughty,
caring for the forest,
is neighbor to the stars.

---

[1] This reading is suggested by my colleague, Idoia Elola, for a phrase that literally translated "chaste as the egg." Another colleague, Sara Guengerich, suggests that the poet may be referring to herself as a laying hen as an allusion to hens being passive in contrast to aggressive cocks. I am grateful for both these ideas.

[2] Again, I thank my colleagues, Idoia Elola and Sara Guengerich, for the translation of a difficult phrase, "viendo el cuerno al ojo."

[3] Olivares and Boyce, 1st ed., postulate that this means "to dream about other men" (365) and seems a valid interpretation.

Y sepa, si no lo sabe,
que más de veinte me han dicho
tal cual vez el ojo has negro,
y aun alguna,[1] el ojo has lindo.
Y después de dar de agrado
a cualquier alma dos chirlos,
queda siempre mi deseo
de polvo y de paja limpio.
Y si alguna vez me pica
algún mosco de buen pico,
con la saliva en ayunas
de la comezón me libro.

FIRST COLUMN
Primo tengo, si vsced prima,
que para todos hay primos
hechos de manga perdida
con vaqueros antiguos.
Déjeme, y Dios no me deje,
y válgame el refrancillo:
de si una puerta se cierra,
ciento se abren de improviso.

SECOND COLUMN
Que la vez que a cuento venga
le cantaré en mi retiro:
escollo armado de cuernos,
yo te conocí edificio.
Et cétera, Martín Porra,
Quod scripsit, escripsit digo;[2]
para ahora y para siempre
que sea mi Dios bendito.

---

[1] Olivares and Boyce, 1st ed., reads "alguno," a logical correction.

[2] A variation on the pronouncement of Pontius Pilate to the Jewish priests who protested against what Pilate wrote on the cross: Jesus, King of the Jews (John 19:22): "*Quod scripsi, scripsi*" (What I have written, I have written). The additional syllable in "escripsit" is to maintain the eight-syllable rhyme scheme (Olivares and Boyce, 1st ed., 366, n. 54).

And know, if you do not already know it,
that more than twenty have told me
that you have black eyes
and another that they are beautiful.
And after giving with pleasure
two deep cuts to some poor soul,
my desire always remains
without responsibility.
And if sometimes a fly
stings me[1] with a fierce bite,
with will power alone[2]
I will get over the itch.

A [male] sucker I have, and you have a patsy [female],
there are fools enough for everyone
shoddy pieces of work,
like people of little importance.
Leave me, but God do not leave me,
and may this little saying do me some good:
for when one door closes,
a hundred open all of a sudden.

So now the time has come,
I will sing to him as I depart:
stumbling block, armed with deceits,
I already knew what you were made of.
Et cetera, Martin Porra,[3]
what is written, is written, I say
so that now and forever
may God be blessed.

---

[1] Metaphorically, "to bother" or "to irritate."
[2] Literally, "fasting on spit."
[3] Olivares and Boyce conjecture that this may be the name of the young man in the poem with the reference to "porra" meaning a bothersome person. They also associate this name with the phrase, "manda a la porra" that means to reject someone with disdain or anger.

97. **Para una novela. Soneto.**[1]

En suspiros y llanto arroje el pecho
la causa que ocasiona mi dolencia,
aunque tras sí con rígida violencia
se lleve el corazón pedazos hecho.
Destiérranme de Clori, a mi despecho,
celos que esta me intiman cruel sentencia,
mas su gusto matando con la ausencia
ha de quedar mi agravio satisfecho.
Pues, a otro dueño concedieron palma
de amor, ¡oh ingrata, aleve!, tus favores,
a tu ruego cual áspid ser intento,
cerrando en mis oídos puerta al alma,
porque bien no se sirve a dos señores
si no es teniendo alguno mal contento.

98. **Décimas para una novela.**[2]   58r

FIRST COLUMN
Fatigado corazón,
¿qué os aqueja? ¿Ver el oro
de vuestro amado tesoro
convertido ya en carbón?
Apelad a la razón,
si descansar pretendéis,
y en ella conoceréis
que ese de mi vida engaño
os libra del desengaño
que en su muerte hallar podréis.
No me admira que sintáis
padecer sin culpa alguna
desaires de mi fortuna
cuando la pena pagáis;
mas si olvidado no estáis
de vos en vuestro desvelo,
pues sabéis que os hizo el cielo
tan valiente en el sufrir,
en parte os pueden servir
las desdichas de consuelo.

---

[1] Serrano y Sanz, 371; Olivares and Boyce, 1st ed., 331.
[2] Serrano y Sanz, 371; Olivares and Boyce, 1st ed., 338–39.

97. Sonnet for a novel.

Let my breast hurl forth sighs and weeping
for the cause of my suffering,
even though afterwards, with harsh violence
my heart may be carried off in pieces.
They banished me from Clori, to my indignation,
jealously imposed a cruel sentence on me,
but her pleasure, killing in its absence,
must satisfy my grievance.
To another lord was conceded the reward
of your loving favors, oh, ungrateful and treacherous one!,
but at your request I try to be like an asp,
closing my eyes, gateway of the soul,
because one cannot serve two masters
without leaving one discontented.[1]

98. Décimas for a novel.

Exhausted heart,
what afflicts you? To see the gold
of your beloved treasure
turned now into coal?
Appeal to reason,
if you want to rest,
and in it you will know
that life is a deception
and it will liberate you to know the lack of deception
that you may find in death.
It does not surprise me that you
suffer without any fault
the slights of my fortune
when you pay the price;
but if you are not forgotten
in your anxiety
you will know that heaven made you
valiant in suffering,
and, in part, this can serve
as a comfort for misfortunes.

---

[1] Reference to Matthew 6:24.

SECOND COLUMN
Esforzad el sufrimiento
consultando a la cordura,
que es suerte, si no ventura,
ver a tiempo un escarmiento.
Sufrid (que según yo siento
grande hazaña viene a ser,)
corazón mío, vencer
con sufrimiento el rigor,
por cuanto es mayor valor
el sufrir que el padecer.
Pues olvidar es forzoso,
determinaos, corazón,
a salir con la razón
de un abismo proceloso.
El triunfo[1] es dificultoso
y en vos poso el valor fuera
si fácil guerra emprendiera.
Si ésta os promete más gloria,
¡ea!, al arma, mi memoria,
muera el enemigo, muera.

99. Villancico a la entrada de dos hermanas hermosas a tomar hábito en la casa Real de la Concepción francisca. Logrando la música del estribillo, segunda vez. 58v

FIRST COLUMN
Hoy al jardín de María,
(madre, virgen pura siempre,)
ofrece amor dos pimpollos
de dos hermosos claveles.
Trasplantarlas de su mano
a Francisco pertenece
que, en fiarse a buena mano,
consiste la buena suerte.
Las flores que el real jardín
en cielo hermoso convierten,
gozosas las dos reciben
con mil festejos alegres.

---

[1] Serrano y Sanz reads "tiempo." This reading was corrected by Olivares and Boyce, 1st ed., 339 and I concur with their correction upon consulting the manuscript.

Be strong in your suffering
consulting your intelligence,
for it is luck, if not fortune,
to learn a lesson in time.
Suffer, for according to what I perceive
this can be a great feat,
heart of mine, to conquer
rigor with suffering,
for it takes more courage
to suffer than to endure.
You must forget,
be determined, heart,
by using reason, to free yourself
from a stormy abyss.
Triumph is difficult
but you have little valor
if you undertake an easy war.
If this [war] promises you more glory,
ay!, to arms, my memory,
may the enemy die, die.

99. Carol for the entrance of two beautiful sisters, taking the habit in the Royal Franciscan House of the Conception. With music for the refrain, a second time.

Today to the garden of Mary,
mother, ever Virgin,
love offers two flower buds
of two beautiful carnations.
Transplanting them with his hand,
they belong to Francis,
for confiding in a good hand
brings good luck.
In the royal garden of heaven
these two flowers are converted
and are received
with a thousand happy celebrations.

Y entre el golfo vistoso de plumas
que el viento matizan cuando las mueve,
voces suenan que dan a Mariana
y a Sebastiana mil parabienes.
Mariana que por María
nombre de gracia merece
en su gracia y en su nombre
a adquirir la gloria viene.

SECOND COLUMN
Sebastiana sigue amante,
aquel joven que valiente
rindió el corazón a flechas,
más del amor que la muerte.
Ambas buscando al esposo
a quien obligar pretenden,
hoy de su culto a las aras
primicias de amor ofrecen.
Y entre el golfo vistoso de plumas
[que el viento matizan cuando las mueve,
voces suenan que dan a Mariana
y a Sebastiana mil parabienes.]

100. Para la misma novela. Romance. Aunque le hice con asunto particular, y no para monja.[1]

FIRST COLUMN
Suspende al arco las flechas,
amor; basten ya tus tiros
que es rigor si no bajeza
quitar la vida a un rendido.
Tu piedad, amor, me valga,
pues eres dios, que es indigno
blasón en deidad tan alta
castigar nobles delitos.
Si te ofendió el sufrimiento
con que ocultar pude siglos
lo fuerte de tus combates,
lo imperioso de tus bríos.

---

[1] Serrano y Sanz, 371–72.

And among the colorful gulf of plumes
that shimmer when the wind moves them
voices ring out that give to Mariana
and to Sebastiana a thousand congratulations.
Mariana who for Mary
deserves the name of grace
in her grace and in her name
comes to claim glory.

Sebastiana follows a lover,
that young brave one
who surrendered his heart to arrows
more of love than of death.
Both looking for the bridegroom
to whom they render their obedience,
today to His cult at the altars
offer their first fruits of love.
And among the colorful gulf of plumes
[that shimmer when the wind moves them
voices ring out that give to Mariana
and to Sebastiana a thousand congratulations.]

100. **Ballad for the same novel. I wrote this for a private matter and not for a nun.**

Suspend the arrows in your bow,
love; enough of your shots
for it is a harsh and base act
to take the life of one who has already surrendered.
Your pity, love, is enough,
since you are a god, for it is an undignified
honor in such a high-placed deity
to punish noble crimes.
If suffering offended you
I would hide it for ages
against the force of your combats
and the imperiousness of your strength.

No fue negar la obediencia
a tu poder mi albedrío,
antes rendirle a tus aras
en honesto sacrificio.
Cuando callé, pude amar,
libre, amor, de tus peligros,
sin temer[1] de ingratitudes
cuidados al alma esquivos.
Mas rotos de la modestia
los lazos, y en el registro
mayor, ostentas, de amante
los afectos encendidos.

SECOND COLUMN
Naufragantes las potencias
entre gustosos delirios,
temer cuando más se logra
el gusto, mortal olvido.
No sé, amor, que triunfo sea,
pues se arguye del principio
de gozar, el fin más cierto
al desengaño propincuo.
Con el discurso luchando
todo el sosiego perdido
y arrestada toda el alma
muero, en fin, de lo que vivo.
Si lo que siento no ignora,
¿qué intentará el dueño mío,
cuando de mi amor prendado
dispone acerbos retiros?
Querer templar mi pasión
hoy con pretextos divinos,
es lo mismo que oponerse
a un rayo de ardientes giros.
Sacarme en prendas de amor
tantos del alma testigos
y en tan estimable empeño
negarme el premio debido.

---

[1] Serrano y Sanz, 372, reads "temor."

My will did not resist obedience
to your power,
before surrendering at your altar
in honest sacrifice.
When I kept quiet, I could love,
love, free of your dangers,
without fearing ingratitude,
stubborn cares of the soul.
But the ties of modesty were broken
and in the great registry,
you boast as a lover
inflaming affections.

But you shipwreck one's forces
among delirious delights,
fearing that when more pleasure
it achieves, it will be fatal forgetting.
I do not know, love, if it is a triumph,
since it can be claimed that from the beginning
of delight, the most certain end
is close to disappointment.
Struggling with words,
all serenity lost
and the soul detained
I die, in the end, from what gives me life.
If I do not ignore what I feel,
what will my master intend
when my captivated love
offers bitter retreat?
Wanting to temper my passion
today with divine pretexts
is the same as opposing
a spinning, burning ray.
Taking from me in pledges of love
so many witnesses of the soul
and in so estimable an endeavor
to deny me the deserved prize.

FIRST COLUMN
Ingratitud denotando
es ya de tibieza indicio,
que el que en gozando se templa
no es amante o es impío.

SECOND COLUMN
Piedad, ¡ay amor!, piedad,
otra y mil veces te pido,
o acabe mi vida luego,
rigor de matantes filos.

101. **A Santa Catalina de Sena. Romance logrando la música del estribillo segunda vez.**

FIRST COLUMN
¡Ay, que se abrasa de amor!
¡Ay, qué fénix de su incendio!
Muriendo de lo que vive
se eterniza en su amor mismo
el corazón más rendido
al amante más perfecto.
Hoy se mira en Catalina
triunfar de su rendimiento;
en la muerte y el amor
gana felices trofeos,
si en la muerte, eterna vida,
en el amor, dulce premio.
Las campanas que hacen la salva
sonoras al alba,
toquen a fuego
que de amor se abrasa muriendo.
Toquen a fuego,
que en vivas llamas

SECOND COLUMN
de amores tiernos
hoy Catalina,
prodigio bello,
fénix muere y renace
para los cielos
por lo hermosa y por lo pura,
rosa y azucena a un tiempo,

Showing ingratitude
signals a lack of warm,
for one who cools off in pleasure
is not a true lover or is cruel.

Pity, oh love!, pity.
I ask a thousand times,
or end my life,
with your severe and killing blades.

101. For Saint Catherine of Siena. Ballad with music for the refrain, the second time.

Oh, she is burning with love!
Oh, what a phoenix in the fire!
Dying for that which she lives
she is eternalized in her love,
with her heart fully surrendered
to a most perfect lover.
Today we see Catherine
triumphant in her submission;
in death and in love
she wins happy rewards,
if in death, eternal life,
in love, a sweet prize.
The bells that ring out the salute
harmonious at dawn,
ring out the fire
that she dies burning with love.
They ring out the fire
that in living flames

of tender love,
today Catherine,
beautiful prodigy,
is a phoenix that dies and is reborn
for the heavens
and in beauty and purity,
rose and white lily at once,

primores cede en el mayo,
fragancias espira al cielo.
Virtud, ciencia, y hermosura
la dan el grado supremo;
que son gracias tan divinas,
de sus glorias argumento,
cinco preciosos rubíes
que en prendas la dio su dueño,
a morir de amor la obligan
con presuroso ardimiento.
Las campanas que hacen [la salva
sonoras al alba,
toquen a fuego
que de amor se abrasa muriendo.]

102. **Al Santísimo Sacramento. Letrilla que se cantó en la santa iglesia de Toledo, año 1643.**

El jazmín que nació de la rosa
hoy nos dice la fe que reposa
en campo de flores
de varios colores,
y entre una azucena
se esconde clavel.
Linda flor se tiene la fe,
pues nos hace creer lo que no se ve.
Dice que es Rey de las flores
clavel que afecta candores
que clavado por amores
de amor maravilla fue.
Linda flor se tiene la fe,
pues nos hace creer lo que no se ve.
Tan bien dice es un bocado
de una flor confeccionado
adonde el gusto cifrado
cuando le coma hallaré.

she cedes delicacies in May,
and exhales fragrances toward heaven.
Virtue, intelligence, and beauty
are given to her in the highest degree;
her graces are so divine
that their story is told with,
five precious rubies[1]
that her master gave her as a reward
who makes her to die of love
rapidly burning.
The bells that ring out [the salute
harmonious at dawn,
ring out the fire
that she dies burning with love.]

102. To the most Holy Sacrament. Letrilla[2] sung in the Holy Church of Toledo in the year 1643.

The jasmine born of the rose
today tells us about faith that reposes
in a field of flowers
of different colors,
and among the lilies
a carnation hides.
Faith is a beautiful flower
that makes us believe what we cannot see.
They say that the king of the flowers
is the carnation that affects innocence
that nailed by love[3]
was a marvel of love.
Faith is a beautiful flower
that makes us believe what we cannot see.
It is well said that a morsel
made from a flower
will bring me great joy
when I eat it.

---

[1] Reference to the stigmata.
[2] Poem of short lines, usually sung, and with a refrain.
[3] The poet is using a play on the words "clavel" meaning carnation and "clavado" meaning nailed, as in Christ nailed to the cross. The red color of the carnation is thus linked with Christ's blood spilt on the cross.

Linda flor se tiene la fe,
[pues nos hace creer lo que no se ve.]
Dice más, que es pan de flor
en que a Dios me da el amor
que le coma con dolor
y salud conseguiré.
Linda flor se tiene la fe,
[pues nos hace creer lo que no se ve.]
Dice es pan de leche pura
que vida eterna asegura
y que yo a Dios y a ventura
le coma y que viviré.
Linda flora se tiene la fe,
[pues nos hace creer lo que no se ve.]
Dice que en esta comida
la gracia está reducida
que de gracia da la vida
y yo, que es gracia, creeré.
Linda flor se tiene la fe,
pues nos hace creer lo que no se ve.
El jazmín que nació de la rosa
hoy nos dice la fe que reposa
en campo de flores
de varios colores
y entre una azucena se esconde clavel.
Linda flor se tiene la fe,
pues nos hace creer lo que no se ve.
Flor dice es flor de perfección
que acogerla en ocasión
llegue con gracia y sazón
y fruto y flor cogeré.
Linda flor se tiene la fe,
[pues nos hace creer lo que no se ve.]
Dice si mi alma desea
ver el dueño en quien se emplea
que en esta forma le vea
y todo mi bien veré.
Linda flor se tiene la fe,
[pues nos hace creer lo que no se ve.]
Dice es galán singular,
tan tierno y fino en amar
que si le llego a obligar
el cielo pondrá a mi pie.

Faith is a beautiful flower
[that makes us believe what we cannot see.]
And it is said that in bread made of flowers
God gives me his love
and if I eat it in pain
afterward I will enjoy good health.
Faith is a beautiful flower
[that makes us believe what we cannot see.]
They say it is bread of pure milk
that assures eternal life
and in it God and good fortune
I eat so that I may live.
Faith is a beautiful flower
[that makes us believe what we cannot see.]
They say that in this food
grace is contained
and that grace gives life
and I will believe that it is grace.
Faith is a beautiful flower
that makes us believe what we cannot see.
The jasmine born of the rose
today tells us about faith that reposes
in a field of flowers
of different colors
and among the lilies hides the carnation.
Faith is a beautiful flower
that makes us believe what we cannot see.
This flower they say is the flower of perfection
and to receive it on occasion
may bring grace and flavor
then I will pick both fruit and flower.
Faith is a beautiful flower
[that makes us believe what we cannot see.]
They say that if my soul desires
to see the Master who uses
this form in which one may see Him
I will see all my well-being.
Faith is a beautiful flower
[that makes us believe what we cannot see.]
They say he is a singularly elegant man,
so tender and fine in loving
that if I ask Him
he will place heaven at my feet.

Linda flor se tiene la fe,
[pues nos hace creer lo que no se ve.]
Dice que es fuego entre nieve,
sol de amor en cielo breve,
luz de luz que el alma bebe
yo a tanto enigma[1] diré:
que linda flor se tiene la fe,
pues nos hace creer lo que no se ve.
El jazmín que nació, [de la rosa
hoy nos dice la fe que reposa
en campo de flores
de varios colores,
y entre una azucena
se esconde clavel.
Linda flor se tiene la fe,
pues nos hace creer lo que no se ve.]

103. Al evangelista San Juan, logrando segunda vez la música del estribo.

Hoy he visto a Juan, zagales,
tan ufano en la tina le vi
que me atrevo a decir que entre flores
y entre plumas de varios colores
la gloria del cielo le asiste allí.
Ay, que no, mas ay que sí,
porque ya advierto
que para alentarle al triunfo
hoy baja a la tierra el cielo.
Vi a Juan salir de la tina
el riesgo fatal venciendo,
que el ser de divino goza
con atributos de eterno,
Juan, que el blasón de divino
mereció, de Cristo al pecho,
si de inmortal le asegura.
No implica al martirio el premio,
contra el fuego y el amor
goza sacros privilegios;
que a un amor otro no vence,
ni un fuego ofende a otro fuego.

---

[1] Manuscript reads "egnima."

Faith is a beautiful flower
[that makes us believe what we cannot see.]
They say He is fire in the snow,
a brief sun of love in the heavens,
light from light that the soul drinks
and to so great an enigma, I say:
Faith is a beautiful flower
that makes us believe what we cannot see.
The jasmine that is born [of the rose
today tells us about faith that reposes
in a field of flowers
of different colors
and among the lilies hides the carnation.
Faith is a beautiful flower
that makes us believe what we cannot see.]

103. To the Evangelist, Saint John, with music for the refrain the second time.

Today I have seen John, lads and lasses,
I saw him so proud in the vat[1]
that I dare to say that among flowers
and among plumes of various colors
the glory of heaven accompanied him there.
Oh, I say no, but, oh, I say yes,
because now I assert
that to magnify his triumph
heaven today comes down to earth.
I saw John come out of the vat
overcoming the fatal danger,
his being enjoying divinity
John attained eternal attributes,
well-deserved by he who, at Christ's breast
was assured immortality.
The reward does not arise from martyrdom,
but love overcomes the fire and
enjoys sacred privileges;
for one love does not conquer another
nor a fire offend another fire.

---

[1] Saint John was tortured in a cauldron of boiling oil.

En recreos amorosos,
engolfado en pensamiento,
convierte en gloria del alma
la pena que siente el cuerpo.   Estribo.[1]
Fue de Cristo tan amado,
Juan, evangelista excelso,
que hoy la ley de agradecido
le puso en tan arduo empeño,
tan valiente como amante,
tan amante como el mismo,
buscando muerte, halla vida,
en el gusto del tormento,
en el tormento, descansa.
Que en un amante perfecto,
la pena es gustoso alivio,
el daño, dulce remedio;
y cual hizo amor a Juan
con Dios, y en ambos contemplo
de la grandeza, dos polos
y del amor, dos extremos.

104. Décimas escritas muy de priesa [sic], en respuesta de otras en que ponderaban la mudanza de las mujeres.[2]   62v

Hombres, no deshonoréis
con título de inconstantes
las mujeres, que diamantes
son si obligarles sabéis.
Si alguna mudable veis,
la mudanza es argumento
de que antes quiso de asiento,
mas en vuestra voluntad,
antes ni después, verdad
no se halló con fundamento.
Si mujer dice mudanza,
el hombre mentira dice;
y si en algo contradice,
es que el juicio no lo alcanza.

---

[1] Indication to the right of the poem.
[2] Serrano y Sanz, 372; Olivares and Boyce, 1st ed., 348; Olivares and Boyce, 2nd ed., 251–52.

In amorous delights,
engulfed in thought,
his soul converts into glory
the pain that the body feels.　　　Refrain.
He was so beloved of Christ,
John, sublime Evangelist,
that today the law of gratitude
placed him in an arduous situation,
so brave as a lover,
such a lover as himself,
who in looking for death, finds life,
joy in the torment,
in the torment, rest.
For, in a perfect lover
pain is joyful relief,
and harm, a sweet remedy;
and just as John was loved
by God, I see in both
two poles of greatness
and two extremes of love.

104. Décimas written in great haste, in response to other poems that consider the fickleness of women.

Men, do not dishonor
with the label of inconstant
women, who are diamonds
if you know how to treat them.
If you see one who is changeable,
the change is an argument
that previously she wanted to be settled;
but in your will,
before or after, truth
could not find a firm foundation.
If to be a woman means fickleness,
then to be a man means to lie;
and if this is a contradiction,
to my judgment, I see none.

Si se ajusta a igual balanza,
por la cuenta se hallaría
en él mentir cada día,
y en mudarse cada mes,
que el mentir vileza es,
mudar de hombres mejoría.

105. Dándome el asunto de un alma a quien Dios hacía singulares favores, hice estos versos.[1]

¡Que deseado tenía
hablar a solas con Vos,
mi dueño, mi bien, mi Dios,
cielo y luz del alma mía!
Que aunque siempre en mi memoria
presente os tengo, Señor,
es de amor
la soledad dulce gloria
donde se logra mejor.
Cuando a vuestros pies me veo
tiernos favores gozando,
de amor me voy exhalando
en un ferviente deseo;
y tan bien hallada estoy
sin mí, cuando más rendida,
que la vida
diera en que muriendo estoy,
por gozar de Vos, mi vida.
El que confiesa adoraros
no excusando el ofenderos,
o no llega a conoceros,
o no se precia de amaros;
que si en el conocimiento
la fuerza de amar consiste,
mal resiste
a amor el entendimiento
donde la razón asiste.
¿Quién para amante y esposo
a Vos, Señor, no apetece,
si sois el que permanece

---

[1] Serrano y Sanz, 372–73; Olivares and Boyce, 1st ed., 371–72; Olivares y Boyce, 2nd ed., 263–64.

If one adjusts the two with equal balance,
in the accounting, it would be found
that men lie every day,
and change every month,
for lying is despicable,
and it is men who need to change.

105. Taking as my theme a soul for whom God did singular favors, I made these verses.

How much I desired
to speak with You alone,
my master, my goodness, my God,
heaven and light of my soul!
And though always in my thoughts
I keep you present, Lord,
it is in love's
sweet, glorious solitude
where I best find You.
When I see myself at Your feet,
enjoying tender favors,
I exhale pure love
in fervent desire;
and I find myself so content,
without myself, when more surrendered to You
that my life
I would give, since I am dying
from the pleasure of You, my everything.
He who professes that he adores You
so as to avoid offending You,
either will never really know You,
or will not take pride in loving You;
for if in knowledge
the force of love consists,
badly resists
one's intellect the force of love
when reason is present.
Who as lover and husband,
for You, Lord, does not pine,
since You are always

galán, fino y poderoso?
Que cuando otro intento vano
de esta verdad le enajena,
dura pena
se ocasiona por su mano,
en que el error le condena.
El mundo gustos concede,
cual por brújula de antojos,
poniendo cerca a los ojos
lo que tocar no se puede.
Pero, mi Dios, vuestros gustos,
a toda satisfacción
del corazón,
dan, sin zozobrarle a sustos,
todo el gusto en perfección.
Yo a vuestros pies, dueño mío,
gozo de un bien sin igual
con que mejoro del mal
que causó mi desvarío;
y en no gozándole anhelo
a gozarle por sana,
sin desear
otro bien que éste del cielo
que jamás puede faltar.

106. Letra humana.[1]

FIRST COLUMN
Bella pastorcica de oro
cuyos ojos de esmeralda
desperdician finas perlas
de dos rosas sobre el nácar.
Dime qué a llorar te obliga,
que la admiración extraña
el ver triste un cielo hermoso
donde se gozan las almas.
Castiga [a] la que te ofende,
y pues que te adoran tantas,
para que adquieran su gloria,
merezcan, niña, tu gracia.

---

[1] Serrano y Sanz, 373; Olivares and Boyce, 1st ed., 357.

gallant, fine and powerful?
That when some other vain intention
takes one away from this truth,
an awful pain
is occasioned by one's own hand,
and the error condemns him.
The world gives us pleasures,
like a compass of whims,
putting near our eyes
that which we cannot touch.
But, my God, Your pleasures
are all satisfaction
and to the heart
give, inspiring fear,
all pleasure in true perfection.
I, at Your feet, my Lord,
enjoy goodness without equal
with which I overcome every evil
that would cause me to falter;
and when I do not enjoy goodness, I desire
to enjoy it and be made well,
without desiring
any other goodness other than this from heaven
that can never fail us.

106. Humane lyric.

Beautiful little shepherdess of gold,
your emerald eyes
squander fine pearls
like two roses on mother-of-pearl.
Tell me what is making you cry,
for it is a strange sight
to see such a beautiful heaven sad
where souls take delight.
Punish her who offends you,
since so many adore you,
so that they may acquire glory,
and deserve your grace, dear child.

Baste el llanto, hermoso hechizo,
que a quien envidia la causa
con fuego de celos, hielas;
con agua de amor, abrasas.

SECOND COLUMN
Aqueste campo que honoras,
archivo fiel de tus ansias,
culto a tu deidad ofrece,
primores cede a tu gala.
Pastorcica de perlas,
si el sol y el alba
en tu vista se gozan,
¿qué harán las plantas?
Las flores enamoras,
porque al tocarlas
alma las comunica
tu mano blanca.

107. **Elogio a un libro de antinomias que escribió el doctor Alfián en favor de la medicina, de cuyas razones se arguye ser insigne estudiante según ellas mismas lo manifiestan y declaran.** 65r

Atentas admiraciones
hoy a tu ingenio consagro
por erudito, milagro
que ha unido contradicciones.
Mas, pues, se da a conocer
su esencia, nada me asombre
siendo de hombre
que de Dios debe tener
entre los dioses renombre.
Si a Esculapio[1] fabuloso
le dan a Apolo por padre,
a ti es más justo te cuadre
doctor insigne y famoso.
Hijo del dios de la ciencia,
todo el orbe te venere,

---

[1] Aesculapius is the Roman god of medicine and healing.

Enough of crying, beautiful enchantress,
for it causes envy in those that
you freeze with the fire of jealousy
and burn with the waters of love.

That field that you honor,
confidant of your anxieties,
offers worship to your godliness,
and its first fruits to your celebration.
Little shepherdess of pearls,
if the sun and the dawn
take joy in your sight,
what will the plants do?
You enamor the flowers
because, touching them,
you give them a soul
with your white hand.

107. Eulogy to a book about contradictions that Doctor Alfián[1] wrote in favor of the science of medicine that attests to his eminence as a scholar.

Attentive admirations
today I consecrate to your intelligence
and your miraculous erudition
that has unified contradictions.
It is well known
that its essence should not surprise since it is
from a man
who has from God
renown among the gods.
If the fabulous god of healing
had Apollo as his father,
it is more just that you be named
a famous and exemplary doctor.
As a son of the god of science,
may all the world venerate you

---

[1] An interesting treatise by Dr. Juan Bautista de Alfián, housed in the BNE, is entitled, *Discurso nuevo y heroico del uso de los baños de agua dulce que se usan en el río y casa particular* (*New and Heroic Discourse about the Use of Fresh Water Baths in the River and in the Private Home*), published by Juan Ruiz de Pereda in Toledo in 1641 (R/4419).

pues, te adquiere
tan alto ser tu elocuencia
que al ser de humano prefiere.
De las más incompatibles
haces razones notorias
porque lo sean las glorias
de hazañas menos factibles.
No tema ya la salud
el tiempo ningún vaivén
que aquí se ven
razones de tal virtud
que el mal trocarán en bien.
No explicando lo que siento,
mas tu alabanza consigo
que aun teme quedar contigo
corto, el mayor sentimiento.
Goza, pues, la edad que el sol
con cuya copia luciente
a tu fuente
corone, ilustre español,
Docto Esculapio excelente.

108. Villancico a Doña María de la Puebla profesando en la Concepción francisca de Toledo y estando el Santísimo Sacramento descubierto.

FIRST COLUMN
Tierna esposa del cordero
en cuyo vellón de plata
tan rico dote interesas
que a tu caudal nadie iguala.
Dime, ¿qué deidad consultas,
qué discreción te acompaña
que así eliges, sabia niña,
esposo que nunca falta?
Mas ya advierto que María,
Reina de este sacro alcázar,
con cuyo nombre te honoras
te concede dicha tanta.
Para esposo te da un hijo,
fiel galán, sabio monarca
con quien tu logro se mira
más allá de la esperanza.

since your eloquence
gains you such renown,
and preference among men.
Of the most incompatible concepts
you make notable arguments
because it is a glorious feat
to bring together unlikely things.
Health now does not fear
the fluctuations of time
because here is seen
reasoning of such virtue
that it turns bad into good.
Although not explaining what I feel,
but to your praise I aspire
although I fear I may sell you
short in expressing even my greatest feeling.
Enjoy, then, the golden age
whose bright reflection
at your spring
crowns you, illustrious Spaniard,
wise and excellent Aesculapius.

108. Carol for Doña María de la Puebla professing at the Franciscan Convent of the Conception in Toledo with the Holy Sacrament displayed.

Tender bride of the lamb
on whose silvery fleece
you bestow such a rich dowry
that no one could equal its worth.
Tell me, what deity do you consult,
and what discretion has led you
to choose, wise child,
a husband who will never fail?
But I remind you that Mary,
Queen of this sacred castle,
with whose name you are honored
concedes this good fortune to you.
For bridegroom she gives you her Son,
faithful and gallant, a wise monarch
with whom one sees you achieve
hope everlasting.

SECOND COLUMN
El gran Francisco es padrino
que con admirable gala
te ofrece rubíes cinco
de perfección soberana.
Ser madrina pertenece
a Beatriz, flor de las gracias,
pues, para esposa de Cristo,
Te ha observado flor intacta.
      Estribo:
Mira hermosa María
si el sol y el alba
de tus dichas se alegran,
¿Qué harán las plantas?
Festéjense las flores
que se acompañan
de esta flor que Dios hizo
con mano franca.

FIRST COLUMN
Puebla hermosa en tus bodas,
grande es la fiesta
y a ilustrarla, el impireo [sic]
hoy se despuebla.
En el cielo y la tierra
aplausos te dan
como a reina escogida
del Rey celestial.
Hoy saldrás, fina amante
de este sol de amor,
porque estás de sus rayos
puesta en el crisol.
Cuanto más te le oculta
la nube blanca,
le franquea a tu gusto
su bella gracia.

The great Francis is your godfather
who with admirable celebration
offers you five rubies[1]
of sovereign perfection.
The godmother
is Beatrice, flower of graces,
and to be a bride of Christ,
she preserves you as an intact flower.
              Refrain:
Beautiful Mary, look and see that
if the sun and the dawn
are happy for your good fortune,
what will the plants do?
May the flowers celebrate
who accompany
this flower that God made
with His generous hand.

Beauty imbues your wedding,
great is the feast
and today to celebrate it, the empire
is depopulated.[2]
On heaven and earth
they applaud you
as a chosen queen
of the celestial King.
Today you go out, fine lover,
from this sun of love,
and with his rays you are
enshrined in crystal.
For however much you may be shadowed by
a white cloud,
it will vanish at your command
by His beautiful grace.

---

[1] The stigmata.
[2] In other words, celestial beings come down from heaven to be guests at this wedding.

Aunque el blanco vestido
paz te promete,
no le ofendas porque usa
mucho el celeste.

SECOND COLUMN
Gózate en el divino
feliz empleo
que son novio y padrino
cosa del cielo.
Niña, hermosa María,
si el sol y el alba
de tus dichas se alegran,
¿Qué harán las plantas?
Festéjense las flores
que se acompañan
de esta flor Dios hizo
con mano franca.

109. A la arrebatada y lastimosa muerte de Doña Ana de Briones, monja de San Clemente de Toledo, de edad de 26.[1]

Fatal rigor ejecutando aleve
la Parca corta el hilo de una vida,
astuta, recelándose vencida,
de su bizarro ardor, en tiempo breve.
Postrada yace al fin de un soplo leve,
lozana planta que en edad florida
a poca tierra infausta reducida,
desengaños causando, a llanto mueve.
Fue Anarda toda gala, entendimiento,
deidad de ingenio, alma y hermosura,
que luego en sí lograrla el cielo quiso.
No atienda no, a su falta de sentimiento
a un punto en que ganó, si por ventura
gloriosa vida en un morir preciso.

---

[1] Serrano y Sanz, 373.

Even though a white gown
promises you peace,
you are content that it is mixed
with much celestial blue.[1]

Take delight in the divine
and happy deed
for the bride and the godfather
are both beings from heaven.
Child, beautiful Mary,
if the sun and the dawn
are happy for your good fortune,
what will the flowers do?
May the flowers celebrate
who accompany
this flower that God made
with His generous hand.

109. For the sudden and grievous death of Doña Ana de Briones, a nun of Saint Clement of Toledo, at the age of 26.

With fatal rigor and treachery
Parca[2] cuts the thread of a life,
wisely since she suspected to be defeated
in a brief time by her fervent ardor.
In the end, she lies prostrate from a light blow,
a vigorous plant in its prime
reduced to a little ill-starred dust,
causing disillusionments that move one to tears.
Anarda was all festive, wise,
a goddess of wit, soul of beauty,
that heaven wanted for itself.
Do not think on her loss
for, by fortune, she earned
in death, a more glorious life.

---

[1] The Conceptionists' habit is white with blue.
[2] One of the Fates in Roman mythology.

110. Letra al Santísimo Sacramento, logrando el estribo humano puesto en música. 67v

Estribo: Triste pensamiento, diles
        a los ojos que más quiero,
        que me muero.

FIRST COLUMN
Dile, pensamiento mío,
a mi fiel amante y dueño
que es triste muerte la vida,
pues, de su vista carezco.
Que aunque galán se concede
a mis ojos encubierto,
gloria no tendré en el alma
hasta gozarle sin velo.
Que, pues, la causa permite
del mal que sin él padezco
que en toda parte me asista
pues, es todo mi remedio.
Triste pensamiento, [diles
a los ojos que más quiero,
que me muero.]
Dile a mi amante que el gusto
en su amor lograr deseo,
que solamente se logra
en Él que es amor perfecto.

SECOND COLUMN
Que el mundo me ofrece dichas
donde, en vez de cumplimiento,
pruebo en desengaño amargo
lo dulce de sus efectos.
Que apenas en sus deleites
a aliviar mis penas llego
cuando me hallo arrepentida
más allá del escarmiento.
Triste pensamiento, diles
a los ojos que más quiero,
que me muero.

110. Poem for the Holy Sacrament, with a secular refrain set to music.

> Refrain: Sad thought, tell
> the eyes that I most love
> that I am dying.

Tell, thought of mine,
my faithful lover and master
that life is a sad death
when I do not see Him.
And even though I glimpse this gallant one
veiled before my eyes,
I will not have glory in my soul
until I enjoy Him unveiled.
Some cause permits
the hardship I suffer without Him,
for everywhere that He may be present
He becomes my sure remedy.
Sad thought, [tell
the eyes that I most love
that I am dying.]
Tell my lover that the pleasure
of His love I long to enjoy,
for it can only be found
in Him who is perfect love.

The world offers me delights
where, instead of joy,
I taste bitter disillusionment
in the sweetness of their effects.
Barely in these delights
do I manage to alleviate my pains,
when I find myself repenting
having learned my lesson.
Sad thought, tell
the eyes that I most love
that I am dying.

111. Villancico a Doña Catalina de Molina, profesando en el convento de San Torcuato de la Orden de San Agustín en la fiesta de la Purificación de Nuestra Señora.

Estribo: Escuchad, zagalejos, las aves,
        cómo cantan con gala y primor
        motetes suaves al alba, María,
        y dulces requiebros y amores al sol.

Jesús, qué favor,
que las bodas celebrar de una hermosa flor;
Jesús, qué dicha,
que el sol, Cristo, se casa con Catalina.
Huyendo la obscura sombra
de las profanas delicias
que a tantas hermosas flores
el puro verdor marchitan,
hoy segunda vez al sol
intacta flor se dedica,
Catalina, Clicie, amante
de los rayos que codicia.[1]
A un rey para esposo elige
que tenga, no es maravilla,
siendo Agustino su padre
pensamientos de entendida.
Si con finezas el alma
para esposo a un rey obliga
ser reina será lo menos
cuando de lo más es digna.
Porque flor pura se observe
al ejemplo de María,
siendo flor de la pureza,
humilde se purifica.
A esta hermosa reina escoge
la novia para madrina,
vinculando en sus favores
todo el colmo de sus dichas.
Su majestad la da en premio
de esta fineza que estima
un Jesús que trae al pecho,

---

[1] "cudicia" in the manuscript.

111. **Carol for Doña Catalina de Molina, professing in the Convent of Saint Torquatus of the Order of Saint Augustine on the Feast of the Purification of Our Lady.**

Refrain: Listen, lads and lasses, to the birds,
            how they marvelously sing with celebration
            gentle motets to the dawn, Mary,
            and sweet endearments and love to the sun.

Jesus, what a favor
to celebrate the wedding of a beautiful flower;
Jesus, what good fortune,
that the sun, Christ, is marrying Catalina.
Fleeing from the dark shadows
of profane delights,
where so many beautiful flowers
have withered while still green,
today a second time to the sun
an unblemished flower dedicates herself,
Catalina, Clytia,[1] lover
who covets its rays.
She elects a king for her groom,
this should not be surprising,
being Augustine her father,
such an intelligent choice.
With graciousness the soul
chooses a king as her spouse
to assure that she who is so deserving
will be no less than a queen.
Because this pure flower has observed
the example of Mary,
being a flower of purity,
she humbly purifies herself.
This beautiful queen
the bride chooses for her godmother,
joining to her favors
the sure promise of good fortune.
She gives her majesty as a reward
for the graciousness that she so esteems
and brings her to Jesus's breast,

---

[1] Nymph enamored of Apollo who, after he abandoned her, turned into a flower that always followed the sun, i.e., a sunflower.

joya más que el cielo, rica.
Con velo a la novia velan
porque velando consiga
toda la gloria sin velo
en el reino adonde aspira.
[Escuchad, zagalejos, las aves,
cómo cantan con gala y primor
  motetes suaves al alba, María,
  y dulces requiebros y amores al sol.]

112. Décimas estrambotadas para una novela.[1] 69r

FIRST COLUMN
Baste el injusto rigor,
tirana[2] de mi albedrío;
permite que ya sea mío,
pues me quitaste tu amor.
Cuando, dueño fiel del alma,
te apreció mi entendimiento,
el rendimiento
era de amor dulce palma
y ya es amargo tormento.
Mudar de dueño procura
mi amor, de ti mal pagado,
que consuela a un desdichado
esto de probar ventura.
Pero tanto dura en mí
la fe del amor primero
que no espero
mejorarme, pues, sin ti,
sin gusto y sin alma, muero.

SECOND COLUMN
No puede el discurso hallar
razón que mi pena enfrene,
que quien pierde el bien que tiene
bien tiene por qué penar.

---

[1] Serrano y Sanz, 374; Olivares and Boyce, 1st ed., 334–35.
[2] Olivares and Boyce, 1st ed. reads "tirano." Serrano y Sanz reads "tirana" as does the manuscript although the lack of agreement with "rigor" warrants Olivares and Boyce's correction.

a jewel richer than heaven.
The bride wears a veil
so that veiled she may obtain
all the unveiled glory
in the kingdom to which she aspires.
[Listen, lads and lasses, to the birds,
how they marvelously sing with celebration
gentle motets to the dawn, Mary,
and sweet endearments and love to the sun.]

112. Extra lines for a song for a novel.

Enough of unjust rigor,
tyrant of my free will;
let my will be mine again
since your love took it from me.
When, faithful master of my soul,
my understanding esteemed you,
the surrender
was a sweet glory of love
but is now a bitter torment.
Wanting a change of master,
my love, by you so badly repaid,
for trying to console misfortune
is to tempt fate.
But so enduring in me is
that faith of my first love,
that I do not expect
to get better, because, without you,
without pleasure and without a soul, I am dying.

Words cannot express any
way to curb my pain,
for one who loses something fine
well has reason to grieve.

Y luego siento piadoso
que mi amor firme has perdido
y, ofendido,
digo: olvidar es forzoso
y solo de mí me olvido.
¡Qué feliz mi suerte fuera,
si antes de llegar la suerte
de gozar el bien de verte,
prevenir el mal pudiera!
Pues así el alma ofendida
no sintiera un dolor tal;
que neutral
está penando la vida
entre aquel bien y este mal.

113. A Santa Catalina di [sic] Esena.

FIRST COLUMN
Esparciendo hermosos rayos
que esferas doran azules,
aquella deidad de Esena
al cielo triunfante sube.
Volante música tropa
de ángeles que la conduce,
eon emulación previene,
lauro eterno a sus virtudes.
El Rey, a quien niña tierna
amante se constituye,
hoy la corona premiando
de su amor las prontitudes.
Bello vergel prodigioso
fue aquesta virgen ilustre,
pues, que de espinas sembrado,
cinco claveles produce.
Finezas de amor logrando
tantas glorias se atribuye
cuantas del esposo penas
a su corazón traduce.

And later I feel kind-hearted
that my steadfast love you have lost
and offended,
I say: one must forget,
but, I only forget myself.
How happy my fate was,
but feeling lucky,
enjoying the sight of you,
was in fact a harbinger of bad luck!
Thus, the offended soul
does not feel such a pain,
being neutral
it is suffering in life
between that goodness and this pain.

113. To Saint Catherine of Siena.

Spreading beautiful rays
that make the blue spheres golden,
that deity of Siena
triumphantly rises to heaven.
A flying musical troupe
of angels conducts her,
with emulation foreseeing
eternal laurels for her virtues.
The King, to whom the tender child
is bound as to a lover,
today, awarding a crown for
the eager willingness of her love.
A beautiful prodigious orchard
was that illustrious virgin
who, sown with thorns
produced five carnations.[1]
Achieving the graces of love,
so many glories are attributed to her,
and the pains of her groom
are transferred to her heart.

---

[1] Reference to the stigmata.

SECOND COLUMN
Celestiales perfecciones,
que en Catalina concurren,
dicen de Dios más grandeza
porque más en ellas luce.
Por deidad soberana
la contribuyen
el aurora, candores,
y el Febo, luces.

114. Otra letra a Santa Catalina de Esena.

FIRST COLUMN
Catalina, en quien el cielo
atesora prendas tantas,
que hermoso prodigio admiras,
discreto milagro pasmas.
Tú, que al esposo que adoras
siempre obligas, siempre agradas;
tan perfecta como bella,
tan amante como sabia.
Tú, pues, que en naciendo fuiste
cándida flor de la gracia,
y ya de amor, mariposa,
mueres en su ardiente llama.
No se diga que comunes
mortales penas te asaltan,[1]
pues, vida en la muerte adquieres,
y gloria en las penas hallas.

SECOND COLUMN
Al enemigo venciste
con resolución bizarra,
ganando a sangre y a fuego
la victoria que hoy te cantan.
Tu triunfo celebra el cielo
con canoras alabanzas
cuando eterna te aseguran
en tu gloria y en tu fama.

---

[1] Manuscript reads "acaltan."

Celestial perfections
that in Catherine concur,
they tell of God's graces
for they so shine in her.
As a sovereign deity
she is given
pure whiteness by the dawn
and lights from Phoebus.

114. Another to Saint Catherine of Siena.

Catherine, in whom heaven
stored up so many gifts as treasure,
you are admired as a beautiful wonder,
and you astonish as a discrete miracle.
You, who so adore your spouse
who you always gratify, always please;
as perfect as you are beautiful,
as loving as you are wise.
You, who when born was
a white flower of grace
and a butterfly of love
who dies in a burning flame.
Do not call common
the mortal pains that assault you,
for you gained life with your death
and you found glory in pain.

You conquered the enemy
with brave resolve,
earning by blood and fire
the victory that today they sing for you.
Heaven celebrates your triumph
with harmonious praises
and they confirm you eternal
in your glory and your fame.

115. A la venida del Espíritu Santo. Cantóse en la Santa Iglesia de Sevilla. Año 1644.

Como bajan rasgando las nubes,
escuadras vistosas de angélicas aves
que volando, corriendo,
rompen el aire
y con canora armonía,
dando nuevas de alegría,
dicen que ya el sol envía
al mundo sus rayos mismos,
que son flechas doradas de amor divino.
Hoy, desde su paralelo,
el sol de amor infinito,
en el cielo de la iglesia
ilumina doce signos.
De la luz de su amor quiere
que remedos siendo activos,
luz de amor al alma influyan
con documentos divinos
fulgente vibra amorosos
rayos de flamantes filos
contra tristezas que al hombre
causó el primer delito.
Lenguas son que al alma enseñan,
de bien amar el estilo
con ternuras[1] fervorosas,
con ardores persuasivos.   Estribo.[2]
Éste, pues, sol increado,
que naciendo de sí mismo,
es ya en su amorosa llama,
fénix de cándido armiño
cuyo calor vivifica
incultas plantas del siglo
porque fructíferas sean
árboles del paraíso,
hecho rayos, hecho lenguas,
dando de su amor indicios
hoy a un fin dichoso empeña
al alma en este principio.

---

[1] "instancias" is underlined and "ternuras" appears below it. There is a note in the left margin of the folio that reads "Uno u otro." I elect here the reading "ternuras."

[2] "estribo" follows "persuasivos" to the right.

115. To the coming of the Holy Spirit. Sung in the Holy Church of Seville in 1644.

How they come down tearing through the clouds,
bright-colored squadrons of angelic birds
that swiftly flying,
cut through the air
and with melodious harmony,
giving happy news,
say that the sun has sent
to earth its own rays
that are golden arrows of divine love.
Today, from its sphere,
the sun of infinite love,
in the church of heaven
illuminates twelve signs.[1]
For the light of His love He wants
active imitations
so that the light of love may influence the soul
with divine instructions
brilliantly and lovingly vibrate
rays of resplendent filaments
against the sadness that mankind
caused with the first sin.
They are tongues that teach the soul
the ways of good love
with fervent[2] tenderness,
and with persuasive ardor.   Refrain.
This sun, eternal, not created,
being born from itself,
is now an amorous flame,
a phoenix of white ermine
whose heat gives life
to the uncultivated plants of the world
so that they might bear fruit
as trees of paradise,
made rays, made tongues,
giving evidence of his love
today he gives a happy ending
to the soul in this beginning.

---

[1] All signs of the zodiac, i.e., the whole sky.
[2] An alternate reading of "fervent authority" is also possible. See note to the Spanish transcription.

116. Al Santísimo Sacramento. Letra vuelta de la humana que queda escrita.

Corazón, pues, halláis el vivir
en lo mismo que os puede matar,
dejadme llorar de vuestro reír,
dejadme reír de vuestro llorar.

FIRST COLUMN
Al convite soberano
venís, corazón, y a fe
que llegaréis con buen pie
si dais al mundo de mano.
Y si acertar a llegar
consiste en saberle huir,
dejadme llorar de vuestro reír,
dejadme reír de vuestro llorar.
Mejorar queréis mi suerte,
comiendo de aqueste pan,
donde cifradas están
pena y gloria, vida y muerte.
Y, pues, gloria en el penar
buscáis, y vida en morir,
dejadme llorar de vuestro reír,
dejadme reír de vuestro llorar.

SECOND COLUMN
El pan con dolor coméis,
fiando de su virtud
que la perdida salud
al alma restituiréis.
Y si en vos para sanar,
es medicina el sentir,
dejadme llorar de vuestro reír,
dejadme reír de vuestro llorar.
En pan de flor os convida
con dulce vida el amor,
andaos, por Dios, a esta flor
y tendremos buena vida.

116. To the Holy Sacrament. Adapted from a secular theme and written as follows.

> Heart, you will find life
> in that which could also kill you,
> let me cry for your laughing,
> let me laugh for your crying.

To the sovereign invitation
you come, heart, and to faith
you will safely arrive
if you put the world aside.[1]
To arrive with certainly
you must know how to flee from it [the world],
let me cry for your laughing,
let me laugh for your crying.
You want to better my luck,
eating of that bread
that encompasses
pain, glory, life, and death.
For you seek glory
in suffering and life in dying,
let me cry for your laughing,
let me laugh for your crying.

The bread that you eat with pain,
confident in its virtue,
for even though health may be lost,
you soul will be restored.
And if you wish to get well,
feeling regret is the medicine,
let me cry for your laughing,
let me laugh for your crying.
In bread of flowers, you are invited
by love with sweet life,
walk, for God's sake, to this flower
and we will have a good life.

---

[1] The pun here consists of a play on "pie" (foot) and "mano" (hand), i.e., if you brush off (literally, with your hands) the ways of the world, your feet will lead you to the way of salvation.

Mas si os habéis a ajustar
solo a comer por[1] vivir,
dejadme llorar de vuestro reír,
dejadme reír de vuestro llorar.

117. **Celebrando la misa nueva un sacerdote en cuya fiesta escribieron algunos toledanos a ruego de un su amigo, y, yo, diciendo así.**

72r

FIRST COLUMN

Con Dios mismo competencia
parece a tener venís,
Pedro, y si buen lo advertís
llana está la consecuencia.
Pues, si aqueste Dios, amante,
os puede subir al cielo,
es constante
que vos, Pedro, en un instante
bajarle podéis al suelo.
Que a su padre exceda un hijo
dicen que jamás se vio
y que vos le excedéis, yo,
de buena razón, colijo
que si al príncipe de fama
vuestro padre le hizo Dios.
Su vicediós
desde hoy a vos Cristo os llama,
Dios transformándose en vos,

SECOND COLUMN

cumplido, pues, cual piedra fuerte
con la obligación del nombre,
no en el negar como hombre
con ser dios que en sí os convierte
que si en cualquiera es traición
negarle a su rey la ley
de razón.

---

[1] "por" is written over "para", an obvious correction in the manuscript.

For you understand that
only by eating will you live,
let me cry for your laughing,
let me laugh for your crying.

117. **For a priest celebrating his first mass,**[1] **some Toledans wrote about this occasion on the request of their friend, and I wrote the following.**

The same competence as God
you seem to have acquired,
Peter, if well you notice
the consequence is natural.
For if that God, lover,
who can raise you up to heaven
is constant
then, Peter, in an instant
you can bring Him down to earth.
That the son exceeds the father
they say is never seen
but you do exceed him,
I infer, with good reason
that the prince of fame
made God your father.
A vice-god
from today forward Christ calls you,
for God has transformed Himself in you,

made like strong rock
in accordance with your name,[2]
and by not denying your humanity
you have been converted into a god
for in anyone it is treason
to deny to his king the law
of reason.

---

[1] The literal translation is "new mass" but it seems more likely that the title refers to a priest's first mass since it occasions the writing of various congratulatory poems as indicated in this poem's title.

[2] Peter, whose name derives from Greek, "petra," boulder or building stone.

Más condenable es la acción
en quien le hace igual el rey,
que piedra, Pedro, seréis
de diamante soberano,
si os labráis de vuestra mano
con el que en ellas tenéis.
Ya vuestra suerte te emulando
qué perfecto os considero.
Pedro, cuando
labrando os vais, o lavando
con sangre de ese cordero.

118. Romance para la novela.[1] 72v

FIRST COLUMN
Pues, gustas, mi dueño hermoso,
que pinte así el sentimiento
el alma va de pintura,
aunque peligre el acierto.
Bien sé que en obedecerte
créditos de amante pierdo,
porque cuanto más te pinte,
mi amor quedará en bosquejo.
Dije mucho y poco dije,
porque de amor los afectos
sólo amor puede decirlos
y él sólo puede entenderlos.
Tus ojos vi por mi dicha
dos soles, digo, en un cielo,
a cuyo imperio el amor
rindió del alma trofeos.
Blasonaba mi albedrío
de leyes de amor exento,
mas ya en cárcel de hermosura
voluntario es prisionero.
Preciado de que me quieras
estoy, pero aun más aprecio

---

[1] Serrano y Sanz, 374–75.

The act is more condemnable
if made by one who the king makes his equal,
for rock, Peter, you will be
of sovereign diamond,
carved by your hand
with your own strength.
Now, emulating your fortune
I consider you perfect,
Peter, when
you are working, washing
with the blood of that lamb.

118. Ballad for the novel.

My beautiful lord, you want
me to paint the feelings
of the soul in a picture
even though I find danger in doing so.
I well know that in obeying you
I lose worth as a lover,
for however much I portray you,
my love remains as a rough sketch.
I said much and I said little,
because the effects of love
only love can tell of them
and love alone can understand them.
For my good fortune, I saw your eyes
as two suns in the sky,
to whose empire love
gave trophies to the soul.
My will boasted
that it was exempt from the laws of love,
but now in a prison of beauty
it is a voluntary prisoner.
I am proud that you love me
but I value even more

SECOND COLUMN
que el amor con que te adoro
deba a mi conocimiento.
No sé, pues, como pintarte
este amor, dígale el pecho,
que anhelos habla en suspiros
y ansias imprime en incendios.
¿No te han dicho ya mis ojos
la pasión de que adolezco?
No, pues, la aumentan tus dudas,
sea el creerla remedio.
Que puesto que en que me quieras
todo bien a adquirir llego
será mal si dificultas,
que amor con amor granjeo.
¿Es posible que no sientes
el riguroso tormento
en que amor mi vida pone
cuando en tus ojos le veo?
¿No es posible que le ignores;
¿mas, qué pretendes? advierto

FIRST COLUMN
en el potro de tus dudas
ver en mí el morir postrero.
Sino es que la pena mía
la mires de ti tan lejos
que no atiendas que en el alma
está, de quien eres dueño.
Bien que si amas como dices,
sentirás lo que padezco
y si de ti no te fías,
pregúntalo a mis desvelos
de quien sabrás que entre glorias
que ocasiona el pensamiento
como en él sólo se logran,
soy Tántalo de deseos.
Y que son en mi memoria
razones tuyas que observo,

73r

that the love with which I adore you
is owing to my own intelligence.
I do not know, then, how to portray
this love for you, so let the heart say it,
sighing with longing
and imprinting anxieties in flames.
Have not my eyes told you
of the passion that I am suffering?
No, then your doubts grow,
because believing is the remedy.
And if you love me
I gain all good fortune
for it will be cruel if you make it difficult
for me to earn love with love.
Is it possible that you do not feel
the rigorous torment
that love causes in my life
when I see your eyes?
It is impossible for you to ignore it;
but, what are you claiming? I see

on the rack of your doubts
my final death.
But my pain
you observe at such a distance
that you do not see it in the soul
of one of whom you are the master.
If you love as you say,
you will feel what I suffer
and if you do not believe it yourself,
ask me about my sleepless nights
and you will learn that glories,
brought on by thought,
only serve
to make me a Tantalus[1] of desire.
And in my memory
I obey your laws,

---

[1] I.e., eternally suffering with the tortures bestowed on Tantalus after his death. See footnote to Poem 30.

discreta vida del alma,
gustosa muerte del cuerpo.
En fin, te quiero; mal dije,
te adoro, no lo encarezco;
lo demás mi amor te diga
que yo explicaré no puedo;

FIRST COLUMN
y si no crees te adoro,
si dudas que por ti muero,
quíteme un puñal la vida
será más dulce instrumento.
Que quien ya no ha de gozarte
en el tranquilo himeneo,
tendrá el morir por lisonja
como el vivir por desprecio.
Mas no, que tuya es la vida;
viva yo a pesar del tiempo,
porque pises más envidias
y goces más rendimientos.

119. A Santa Teresa, Romance.[1]

FIRST COLUMN
Óiganme, que a cantar vengo
maravillas de Teresa;
atención, que ya me arrojo
al mar de sus excelencias.
Oigan, de Teresa digo,
flor cándida, hermosa aquella
que admirada fue por sola
y fue por muchas perfecta.
La que armada de rigores,
pertrechada de asperezas,
no hay contraste que la aflija
ni victoria que no emprenda.
Todo a su valor se postra,
a su primor se sujeta;
y aun el mismo Dios de amor
murió por amores de ella.

---

[1] Olivares and Boyce, 1st ed., 385–86; Olivares and Boyce, 2nd ed., 269–70.

of the discreet life of my soul,
and the pleasurable death of the body.
All and all, I love you; I said that badly,
I adore you, I do not exaggerate it;
more about my love
I will not be able to explain;

if you do not believe that I adore you,
if you doubt that I am dying for you,
kill me now with a knife,
for it will be the sweetest way.
For one who cannot now enjoy you
in serene nuptials,
will die from flattery
as one who lives with disdain.
But no, my life is yours
regardless of the years that pass,
giving you more time to tread jealousy
and to enjoy more rewards.

119. Ballad For Saint Theresa.

Listen to me, for I have come to sing
the marvels of Theresa;
attention, I shall throw myself
into the sea of her excellence.
Listen, of Theresa, I speak,
that white, beautiful flower
who was singularly admired
and who was, for many, perfect.
She who armed with rigors,
bolstered by austerity,
no conflict was too great for her,
no victory that she did not win.
To her valor all should bow down,
and to her skill subject oneself;
for even the God of love
died for love of her.

A su corazón apunta
dulces si doradas flechas,
y en tanto fuego templadas,
luego más vivas penetran.
Tanto su ser diviniza
la unión que en Dios manifiesta
que no muriera de humana,
que de amante no muriera.[1]

SECOND COLUMN
En Teresa el cielo influye
soberana inteligencia,
porque ángel le constituya,
almas que reduzca estrellas.[2]
Mas, ¿qué digo, señores?
¡Ay!, que se anega
mi discurso en el golfo
de sus grandezas.
Más, ¡ay!, ¿qué digo?
No es acierto alabarla
sino delito.

120. Décimas por cantadas, dándome el asunto al que las había de cantar.[3]

FIRST COLUMN
Juré, Filis, de no verte
porque de verte moría;
aquesto jurar podía,
más no dejar de quererte.
Confieso que es pena fuerte
que dos distantes estén,
Filis, queriéndose bien;
pero es gusto sin igual
salir tan bien de ese mal
que se pueda dar por bien.

---

[1] Olivares and Boyce begin this line with "de," but there is a word, probably "que" preceding "de." Also, another syllable is needed for the required eight syllables per line.
[2] Olivares and Boyce supply an "a" before "estrellas."
[3] Serrano y Sanz, 375; Olivares and Boyce, 1st ed., 342–43.

He aimed at her heart
sweet, golden arrows,
tempered in fire
so that they penetrated more deeply.
Her being is sanctified
and manifests union with God,
not by suffering a human death,
because such a lover never dies.

Heaven granted Theresa
sovereign intelligence,
because, being like an angel,
her soul becomes another star.[1]
But, what am I saying, ladies and gentlemen?
Ay! my discourse
is drowning in the gulf
of her greatness.
But, ay! What am I saying?
To merely praise her is impossible
and even a crime.

120. Décimas to be sung, having charged me with the subject about which they were to sing.

I swore, Phyllis, not to see you
because I was dying from seeing you;
I could make that oath,
but not stop loving you.
I confess that it is severe pain
to suffer these two dilemmas,
Phyllis, loving so deeply;
but it is pleasure without equal
to well escape from this pain
that can also be for my good.[2]

---

[1] Intelligence here is considered an angel and, like other fortunate beings, Theresa's soul becomes another star in the firmament (Olivares and Boyce, 2nd ed., 270).

[2] The poet is playing with opposites: "bien" and "mal," literally "good" and "bad." But "mal" can also mean pain or suffering and "bien" may be used as the adverb meaning "well." That is, it is good to escape bad but, even the bad can be considered good since suffering for love is, according to the poet, a necessary component of loving "well."

Cuerda fue en mí la locura
de no cumplir lo jurado,
porque amor no está obligado
a cumplir lo que se jura;
y porque así mi ventura
logró la mayor victoria,
hallándome en tu memoria
cuando te juzgaba ajena,
con que salí de la pena
para entrar luego en la gloria.

SECOND COLUMN
De valiente haciendo alarde,
vencer quise en mí al amor,
y postrado a su valor,
nunca me vi más cobarde.
Sus leyes quiere que guarde
con decoro de rendido,
pues llego otra vez herido
de sus flechas a tus plantas,
donde vencedor levantas
al que se da por vencido.
Ya no tengo de librarme
de más peligro de muerte
que el que ocasiona no verte,
pues sólo basta a matarme;
que aunque puedan obligarme
celos a huir tu favor,
no mi quitará el rigor
que amarte, señora, pueda;
que adonde [sic][1] ceniza queda,
si no llamas, hay calor.

---

[1] Corrected by Olivares and Boyce, 1st ed. to "donde." "Adonde" in Serrrano y Sanz. The manuscript reads "adonde," but Olivares and Boyce's correction is the better choice semantically.

It was wise of me, in my madness,
not to comply with my oath,
because love is not obliged
to comply with what it swears;
for thus my fortune
achieved a great victory,
finding myself in your memory
when I judged that I had been forgotten,
and with this knowledge, I left behind pain
and entered into glory.

Showing off as brave,
I tried to conquer love,
and prostrated by his [love's] valor,
I never saw myself a bigger coward.
He wants me to obey his laws
with the decorum of the submissive,
so I am again wounded
by his arrows and at his feet,
where you lift me up, as a conqueror,
and I as one who admits defeat.
Now I do not have to free myself
from the great danger of death,
occasioned by not seeing you,
since it is enough to kill me;
that even though I may be forced
by jealousy to flee from your favor,
harshness cannot prevent me from
loving you, my lady;
for where ashes remain,
if there are no flames, there is still heat.

121. Vuelta de humana en divina por lograr el tono.[1]   74v

A la gaita cantó Gila
que tocaba Antón Pasqual,
viendo el rey de cielo y tierra
disfrazado en blanco pan.
¿Cómo tu grandeza dice
en tal pequeñez está
que te comerá cualquiera
y de un bocado no más?
¿Cómo el hombre, a quien tu aliento,
alma, vida y ser le da,
te hace venir a las manos,
Señor, sin dificultad?
Siendo Dios de amor que puedes
de todos hacerte amar,
¿cómo en un bocado hechizas
suavizando el amor más?
¿Cómo en este manjar dulce
vida ofreces inmortal,
si a un descuido de él que come
muerte suele dar?
Tanto blasonas de fino,
tanto obligas de galán,
que todos se ajusten quieres
a sola tu voluntad.

122. Romance muy celebrado y cantado con razón.[2]   75r

FIRST COLUMN
De las mudanzas de Gila
qué enfermo que anda Pascual,
¿cómo ha de sanar, si es ella
la cura y la enfermedad?

---

[1] This poem is not in Serrano y Sanz's inventory.

[2] Serrano y Sanz, 375–76. This poem occupies the first column of 75r while the following poem, "Mi respuesta oyendo los últimos versos" occupies the second column of 75r and continues with the last four lines, in a single column, on 75v. The rest of 75v is blank. I include this romance among Belisarda's poems because she does not attribute it to another poet, even though the following poem is labeled as her response to this one. The poet may be playing with different poetic voices and responding to her own composition.

121. Taking a secular subject and making it divine but retaining the tone [of the original].

Gil sang along with the bagpipes
that Anton Pasqual was playing,
seeing the King of Heaven and Earth
disguised as white bread.
How can your greatness be told
in such a small thing
that anyone could eat
in a single mouthful?
How is it that man, to whom Your breath
gives soul and life,
can come into our hands,
Lord, with no difficulty?
Being the God of love who can
make everyone love You,
how can You enchant a single mouthful
making Your love more tender still?
How in this sweet food
can You offer immortal life,
and those who neglect to eat it
You condemn to death?
You display such elegance,
You require such gallantry,
for You want to reconcile all
to Your will alone.

122. A very celebrated ballad rightly to be sung.

From the fickleness of Gila
Pascual is very ill,
how is he to get well, if she is
both the cure and the illness?

Opilado de desdenes,
la manda el doctor tomar
acero de desengaños
que obran bien y saben mal.
Yo sé que le recetara
una larga ausencia a Bras,
si a la cabaña no hubiera
vuelto a sufrir y a adorar.
Gila es su muerte y su vida,
y no se la quiere dar;
¡desdichado de él que vive
por ajena voluntad!
Nadie se fíe de sí
cuando tan rendido está,
que en los achaques de amor,
el remedio enferma más.
Pues, no se supo del riesgo
de sus ojuelos librar,
quien tal hace, que tal pague;
muera por ella Pascual.
Pastores, guardáos de Gila,
que es veneno del lugar,
y con dos áspides verdes
basilisco de cristal.

SECOND COLUMN
123. Mi respuesta, oyendo los últimos versos.[1]

De las mudanzas de Gila
dicen que enfermó Pascual;
su discreción califica
con la mayor necedad.
Con desengaños le curan,
que son remedio eficaz,
y el que no sana con ellos,
no obra bien y sabe mal.
El desdén pasa a desprecio
si amor cansándose va,

---

[1] Serrano y Sanz, 376; Olivares and Boyce 1st ed., 359–60; Olivares and Boyce, 2nd ed., 256–57.

Thwarted by disdain,
the doctor instructs him to take
the steel of disillusionment
that works well but tastes bad.
I know that he would have prescribed
a long absence for Bras,
if he had not returned home[1]
to suffer and adore.
Gila is his death and his life,
and she does not want to give either to him;
how unfortunate is he who lives
at the whim of another's will!
No one has confidence in himself
when he is so surrendered,
for in ailments of love,
the remedy makes one sicker.
But he does know of the risk
of freeing himself from her sparkling eyes
for as one reaps, so will he sow;
Pascual may well die for her.
Shepherds, watch out for Gila,
who is poison to this place,
and with two green asps[2]
a crystal basilisk.

123. My response after hearing the last verses.

From the fickleness of Gila,
they say that Pascual became ill;
his discretion would qualify
as the greatest folly.
They cure him with disillusionments,
that are an effective remedy,
and he who is not cured by them,
errs and knows nothing.[3]
Disdain becomes contempt
if love becomes tired,

---

[1] Literally, "to return to the cabin."
[2] I.e., Gila's two green eyes.
[3] This is a play on words with the meaning of "saber" in the previous poem, since "saber" can mean "to taste" or "to know."

y así nunca a la cabaña
vuelva a sufrir y a adorar.
Nadie se fíe de sí
cuando tan rendido está,
que penando vive o muere
por ajena voluntad.
Si Gila es su muerte y vida,
¿para qué se la ha de dar,
si da la vida el remedio
y el remedio enferma más?
Pues Pascual con las finezas
más que obliga, ofende ya;
huya al riesgo a la vista
muera por ella Pascual.
Que las mudanzas aprenda,
le receto, y que al compás
baile del son que le hicieran,
y a buen aire sanará.
Pascual sanará en queriendo
si en dejar de querer da,
que en los amantes es tema
la cura y la enfermedad.

124. A San Vicente mártir logrando segunda vez la música del estribillo.[1]

FIRST COLUMN
Aquel mártir valeroso
a quien España celebra
por corona de sus glorias,
por timbre de sus grandezas.
Vicente, aquel cuyo amor
a Dios en su ayuda empeña
tanto, que en valiente lucha
hoy vence la muerte fiera.
Consumirle en vivas llamas
el tirano cruel intenta,
pero las de amor más vivas
asisten a su defensa.

---

[1] A note at the top of this folio reads: "Viva usía tanto como su fama Capellán que S.P.V." [Long live your worship as well your fame as chaplain who S.P.V.]. I am not aware of the meaning of the initials S.P.V.

and never returns home [1]
to suffer and adore.
No one has confidence in himself
when he is so surrendered,
suffering, he lives or dies
by someone else's will.
If Gila is his death and his life,
why give one's will over to another,
if the remedy gives life
but the remedy also makes one sicker?
So, Pascual with gallantry
more than obliges, now offends;
may he flee the risk since it appears
that Pascual may die because of her.
Knowledge of fickleness,
I prescribe for him, and to that rhythm
may he dance to the sound that it makes
and soon he will be well.
Pascual will get well from loving
when he truly desires to stop loving,
but, for lovers, the cure and the illness
are the same thing.

124. For Saint Vincent, martyr, with music for the second refrain.

That valorous martyr
whom Spain celebrates
for the crown of his glories,
for the timbre of his greatness.
Vincent, he whose love
persists in helping God
so much that in the valiant struggle
he today defeats cruel death.
To consume him in bright flames
the cruel tyrant intends,
but the flames of love are brighter
and attend to his defense.

---

[1] Again the literal meaning is "returns to the cabin" as in the previous poem.

Estribillo: 1º A Vicente embiste
la llama fiera,
toquen a milagro
pues, no se quema.
2º No se ven aquí campanas
con que a milagros toquemos.
1º Pues hay música de a doce
súplanlas los instrumentos.
Todos: Tan, Tan, Tan.
2º Y si no envidian las voces,
canten alegres con ellos.
Todos: Tan, tan, tan.

SECOND COLUMN
Los fatales instrumentos
donde su muerte resuena
más dulce le comunican
vida que al alma recrea.
Con peines sus carnes surcan[1]
si con garfios las penetran,
y unos a amor sirven alas;
otros al deseo, espuelas.
De hierro entre ardientes hojas
le fijan que bien lo piensan,
porque su valor escrito
quede en impresión eterna.
Ya tarjetas son las hojas
donde fijo se contempla
jeroglífico de amor
que glorioso está en la pena.
A Vicente embiste
la llama fiera;
Toquen a milagro,
pues, no se quema.

125. Otra, volviéndola de humana, divina, a Santa Catalina de Esena. 76v

A la gaita cantó Gila
que tocaba Antón Pascual,
celebrando en voz festiva
las glorias de una deidad.

---

[1] Manuscript reads "sulcan."

Refrain : 1st. Vincent is assaulted
by a cruel flame,
ring out the miracle
for he is not burned.
2nd We cannot find any bells here
with which to ring out his miracles.
1st There is music for twelve,
substitute instruments for them [the bells].
All: Rum, pum, pum.
2nd And the voices are not jealous
and sing along happily with them.
All: La, la, la.

The fatal instruments
that played for his death
now sound out more sweetly
life restored to his soul.
His flesh is torn on torture racks
and hooks penetrate it,
but they become wings of love;
others spurs of desire.
Between red-hot plates of iron
they place him, how well they plan it,
so that his valor be written
and imprinted eternally.
These plates are now sheets
where one can contemplate
this hieroglyph of love
who is glorious in his suffering.
Vincent was attacked
by a cruel flame;
ring out the miracle
for he is not burned.

125. Taking a secular song and making a divine one for Saint Catherine of Siena.

Gil sang to the bagpipes
that Anton Pascual played,
celebrating in a festive voice
the glories of a deity.

Feliz Catalina dice,
a quien hoy los cielos dan
justo premio a tus virtudes
en el lauro de inmortal.
Como a estrella que más luce,
como a flor de más beldad,
las que cielo y tierra ostentan,
aplausos te rinden ya.
Suele nubecilla leve
las estrellas eclipsar,
mas aún no amancillan nubes[1]
mortales tu claridad.
La rosa que tus candores
caduca quiso imitar
en naciendo, vive menos,
tú en muriendo, vives más.
Premia afectos con favores,
pues, tu valimiento estar
que el rey como a esposa amada
te sube a su trono real.[2]

126. A la transfiguración de Cristo en el Tabor.[3]

77r

FIRST COLUMN

Con los tres a quien la fama
dio más glorioso renombre,
el monarca y rey supremo
llega a Tabor una noche.
Ya la eminencia termina,
y sin dejar de ser hombre,
en el ser de Dios ostenta
sus atributos mayores.
Los tres validos se duermen
y aunque leales los conoce
en tanto rey ejecuta
lo que sabio en sí dispone.
Con dos amigos consulta
que uno de su ley fue norte,

---

[1] Manuscript reads "nuebes."
[2] "real" here is my best guess since an "r" is clearly visible as the first letter of the last word in this line but the rest of the word is covered by the tight binding.
[3] Mountain in Galilee where it is believed the Transfiguration of Christ took place.

He tells of happy Catherine,
to whom today the heavens give
just reward for your virtues
in laurels of immortality.
Like a star that shines brightly,
like a most beautiful flower,
of which heaven and earth boast,
they now give you applause.
Usually a thin cloud
can eclipse the stars,
but even dark clouds cannot tarnish
your clarity.
The rose that tried to imitate
your purity, withers and
at the moment of its birth, lives less,
while you, at the moment of death, live more.
Awarding affections with favors,
and to be your refuge
as his beloved bride,
the king raises you up to his royal throne.

126. For the Transfiguration of Christ on Tabor.

With the three[1] to whom fame
bestowed most glorious renown,
the supreme monarch and king
arrives to Tabor one night.
His eminence ends,
and without ceasing to be man,
shows himself to be God
in His greatest attributes.
The three favorites fall asleep
and even though He knows them to be loyal
the king will carry out
whatever wisdom itself decrees.
He consults with two friends
one of whom was the guide of His law,[2]

---

[1] The apostles Peter, James, and John, who witnessed Christ's transfiguration on the mount of Tabor in Galilee.

[2] Moses.

otro quien con celo ardiente
su honor defendió a rigores.
Allí, a los dos, comunica
glorias que a su lado gocen,
que quien tanto amarle supo
tan altos adquiere honores.
Benignamente les habla
cuando por el aire se oye
voz que de Juan, Diego y Pedro
acredita presunciones.

SECOND COLUMN
Oíd a mi hijo, dice,
así demostrando el orden
con que el hombre a Dios siguiendo
suba asperezas del monte.Vestidura que dichosa
fue material hasta entonces,
candores inmensos brilla
de luz inundando el orbe.
Nube que paz asegura
al sol de justicia esconde,
porque verle en gloria tanta
no impidan sus resplandores.
Pasmado a tanto misterio,
a glorias tantas inmoble,
Pedro, ignorando la eterna
la que mira, ciego escoge.
Que turbado Pedro elige
que deslumbrado propone
cuando glorias no hay sin penas,
ni sin finezas favores.
   Estribo:
Cómo baten las alas
que el aire rompen
serafines de amor abrasados,
que a Dios en la tierra repiten amores.
Ya vuelan, ya paran,
ya cantan tan acordes,
Con dulce armonía,

and the other with ardent zeal
rigorously defended His honor.[1]
There those two receive
glories that they enjoy at His side,
for he who knew how to love Him so well
acquires the highest honors.
Kindly He speaks to them
when in the air is heard
a voice that for John, James, and Peter
confirms suspicions.

Listen to my Son, it says,
thus giving the command
that man must follow God and
scale the harshest of mountains.
The fortunate clothing that
was but material until then,
now shines so brilliantly white
that its light floods the world.
A cloud that assures peace
obscures the sun of justice,
so that its brilliance will not impede
seeing him in all his glory.
Stunned by such a mystery,
immobilized by such glories,
Peter, unaware of the eternal
that he is seeing, blindly chooses.
Peter, confused and dazzled,
proposes and proclaims
that there are no glories without pain
nor favors without perfection.
      Refrain:
How their wings beat
and cut through the air
the seraphim afire with love,
that to God on earth repeat their love.
Now they fly, now they stop,
now they sing so well together
with sweet harmony,

---

[1] Elijah.

festivas canciones
celebrando el prodigio que admiran
de Cristo glorioso entre los hombres.

127. Orta.[1]

FIRST COLUMN
Al postrero parasismo
con que fenece la noche,
la aurora bosteza luces,
la selva respira olores.
Despierta el pájaro amante,
explicando en sus redobles
finezas de amor que sirven
de reclamo a su consorte.
Lozano se mira el lirio,
galán de todas las flores,
que en la de su amor librea
perfiles de oro interpone.
Los alhelíes[2] dan muestra,
y equivocando colores,
lisonjero a dos sentidos,
bello ejército disponen.

SECOND COLUMN
La rosa, que manso viento
del verde botón descoge,
pródiga dispensa al día
fragantes adulaciones.
Mosqueta, del desaliño
gala haciendo a sus primores,
mariposa del sol muere,
cándido aroma del monte.
Todo en el mayo se alegra;
sólo a mis tristes pasiones
no hay medio que las alivie,
ni alivio que las minore.

---

[1] Serrano y Sanz, 376; Olivares and Boyce, 1st ed., 356.
[2] Gillyflowers, flowers of many colors; "alhelíe" is also a general name for violets.

festive songs
celebrating the miracle that they witness
of Christ glorious among men.

127. Another.

At the last spasm
with which the night dies,
the first lights of dawn break,
the forest gives off smells.
The lovebird awakens,
explaining with warbling sounds
the fineness of love that serves
as a call to his consort.
Proudly the lily sees itself,
elegant among all the flowers,
and weighs the elegance of love
as if weighing gold.
The gillyflowers show themselves,
in all their colors,
pleasing to two senses,
they display a beautiful array.

With the soft wind, the rose's
green bud spreads,
prodigiously privileging the day
with its fragrant flattery.
The scruffy white musk rose
shows off its first fruits,
dying like a butterfly to the sun,
giving off pure aroma to the countryside.
Everything in May is happy;
but, for my sad passions,
there is no cure,
nor any relief that lessens them.

128. Décimas apoyando que los celos declarados son más insufribles que los recelos.[1]

FIRST COLUMN
De un recelo imaginado
y una celosa evidencia,
hay la misma diferencia
que entre lo vivo y pintado.
Un agravio declarado
vivo dolor a ser viene
del alma en quien siempre tiene
muerta toda la esperanza;
y como alivio no alcanza,
es su tormento perenne.
Cuando el agravio es dudoso,
pinta el temor una calma
adonde padece el alma
de un *qué será* rigoroso;
mas en el sentir penoso
de la duda se alimenta;
y si salir de ella intenta,
porque enfermo el gusto advierte,
luego teme que su muerte
cause ejecución violenta.

SECOND COLUMN
No diga que tiene amor
quien no tiene sufrimiento,
que esperar es argumento
de la fineza mayor.
Perder el gusto en rigor
por un disgusto temido
siempre es remedio mentido
que busca amor agraviado;
y después, desesperado,
llora el sosiego perdido.
Perseverar en querer,
aunque se oponga el recelo,
es a costa de un desvelo
granjearse el merecer;

---

[1] Serrano y Sanz, 376–77; Olivares and Boyce, 1st ed., 340–41. There is one line missing in Serrano y Sanz that Olivares and Boyce correctly include.

128. Décimas, supporting that declared jealousies are more insufferable than suspicions.

Between imagined suspicion
and jealousy with evidence,
there is the same difference
as between a living being and its painted image.
A declared offense
becomes a sharp pain
of the soul, for one for whom
all hoped has died;
and, since relief cannot be found,
it is perennial torment.
When the offense is doubtful,
fear conjures up a calmness
where the soul suffers
from a harsh question: Could it be?
and, feeling aggrieved,
it feeds on doubt;
and if it tries to rid itself of it,
because desire warns of sickness,
and then fears that its [doubt's] death,
may cause a violent reaction.

Do not say that one loves
who does not suffer,
for hoping is a matter
of finest elegance.
At most, losing happiness
for a feared unpleasantness
is always a lying remedy
that aggrieved love seeks;
and later, desperate,
cries out for its lost serenity.
Persevering in love,
even though suspicion may oppose it,
is the cost of watchfulness,
worthy of winning;

y por salir de temer
dar por bien que llegue el mal,
es de amor desaire tal,
que aquí establecer querría
que amor tan sin bizarría
no es de amante racional.

78v [Blank]

129. A la Señora fundadora del convento de la Concepción Real de Toledo. Villancico.

79r

Estribillo: Ay, cómo vuela, mas ay, cómo corre
          una blanca paloma bizarra
          que ostenta hermosura, que afecta candores
          y a los cielos dichosa camina.

FIRST COLUMN
El aire rompiendo con alas veloces,
Beatriz, que del mundo huyendo,
hermosa paloma escoge
seguro nido en que amante
ni peligre ni zozobre.
A sus amores
busca empleo que dure,
premio que honore,
cándida paloma siendo
fénix de amor se dispone,
al incendio que codician[1]
tiernas del alma ambiciones
que en sus ardores
se eterniza, adquiriendo
glorioso nombre.

SECOND COLUMN
De los afectos comunes
negada al loco desorden,
sólo al gozo se permite
de su divino consorte.
Que sus primores,
siendo tantos, es justo
que en Dios se logren.

---

[1] Manuscript reads "cudician."

and in order to stop fearing
and to take the good that may come from bad,
is a rebuff to love,
and I would like here to assert
that love without valor
is not for a rational lover.

129. Carol to the lady, founder of the Royal Convent of the Conception of Toledo.

Refrain: Oh, how she flies, and oh. how she runs,
    a valiant white dove
    that boasts beauty of pure innocence
    and happily flies toward the heavens.

Tearing through the air on fast wings,
Beatrice, fleeing from the world,
chooses, like a beautiful dove,
a sure nest where a lover
suffers no danger nor from which one can fall.
For her love
she looks for an enterprise that will last,
a reward that will honor
a pure white dove being
the phoenix of love that prepares itself
for the fire coveted by
the tender ambitions of the soul
who, in their ardor
become eternal, acquiring
a glorious name.

Dismissing common desires
as insane chaos,
she only permits herself the enjoyment
of the most divine consort.
For her marvels
are so many that it is just
that they be fulfilled in God.

Cuando poderosa envidia
a su luz clara se opone,
se manifiesta más puro
sol de hermosos esplendores,
que ni aún la noche
a este sol de belleza
la luz esconde.[1]

130. A Santiago, patrón de España.

79v

Florecillas que traviesas, [sic][2]
entre los aires jugáis,
cuya hermosa competencia
festejando a Diego está.
Celebrad, celebrad
la victoria que os logra
el gran capitán.
Aves, que tocáis alegres
instrumentos de coral,
dulce salva haciendo a Diego
que al cielo triunfante va.
Publicad, publicad
que el primero ha ganado
silla celestial.
Arroyos, que fugitivos
chítaras [sic] sois de cristal
que con voz de plata a Diego
armónico aplauso dais.
Festejad, festejad
, , , , , ,[3] sol que en su ocaso
, , , , , , inmortal.
Serafines que a la esfera

80r

de amor a Diego lleváis
donde entre todos se mire
con suma felicidad.
Repetid y cantad,

---

[1] The ink is very faded at the end of this line. "Esconde" seems a likely possibility based on a visible "e" to begin the word and the rhyme scheme in o-e.

[2] More commonly "atraviesas."

[3] Indication of missing paper. The last folios of the manuscript are in extremely poor condition. I have supplied the visible words. Vinatea Recoba reconstructs the lines as "a este sol que en su ocaso / renace inmortal" [at this sun that in its setting / is reborn immortal].

When powerful envy
opposes her clear light,
she shines with more purity
as a sun of beautiful splendor,
for not even the night
cannot hide the light
of this sun of beauty.

130. To Saint James, Patron of Spain.

Little flowers crisscrossing,
playing in the air,
in beautiful competition,
are celebrating James.
Celebrate, celebrate
the victory that is won for you
by the great captain.
Birds, happily playing
choral instruments,
make a sweet salute to James,
who triumphantly rises up to heaven.
Make known, make known
that the victor has earned
a celestial throne.
Streams like fugitive
crystalline zithers,
with silvery voice
give harmonious applause to James.
Make merry, make merry,
, , , , , ,[1] sun that at its setting
, , , , , , immortal.
Seraphim to the sphere
of love carry James
where, among all, he may be seen
with great happiness.

---

[1] Indication of missing paper. Please see Spanish transcription for more information. I have supplied a translation of the legible words for the incomplete lines.

que ninguno es más puro
ni es amante más.
Estribo: Pajarillos sonoros,
al arma, tocad,
que vistosa escaramuza
las flores hacen ya.
Tocad, tocad,
al arma, guerra, guerra.
¡Qué se embisten!¡ Qué se encuentran!
Más ya poniendo paz,
los arroyos risueños
corren sin parar
y serafines canoros
en dulces suaves coros
por el aire diciendo van:
viva Diego, pues, hoy de la muerte
tan valeroso ha sabido triunfar.
Coplas:[1]
Victorioso sale Diego
de la batalla fatal,
donde hallar supo más vida
la muerte buscando audaz.
Vivo y muerto, a Dios imita,
tan milagroso en obrar,
que fe plantando en las almas,
flor y fruto al cielo da.
cielos, franquead las puertas
que un prodigio llega ya,
toda[2] nieve en la pureza,
todo fuego en el amar.
El pavimento azul dora
con tan inmenso brillar
que los astros que enriquece,
turbados de luz están.

---

[1] Vinatea Recoba reads the "coplas" as a separate poem, but, here, as in other *villancicos*, Belisarda clearly indica el ponts portion of the poem that is the "estribillo," or "estribo" and the section that forms the "coplas"—the two components of traditional *villancicos*. For purposes of comparison, see another *villancico* in this collection, no. 49.

[2] "Todo" in the manuscript, an obvious error.

Repeat and sing,
for none is purer
nor greater a lover.
Refrain: Sonorous birds
to arms, sing,
for a lively skirmish
is being made by the flowers.
Sing, sing,
to arms, war, war.
How they charge! How they meet!
But now, making peace,
the gurgling streams
flow without stopping
and melodious seraphim
in sweet, soft choruses
fly through the air singing:
long live James who today over death
has so valiantly triumphed.
Stanzas:
James comes out victorious
from the fatal battle,
where he found more life
in boldly looking for death.
Alive and dead, he imitates God,
miraculously working
to plant faith in souls
that produces flower and fruit for heaven.
Heavens, open the gates
for a marvel is now arriving,
all like snow in purity,
all like fire in loving.
The blue firmament becomes golden
and with such intense brilliance
the stars are enriched,
disturbed by such light.

131. Persuadiendo a una dama que amase, escribieron cuatro poetas glosando esta copla, y yo respondí sobre la misma glosa por la dama, conforme a su dictamen.[1]

81r

Glosa: Ama el delfín en el río,
    el pajarillo en el viento,
    en las montañas la fiera,
    que el amor de todo es dueño.

FIRST COLUMN
Prevenida al desengaño,
juzgo, aunque dios al amor
niño, al fin, cuyo favor
es de la [sic] alma loco engaño.
Y aunque su poder no extraño,
tengo por gran desvarío
que de este rapaz el brío
un escarmiento no enfrene
pues, porque razón no tiene,
ama el delfín en el río.
Es de la afición el gusto
recreo de las potencias,
y en más cuerdas advertencias
de ellas un tirano injusto.
No, pues a su ley me ajusto,
porque vivamente siento[2]

SECOND COLUMN
que excede al mayor contento
siempre el pesar más ligero;
y, así libre imitar quiero
el pajarillo en el viento.
Sólo en fieras y montañas
la firmeza está segura,
adonde al amor pro*cura*[3]
dulce premio a sus *hazañas*

---

[1] Partially transcribed by Serrano y Sanz, 377. Olivares and Boyce, 1st ed., 344–45 offer a complete transcription.

[2] I correct Olivares's and Boyce's transcription of line 16 which they read as "Porque vivamente siente, siento." The introduction of "siente" disrupts the eight-syllable per line rhyme scheme.

[3] Italics here and for subsequent words or parts of words indicates that the paper is missing or illegible. For this reconstruction I follow Serrano y Sanz's transcription (as do

131. Persuading a lady to fall in love, four poets wrote glossing a couplet and I responded to the same gloss for the lady, according to her dictate.

    Gloss: The dolphin loves in the river,
           the little bird in the wind,
           the wild beast in the mountains,
           for love is the master of all.

Anticipating disappointment,
I judge that the god of love
is a child whose favor, in the end,
is a mad deception for the soul.
And, even though his power does not surprise me,
I take it for a great madness
that the spirit of this kid
cannot be reined in with a warning
and, because he is wrong,
the dolphin loves in the river.
The fondness of affection
is a delight for one's faculties,
but it is wise to be warned
that it is an unjust tyrant to them.
I do not conform to your law
because I truly feel

that greatest contentment
is always the lighter burden;
and, thus, free, I want to imitate
the little bird in the wind.
Only in wild beasts and the wilderness
is stability certain,
where love secures
the sweet prize for its deeds

y en los hombres son *extrañas*
las mudanzas que pon*dera*
mi imaginación *severa*
donde llego a examinar
que ya sólo puede am*ar*
en las montañas la fiera.

FIRST COLUMN
Si en cautivar mi albedrío
gloria pretendes tener,
yo la pienso poseer
en que siempre sea mío.
De mi amor sólo confío;
y así, haciendo en mí el empeño,
tu consejo no desdeño,
si de amor no he de librarme,
pues yo misma quiero amarme,
que el amor de todo es dueño.

132. Letra al bautismo de Cristo.

Con silencio tan profundo
el Jordán los pasos mueve
que los troncos no le escuchan,
las arenas no le sienten.
Al mirarse cielo hermoso
el suspenso le tiene
que[1] un lucero y un sol
hoy las estrellas llueven.
Con la que maneja Juan
a los cristales convierte,
en margaritas que hermosas
siembran[2] los margines verdes.

SECOND COLUMN
Las hebras de oro que adornan

Olivares and Boyce). The page may have been complete when Serrano y Sanz made his transcription in 1905.

[1] The first word(s) of this and the following two lines are extremely faded. I have tried to reconstruct from the letters that are visible, indicated in italics.

[2] The first word(s) of this line are completely missing. I supply "siembran" as a possible reading because it seems to fit the meaning and the rhyme scheme of eight-syllables per line.

and, in men, strange are
the inconstancies that are pondered
by my vivid imagination;
I have come to believe
that the only one capable of love is
the wild beast in the mountains.

If in capturing my will
you think that you will gain glory,
I try to possess it,
so that it may always be mine.
I am only confident in my love
and, being so determined,
I do not disdain your advice,
if I cannot free myself from love,
I want to love myself,
for love is the master of all.

132. Lyrics for the Baptism of Christ.

With such profound silence
the Jordan flows along,
and the tree trunks do not listen to it,
the sands do not notice it.
Beautiful heaven looking down
watches in suspense
as a bright star and a sun
today the stars rain down.
With the one [star] that John touches
he converts it to crystals,
in beautiful daises
sown on the green banks.

On the golden threads[1] that adorn
the divine temples of the Word,
John sprinkles pure drops of dew,

---

[1] I.e., golden hair.

del Verbo divinas sienes
siembra Juan de aljófar puro,
quedando de ellas pendiente.
Antes que nazca el baptista
de gracia Dios le enriquece
que puesto que ha de pedirla,
solo Juan dársele puede.
El Verbo divino en carne
a los pies de Juan se ofrece
que para luchar con culpas,
desnudarse es conveniente.
A los balcones del cielo
el Padre ostenta eminente
quien es Dios, porque con Juan,
no le equivoquen dos veces.
Blanca paloma divina
paces al alma promete,
si en el Jordán de la gracia
hoy eterna vida adquiere.
Cristales risueños
que con dulce voz
publicáis las dichas
del gran precursor.
Celebrad alegres
que hoy bautiza a Dios.

133. Esta glosa que escribió una religiosa carmelita de Ocaña, puse aquí por digna de ser celebrada en primer lugar y por leerla yo algunas veces. El asunto fue una pintura de Cristo crucificado de cuyo costado salían dos fuentes, una de sangre, otra de agua, que venían a parar a un corazón que tenía a los pies. Y de él nacían dos pimpollos, uno con tres azucenas y otro con tres rosas y la redondilla que la dieron dice así:

>
> Es el indicio tan cierto
> que para Dios jardín fue
> tu corazón, hombre, que
> le riega aun después de muerto.

Glosa.

suspended in His locks.
Before the Baptist was born
God enriched him with grace
and when He [Christ] came to ask for it [grace],
only John could bestow it.
The Divine Word made flesh
offers Himself at John's feet
for to struggle with faults,
one must first bare oneself.[1]
From the balcony of heaven
the eminent Father shows
who is God, so that with John,
they do not confuse Him [Christ].
The divine, white dove
who promises peace to the soul,
in waters of the Jordan
today gains eternal life.
Cheerful crystals
with sweet voice
announce the good fortune
of the great precursor.[2]
Happily celebrate
for today he baptizes God.

133. This is a gloss that a Carmelite nun from Ocaña wrote; I include it here because it is worthy of being celebrated, and I have read it several times. It is about a picture of Christ crucified from whose side gushed two springs—one of blood and another of water—that flowed together into a heart at His feet. From the heart were born two buds—one with three white lilies and another with three roses. And the quatrain that they gave her reads:

>It is certain proof
>that God made your heart
>a garden, mankind, for
>He waters it even after His death.

Gloss.

---

[1] The idea is to present oneself naked before God, i.e., hiding nothing from Him.
[2] I.e., John the Baptist.

FIRST COLUMN
Pasajero caminante,
pues ya despierto del sueño
das el corazón amante
a las plantas de su dueño;
no pases más adelante,
mírale por amor muerto
y que es tu seguro puerto
lo dice clavado allí,
de donde el morir por ti
es el indicio tan cierto.

SECOND COLUMN
En tan lúcidos abriles
de divinizadas flores,
cobra perdidos pensiles
entre jazmines[1], camelias,[2]
violetas, claveles,
coge flores que yo sé
que broten tu amor y fe.
Las de la gracia primera,
mostrando esta primavera.
que para Dios jardín fue,

FIRST COLUMN
libre del propio interés
sigue amando tu elección,
pues, Dios, en sus rotos pies
da trono a tu corazón
porque centro suyo es.
A luces tantas se ve
lo que Dios contigo fue;
dale en mucho ponderar
que, en fondo tal, podrá hallar
tu corazón, hombre, que

---

[1] "jazmíneos" in the manuscript.
[2] "Camellias" is a reconstruction since only the letters "ca" are legible; "camellias" also maintains the eight-syllable line.

Passerby,
now awakened from sleep
you lay your loving heart
at the feet of its master;
do not pass on by,
look at Him dead for love's sake,
a secure port He
attests, nailed there,
where He died for you
as certain proof.

In such splendid Aprils
with divine flowers,
He collects lost, beautiful gardens
among jasmine, camellias,
violets, carnations,
He picks flowers that I know
will bloom with your love and faith.
Those of first grace,
showing that this spring
was a garden for God,

freed from your own interests
you continue loving whom you have chosen
for God, at His broken feet,
gives a throne to your heart
where He is at its center.
And with so much light, one sees
what God did for you;
it gives us much to ponder
for you will find, in the depths
of your heart, mankind, that

SECOND COLUMN
de aquel abierto costado
te explaya[1] Dios dos raudales:
de bermellón[2] desatado
es éste, aquel de cristales.
Extremos de enamorado,
ya es tu corazón su huerto,
dejóse inundar, que a cierto
si dio azucenas y rosas,
Dios porque duren hermosas,
las riega aun después de muerto.

134. Soneto que hice en alabanza de esta glosa.

Quien alabar a vuestro autor pretende
que se atreve a la luz del sol recelo,
si al incesante de la fama vuelo,
una pluma sutil cortar no emprende.
Cuando a vuestros primores más se atiende,
y que al dueño que os dan oculta un velo
parece, versos, que si no es el cielo,
es deidad que lo que hay en él comprende.
Sois de un ingenio peregrino
de una mujer, prodigio entre mortales,
a quien Dios adecuó con franca mano.
Es ángel a creer me determino,
puesto que con hacer milagros tales,
se acredita lo que es tan soberano.

135. Romance, y el asunto ver un galán que su dama le ofendía y porque se quejaba de ella, darse por agraviada de él.

83r

FIRST COLUMN
Que de ver celoso a Lisio
quejosa Filis esté;
no amor, pero confianza,
no piedad que rigor es.
Negar causas al recelo
anima el amor tal vez,
y muchas le ofende una
que de celos llega a ser.

---

[1] "esplaya" in the manuscript.
[2] "mermellón" in the manuscript.

from that open side,
God pours out two torrents:
one of unbound vermilion,
the other crystalline.
Extremes of the lover,
your heart is His garden
that He waters, and as proof,
white lilies and roses bloom,
and so that they may stay beautiful
God waters them even after His death.

134. Sonnet that I wrote in praise of this gloss.

Whoever tries to praise your author
dares to mistrust the light of the sun,
flying incessantly toward fame
no subtle pen should dare to engrave.
When one pays close attention to your skill,
even though the master is hidden behind a veil
it seems that you, verses, if not from heaven,
nonetheless reveal divine understanding.
You [verses] are from a rare genius,
made by a woman, a prodigy among mortals,
that God endowed with a generous hand.
I can well believe that she is an angel,
since in accomplishing such miracles,
she gives credit to what is so sovereign.

135. Ballad about a young man whose lady offended him and because he complained about her, she got angry with him.

Seeing Lisio jealous,
Phyllis complains;
not of love, but of confidence,
and not of pity that is harshness.
Denying causes for mistrust,
perhaps encourages love,
and of many [causes], one offends her
and that one is jealousy.

Juzgóse Lisio en la cumbre
de más dichosa altivez,
pero, ¿qué fin de subir
no es principio de caer?
Con dulces halagos Filis
empeñó a su amor cortés
a que en prendas de servicio
la rindiese un alma fiel.
Finezas que amante ostenta
tantas Lisio en Filis ve
que un temor desmentir pudo,
que ya es evidencia cruel.

SECOND COLUMN
Si se cree que amor firme
por el efecto y por fe
a la vista de un agravio,
¿cómo se podrá creer?
Por la pena que es de Filis,
penan los dos? ¡Ay, de quién
el remedio está en su mano
y muriendo está sin él!
La ofensa que llora en Lisio
no excusa Filis y es que
por razón de estado ofende
por razón infiel.
Celos enemigos,
Al rigor sus , , , ,[1]
Que es in , , , ,
El dar mal por bien.[2]

136. Letra, para cantada.

83v

FIRST COLUMN
Los ojos de Fili [sic],
ay, Dios, cómo lloran
diluvios de perlas
donde amor se engolfa.

---

[1] Paper is missing at the end of this and the following line.
[2] "El dar mal por" is legible; therefore "bien" is the most logical reconstruction.

Lisio thought himself at the peak
of his most lofty pride,
but, what does it mean to climb high
if it is the beginning of your downfall?
Phyllis, with sweet flattery,
obliged by courtly love,
in favors of service
surrendered her faithful soul.
Elegance that a lover displays
Lisio appreciates in Phyllis,
but fear could refute it,
and the evidence is cruel.

If one believes love remains constant
in both effect and faith
when a grievance occurs,
how can one believe?
Due to the pain that Phyllis feels,
they both suffer? Woe to one who has
the remedy in hand
and is dying without it!
The offense that Lisio committed
Phyllis will not excuse, and for this
state of affairs, she offends
by unfaithful reason.
Enemy jealousies
The rigor   ,   ,   ,   ,   ,
that is   ,   ,   ,   ,   ,
giving bad for good.

136. Lyrics to be sung.

Phyllis's eyes,
oh, God, how they cry
rivers of pearls
that are engulfed in love.

En quien su luz mira,
es si bien, señora,
el vivir, agravio,
el morir, lisonja.
De amor y de celos
Fili, un mar zozobra
y en otro más cierto
peligro se arroja.
Que muera repite
quien sin lo que adora,
el alma le falta,
la vida le sobra.
Por ambiciosos,
mayores glorias
en sus ojos hace
su mansión dichosa.

SECOND COLUMN
Valiéndose de ellos,
llorando, enamora,
y mirando, mata
con perlas hermosas.
Tírame el amor
las lágrimas que llora
si lágrimas son perlas,
tíremelas todas.

137. Romance a un retrato de Nuestra Señora de Monserrate [sic]   84r
que celebran las devotas religiosas de la Concepción de Toledo.

FIRST COLUMN
A la más hermosa aurora,
a la más luciente estrella,
que por madre tiene el mundo,
que el cielo tiene por reina.
A la que es la mejor hija,
y la esposa más perfecta,
donde el Dios, que es trino y uno,
amoroso se recrea.[1]

---

[1] This is a play on words since "recrearse" can mean "to take delight or pleasure" in something or someone, but it can also mean "to be recreated" in the sense that God was recreated, made incarnate, as man through the Virgin.

Whoever looks at their light.
knows well, my Lady,
that living offends and
dying flatters.
From both love and jealousy
Phyllis founders at sea
or into more certain
danger throws herself.
She repeats that she is dying
without whom she adores,
her soul falters,
and life is too burdensome.
For ambitious,
greater glories
in her eyes, she builds
a fortunate mansion.

Using them [her eyes],
crying, she falls in love,
and gazing at them, kills
with the beautiful pearls.
Love tosses to me
the tears that she sheds
and if tears are pearls,
toss them all to me.

137. Ballad to a portrait of Our Lady of Montserrat that the devout nuns of the Conception of Toledo celebrate.

To the most beautiful dawn,
to the most brilliant star
that the world has as its mother
and that heaven has as its queen.
To her who is the best daughter,
and the most perfect spouse,
of whom God, triune and one,
amorously takes delight.

A María, que este nombre
dice es un mar de excelencias,
copia de aquélla que el orbe
en Monserrate venera.
Hoy en aqueste palacio,
que siempre glorioso ostenta,
de su concepción el timbre,
la sacra imagen festejan.
Oculta no se permite,
puesto que de la tiniebla,

SECOND COLUMN
en que el olvido la puso,
que la sacasen dispensa.
Qué milagrosa dispone,
qué prodigiosa, qué alienta
corazones que a su culto
tantas dedican finezas.
No hay voluntad que no rinda,
dificultad que no venza
quien mandar a un hijo puro,
que es dueño del cielo y tierra.
A la flor de las flores,
háganle fiestas,
que es maravilla
siendo azucena.
Canten , , , , ,[1]
motetes dulces sonoros
avecillas que el aire
rompiendo vuelan.
A esta avecilla
, , , , , ,[2]

138. Villancico de la Ascensión que se cantó en la Santa Iglesia de Sevilla, año de 1646.

84v

FIRST COLUMN
1º ¡Ah, del cielo, ah, del cielo,
Ah, de la región suprema!

---

[1] Paper is missing; the repair of a tear here obscures the rest of this line.
[2] There appears to be at least one more line, but the paper here is torn away and it is impossible to be sure.

To Mary, whose name
speaks of a sea of excellences,
to a copy of her that the world
venerates in Montserrat.
Today in that palace,
where it is gloriously displayed,
and to honor her conception,
they celebrate her sacred image.
She should not be hidden,
and from the darkness

where she might be forgotten,
they bring her out to honor her.
How miraculously displayed,
how prodigious, how she inspires
hearts, that to her worship
dedicate such eloquence.
There is no will that does not surrender [to her],
there is no difficulty she cannot overcome
for He who sent His pure Son,
to be the master of heaven and earth.
This flower of flowers,
let us celebrate her,
for she is marvelous
being a white lily.
Sing , , , , ,[1]
sweet, melodious motets
little birds who fly
breaking through the air.
To this little bird
, , , , , , , , , , , , , , , ,[2]

138. Carol of the Ascension sung in the Holy Church in Seville in 1646.

1st Oh, of heaven! Oh, of heaven!
Oh, of the supreme realm!

---

[1] Paper here is missing but the meaning is still clear.
[2] One line is apparently missing.

Oid, los que sois de amor
vigilantes centinelas.
2º ¿Quién en tales voces llama
al cielo desde la tierra,
sabiendo que instancias mudas
más veloces le penetran?
1º ¡Ah, del cielo jerarquías
que ocupáis sillas eternas,
las puertas, abrid! 2º No hay voces
que basten a abrir las puertas
cuando[1] a méritos del alma
el cielo[2] no las franquea.
Abrid, que triunfante
el que[3] a la gloria llega,
Dios enseña en sí mismo
con misteriosa evidencia.
Quienes[4] llegan a la gloria
no entran si[5] no pasan penas.

SECOND COLUMN
1º Tantas pasó por el hombre
que ya victorioso queda.
2º Cántenle, pues, la victoria
en la militante iglesia.
1º2º Y háganle al entrar en el cielo la salva
dulzainas, chirimías, y vihuelas,[6]
y, entre los ecos sonoros,
repitan a coros
las voces diversas
a este Rey, vencedor de la culpa.
Tollite portas, principes, vestras,
[*et elevamini, portæ æternales,*
et introibit rex gloriæ.]

---

[1] "Cuando" is my reconstruction; paper missing.
[2] "El cielo" is my reconstruction; paper missing.
[3] "El que" is my reconstruction; paper missing.
[4] "Quienes" is my reconstruction; paper missing.
[5] "No entran si" is my reconstruction; paper missing.
[6] "biguelas" in the manuscript.

Listen, those of you who are
vigilant sentinels of love.
2ⁿᵈ Who calls out with such voices
to heaven from the earth,
knowing that silent petitions,
penetrate it more quickly?
1ˢᵗ Oh, hierarchies of heaven
who occupy eternal thrones,
open the doors! 2ⁿᵈ There are not enough voices
to open the doors
for only the merits of one's soul
open the doors of heaven.
Open them, triumphantly
to Him who arrives in glory
for God shows himself
with mysterious proof.
Those who arrive to glory
do not do so without suffering.

1ˢᵗ So many pains He suffered for man,
He who now reigns in victory.
2ⁿᵈ Sing of His victory
in the militant church.
1ˢᵗ 2ⁿᵈ And when He enters heaven, salute Him
with woodwinds and vihuelas,
and amidst the harmonious echoes,
repeat in choirs
diverse voices
to this King, conqueror of sin.
Tollite portas, principes, vestras,
[et elevamini, portæ æternales,
et introibit rex gloriæ.][1]

---

[1] Psalm 23:7 in the Vulgate used as a gradual in Advent and in the offertory of the Christmas vigil. In English, "Lift up your heads, O ye gates! and be lifted up, O ancient doors! that the King of glory may come in."

Coplas:[1]
Quedó al fin de Dios vencida
Aquella culpa primera,
fiero enemigo que al alma
ruina amenazaba eterna.
Saca del cóncavo triste
aquéllos en quien nos muestra
que posesión afianzan
esperanzas nunca inciertas.

FIRST COLUMN
Sube al cielo, deja el mundo
porque, sin su vista tenga,
el hombre la fe más firme
donde estribe su grandeza,
del reino que para el alma
ha ganado en buena guerra;
hoy en nombre suyo toma
la posesión de que es reina.

139. Otro a la venida del Espíritu Santo que se cantó en la misma iglesia.

Estribo:
Si de Dios el dulce favor,
alma, pretendéis gozar,
sabedle buscar
con amante fervor
porque sólo se paga de amor
quien sabe mejor
el estilo de amar.
El espíritu divino
hoy en lenguas se convierte
que quiere de aquesta suerte
mostrar de amor el camino.

---

[1] Vinatea Recoba reads these "coplas" as a separate poem. See footnote 1 on p. 332.

Stanzas:
Finally conquered by God
that first sin,
cruel enemy of the soul
that threatened eternal damnation.
From the sad cave,[1] He rescues
those whom He shows us
as examples to maintain
hope ever certain.

He flies up to heaven, He leaves the earth
because, even without sight of Him,
man may have firm faith
that testifies to the greatness
of the kingdom that, for the soul,
He won in the good fight;
today, in His name, He takes
possession of all that He rules.

139. Another for the coming of the Holy Spirit that was sung in the same church.

Refrain:
If God's sweet favor,
soul, you hope to enjoy,
know how to look for Him
as a fervent lover,
because love is only awarded
to one who knows best
the art of love.
The divine spirit
today comes in tongues [of fire],[2]
and wants, in this guise,
to show us the way to love.

---

[1] I.e., purgatory.
[2] I.e., the Holy Spirit.

SECOND COLUMN
Si a Dios pretendéis hallar,
este es el rumbo de vigor,
con tierno amante desveló
un incendio de amor hecho.
Busca Dios en vuestro pecho,
su habitación y su cielo,
vos le debéis hospedar
alma con activo ardor.
Porque sólo se paga [de amor
quien sabe mejor
el estilo de amar.]
Con lenguas de fuego mudo[1]
su amor os está intimando
porque más le explica   ,   ,   ,   ,   ,
son callando m   ,   ,   ,   ,   ,
amad, para   ,   ,   ,   , .
finezas   ,   ,   ,   ,   ,
porque [sólo se paga de amor]
quien [sabe mejor]
[el estilo de amar.][2]

FIRST COLUMN   85v
De la esfera luminosa,
de Cristo si se repara
su amor en rayos dispara
una [sic] enigma[3] misteriosa [sic]
cuyo sentido, ganar
pueda el afecto interior.
Porque sólo se paga [de amor
quien sabe mejor
el estilo de amar.]
Su ley a imprimiros viene
con fuego en el corazón
que no hay ley con perfección
en quien vivo amor no tiene.

---

[1] "Mudo" is partially a reconstruction since only "mud" is legible and the paper it torn away.
[2] These last three lines can be inferred since they are part of the refrain and the initial words are visible
[3] Manuscript reads "egnima."

If you want to find God,
this is the only way,
with a tender lover He revealed
a fire made of love.
Look for God in your heart,
His home and His heaven,
where you should give Him lodging
in your soul with active ardor,
because love is only awarded
[to one who knows best
the art of love.]
With tongues of silent fire
His love draws close to you
because more He explains , , , , , , , ,
are keeping quiet , , , , , , .
love, for , , , , , , ,
elegance , , , , , , ,
because love is only awarded
to one who knows best
the art of love.

From the luminous sphere
of Christ we can see how He
spreads out His love in rays,
a mysterious enigma
whose meaning we learn
only with the soul's affection,
because love is only awarded
[to one who knows best
the art of love.]
He comes to engrave His law
in your heart with fire
for there is no perfect law
in one who does not burn with the fire of love.

Con esto os quiere empeñar
a que le améis con primor.
Porque sólo [se paga de amor
quien sabe mejor
el estilo de amar.]
Todo su Amor y su gracia
, , , que la améis Dios envía
, , , , , gracia sería
, , , , , que desgracia
, , , , , no hay llegar
, , , , , superior
, , , , , , , de amor.

SECOND COLUMN
140. A San Joseph, letra.

Al Olimpo eterno sube
Joseph, tan resplandeciente,
que pasmando el cielo a luces
su curso el móvil suspende.
El Dios, que por hijo tuvo,
silla excelsa le concede,
que a finezas de tal Padre
tanto honor tal hijo debe.
Ya los amantes cherubes[1]
a este serafín de nieve,
por lo amoroso y lo puro,
lugar más sublime ofrecen.
Todo valimiento alcanza
y toda dicha posee,
éste que fue digno esposo
de aquella reina eminente.
Como amarla tanto supo
bien que injustos celos tiene,
porque poco amor se arguye
en quien celos no le ofenden.

FIRST COLUMN

86r

Que es el mayor de los santos
Joseph lo acredita siempre,

---

[1] Manuscript reads "cherubes" for "querubines" in order to maintain the eight-syllable rhyme scheme.

With this he wants to bind you
so that you may love more perfectly
because love [is only awarded
to one who knows best
the art of love.]
All His love and His grace
God sent, so that you might love
, , , , , , , grace would be
, , , , , , , , , that disgrace
, , , , , , , , , , does not arrive
, , , , , , , , , , superior
, , , , , , , , , of love.

140. Lyrics to Saint Joseph.

To the eternal Olympus rises
Joseph, so resplendent,
that his light astounds the sky
that ceases the course of its movement.
God, who considered him as His son,
gives him an exalted throne
because the graces of such a Father
are a deserving honor for such a son.
Now the loving cherubs
to this seraph of snow,
because of his love and his purity,
offer him the most sublime place.
He attains all advantage
and possesses all good fortune,
he who was the dignified spouse
of that eminent Queen.
He knew how to love her well
since showing unjust jealousy,
only argues for little love
in whom jealousy does not offend.

As the greatest of saints
Joseph is always rewarded,
for he raised Him[1] who raised them [the other saints]

---

[1] I.e., Christ.

pues que crió a quien los cría
y mandó a quien obedecen.
Querubes hermosos
que con dulce voz,
publicáis las glorias
que de Joseph son.
Repetid: que es grande,
pues, a Dios crió.

141. A señor Santiago.

O vista rayos, o plumas,
esferas matice o dore,
Diego, cisne y sol a un tiempo,
los aires que surca,[1] rompe.
Y a rayo animado llega
a los celestiales orbes,
ave que si no su muerte,
vida canta más acorde.

SECOND COLUMN
A su zenit le conducen
angélicos escuadrones
donde lúcidos desvelos
premien eternos favores.
O, qué brillante domina,
y qué canoro interrumpe
luces que rinde a gorjeos,
aves que vence a candores.
Salió del sangriento ocaso
cual suele el sol de la noche
cuando se desembaraza
de purpúreos arreboles.
La primavera   ,   ,   ,   ,
Diego es flor de los   ,   ,
el cielo dice que es   ,   ,   ,
pues, nació   ,   ,   ,   .
Afuera a   ,   ,   ,   ,   ,
retire el   ,   ,   ,   ,   ,
pues que   ,   ,   ,   ,
corona   ,   ,   ,   ,   ,

---

[1] Manuscript reads "sulca."

and he commanded Him whom they obey.
Beautiful cherubs
with sweet voice,
proclaim the glories
of Joseph.
Repeat: He is great
since he raised God.

141. To Saint James.

Oh dress with rays and plumes,
tinge and make golden the spheres,
James, swan and sun at one time,
breaks through the air that he plows.
And arrives on a bright ray
to the celestial orbs,
a bird, singing not of death,
but melodiously of life.

He is conducted to his zenith
by angelic squadrons
where lucid wakefulness
is rewarded with eternal favors.
Oh, how brilliantly he dominates,
and how harmoniously he interrupts
the lights that surrender to the chirping
of birds that defeat pure white [lights].
He came out of the bloody darkness
like a sun in the night
that clears darkness away
with a purplish-red glow.[1]
The Spring   ,   ,   ,   ,
James is the flower of the   ,   ,   ,   ,   ,
heaven says that he is   ,   ,   ,   ,   ,   ,
since he was born   ,   ,   ,   ,   ,   ,   , .
Outside   ,   ,   ,   ,   ,
pulls back   ,   ,   ,   ,   ,
so that   ,   ,   ,   ,   ,   ,
crown   ,   ,   ,   ,   ,   ,   ,
and among   ,   ,   ,   ,

---

[1] The remainder of the poem's lines are only partially legible due to paper torn away.

y entre , , , , ,
ves , , , , , ,
hay , , , , , .

142. Villancico a la profesión de una monja de San Clemente de Toledo, hija de San Benito y San Bernardo, devota del evangelista San Juan, estando el Santísimo Sacramento descubierto en la octava de la Asunción de Nuestra Señora.

FIRST COLUMN
1º Vengan, lleguen, señores:
verán las fiestas
que a unas bodas hacen
cielos y tierra.
Pregunta: Di, ¿quién en el mundo
habrá que merezca
que en sus desposorios
el cielo intervenga?
Respuesta: ¿es que me lo preguntas
, , , , , nueva
, , , , , de aquel prodigio[1]

SECOND COLUMN
1º Es un rey que tan fino,
galán se ostenta,
que hoy en cuerpo ha salido
porque le vean.
2º Oigan, atiendan,
que la palma y corona
le dan de reina
Estribo ambos:
1º2º Y repiten los cielos,
venga, venga enhorabuena,
de Cristo la esposa,
la cándida rosa.
Blanca mariposa
que al sol se acerca
cuando en él se abrasa,
más vida queda.
Coplas.

---

[1] It appears that four lines are missing due to torn paper.

BNE MS. 7469

you see , , , , , ,
there are , , , , , , , .

142. Carol for the profession of a nun of Saint Clement of Toledo, daughter of Saint Benedict and Saint Bernard, a devotee of the Evangelist Saint John, with the Holy Sacrament displayed on the octave of the Assumption of Our Lady.

1st Come, ladies and gentlemen, come:
you will see the celebration
of a marriage made
on heaven and earth.
Question: Tell, who in the world
might deserve
that in her wedding
heaven intervenes?
Answer: Is what you are asking
 , , , , , , new
 , , , , , , of that prodigy?

1st He is so fine a king,
proudly gallant,
who today in flesh has appeared
so that we might see Him.
2nd Listen, pay attention,
for they give her the palm and crown
as a queen.
Refrain for two voices:
1st 2nd And the heavens repeat,
come, come, congratulations
to the bride of Christ,
the pure rose.
A white butterfly
that draws near to the sun
and, when she is consumed in fire,
she has more life.
Stanzas.

FIRST COLUMN
Entre los dos:[1]
Hoy con denuedo bizarro
del mundo burla Manuela,
dando con un San Benito
nuevo lustre a su ascendencia.
Tan hija ya de Bernardo
que quien no le imita piensa,
que se queda en Bernardina
y a ser Bernarda no llega.
El velo con que hace alarde
de que ha de velar da señas
que de desvelos se paga,
di, ¿es que en su amor se desvela?
Fe promete al dulce esposo,
que no hay firme amor sin ella,
y para sólo un amante,
le pide y la da licencia.
Aquel águila es sin duda
que al radiante examen lleva,
hoy este alumno que al sol
busca amante y mira atenta.

, , , , , ,

SECOND COLUMN
El Ganimed[es]   ,   ,   ,[2]
que voló en sus alas
a servir copa al amante[3]
de la deidad más suprema.

---

[1] Vinatea Recoba again reads these "coplas" as a separate poem but they are part of the *villancio*, and the subject matter of the "coplas" is directly related to the title of the *villancico*.

[2] Remainder of line is missing. Ganymede was stolen by Zeus to be his cup-bearer and lover by hiding him in the wings of an eagle (Vinetea Recoba, 467).

[3] "Amante" is a reconstruction since only "ama" appears due to torn paper.

For two voices:
Today with valiant courage
Manuela makes fun of the world
giving a Saint Benedict[1]
new luster to her ascendency.
Such a daughter of Bernard,
whom she hopes to imitate,
may she remain as Bernardina
since she is not Bernarda.[2]
The veil that she wears
to hide herself is a sign
that she will be repaid with unveilings,[3]
say, does it [her veil] reveal her love?
The faithful promise she makes to her sweet bridegroom,
for there is no steadfast love without it [faith]
and only to be His lover,
she asks Him and He grants it to her.
Without doubt, that eagle
who carries [her] to the radiant exam,[4]
today this student looks to the sun
attentively, searching for her lover,
He who encourages her[5]

Ganymede , , , , , ,
who flew on his wings
to serve the cup to the lover
of the most supreme deity.

---

[1] This could be a play on words with "Sambenito," meaning penitential garb, later used as a sign of disgrace for those accused by the Inquisition. Here the implication would be that, by donning the nun's habit she is reversing ("making fun of") the dishonor such an outfit would usually signify.

[2] A play on words. "Bernadina," a diminutive noun, implies her new status as a nun, i.e., as a novice. "Bernadina" could also be an adjective since she is entering the order of St. Bernard.

[3] Another play on "velar," to veil or hide away, and "desvelar," to reveal or remove the veil from. The idea is that, by taking on the veil, she will be privy to revelations from God.

[4] I.e., taking her vows as a nun.

[5] Reconstruction for meaning; paper missing.

Con sólo un plato convida
a todos, que a todo sepa
de tal gracia que la novia
coma en el plato cuanto apetezca.
Feliz desposorio en tierra[1]
Que de la madrina , , , , ,
la coronación divina
festivó el cielo , , , .[2]

143. A San Bernardo, Romance.

FIRST COLUMN
Oh, tú que mueres de amores,[3]
imitador celestial
de los que en dulces capillas
siempre a Dios cantando están.
Entre suaves acentos,
la vida rendiste ya,
siendo de amor en el fuego,[4]
si cisne inmortal.
Nave del aire a los cielos,
, , , , , galán[5]
, , , , , entre golfos de luces
, , , , tus candores más.
, , , te envidia la muerte
, , , , su rígido afán
, , , , el morir, la gloria.
, , , , vida eterna da.
, , , , , de aquel ave
, , , , , está
, , , , , fuiste
, , , , , deidad.[6]

---

[1] This and the following four lines are only partial due to the torn folio. I have transcribed, with some supposition, all that is visible.

[2] There is at least one word missing from the end of this line in order to maintain the eight-syllable rhyme, but paper here is torn.

[3] This folio is torn, and I reconstruct these first two lines as per their transcription on p. 378 of Serrano y Sanz's inventory.

[4] Serrano y Sanz, 376–77.

[5] All the remaining lines of this poem are only partially visible or missing entirely.

[6] There are two more lines to this poem but only the last few letters of the last word of each line are visible.

With only one dish He invites
all, so that all will know
that the bride is of such grace
that she may eat all that she wants from the plate.
A happy wedding on earth[1]
that the bridesmaid , ,
the divine coronation
celebrated in heaven , , , , .

143. Ballad for Saint Bernard.

Oh, you who die from love,
celestial imitator
of those who in sweet chapels
are always singing to God.
Among melodious accents,
you surrendered your life,
being love in the fire,
a phoenix, an immortal swan.
A ship on air to the heavens,[2]
, , , , , , , gallant one
, , , , , , , , , among gulf of lights
, , , , , , , , your candors more.
, , , , , , , , death is jealous of you
, , , , , , , , his strong eagerness
, , , , , , , , dying, the glory.
, , , , , , , , gives eternal life
, , , , , , , , of that bird
, , , , , , , , is
, , , , , , , , was
, , , , , , , , , deity.

---

[1] "Earth" is my reconstruction. The following four lines are incomplete due to torn paper, but I have tried to reconstruct some meaning from them.

[2] The rest of this folio is torn and the remaining lines are only partially visible. To try to reconstruct a translation is not feasible.

144. Al Santísimo Sacramento.[1]

SECOND COLUMN

Poco importa, sol divino,
que blanca nube os disfrace
si en conocer vuestras luces
la fe es lince penetrante.
Flechas son que amor fulmina
tantos rayos celestiales
que a impresiones acreditan
lo que a incendios persuaden.
Aunque amor y fe son ciegos,
al blanco aciertan constantes,
y, a lo que la vista ignora,
los afectos dan alcance.
Que sois sol de la alma [sic] mía
lo dice el luciente examen
con que sacáis de mis sombras
amorosas claridades.
Cobarde espero mis dichas,
Señor, de vuestras piedades
que teme al ofendido[2]
es merecer por cobarde.
Rayos que el sol esparce
para que el alma viva de amor matado
que entre ardientes desmayos
dulce acierto seréis donde más vives.[3]

145. Dándome por asunto cortarse un dedo llegando a cortar un jazmín. Soneto.[4]   88r

Filis, de amor hechizo soberano,
cortar quiso un jazmín desvanecido,

---

[1] This poem does not appear in Serrano y Sanz's inventory.
[2] The ink here is very faded.
[3] Last word is illegible, but I reconstruct it as "vives."
[4] Serrano y Sanz, 78; Olivares and Boyce, 1st ed., 333; Olivares and Boyce, 2nd ed., 249–50. This page (the last of the manuscript) has been repaired, but several words are missing. I follow Serrano y Sanz's transcription, as do Olivares and Boyce in both editions. It is impossible to know if the missing words were legible when Serrano y Sanz made his inventory in 1905 or whether he was supplying them for meaning and rhyme scheme. I have italicized in the transcription the words supplied by Serrano y Sanz that are no longer visible in the manuscript.

144. To the Holy Sacrament.

Divine sun, it is of no consequence
that a white cloud conceals you
if, knowing of your lights,
faith has sharp vision.
[Your lights] are arrows of love that emit
so many celestial rays
that they give the impression
of being on fire.
Even though love and faith are blind,
they always hit their target,
for what one cannot see,
affections can attain.
You are the sun of my soul
and the bright test proves it,
for You take me out of the shadows
with amorous clarities.
Cowardly I await the good fortune,
Lord, may I enjoy Your mercies
but I fear of offending,
or receiving what I deserve as a coward.
Rays that the sun emits
so that the soul may live, killed by love,
that among ardent swoons
a sweet victory where you are more alive.

145. Sonnet, taking as my theme cutting one's finger while trying to cut a jasmine.

Phyllis,[1] of sovereign love's spell
wanted to cut a vain jasmine,

---

[1] Phyllis was the daughter of a Thracian king. who married Demophon, king of Athens, when he passed through Thrace on his way back from the Trojan War. Demophon abandoned Phyllis out of a sense of duty to help his father, Theseus, in Greece. Phyllis, believing he would never return, committed suicide, and an almond (or hazelnut) tree grew on the spot. When Demophon returned at last, the tree blossomed in response.

    y de cinco mirándose excedido,
quedó del vencimiento más ufano.
    No bien corta el jazmín cuando tirano
acero un rojo humor otro ha teñido,
mintiendo ramillete entretejido
de jazmín y clavel la hermosa ma*no*.
    Átropos bella a la tijera cede,
piadosa ejecución si inad*vertida*,
a su mano dolor ocasionando;
que si alma con su sangre dar no puede,
en vez de muerte dio, al jazmín la vida,[1]
de amor el duce imperio *dilatando*.

---

[1] Olivares and Boyce add "la" to maintain the eleven-syllable rhyme scheme. Serrano y Sanz omits "la" in his transcription.

and of five, seeing themselves exceeded,
the proudest one fell conquered.
No sooner than she cuts the jasmine, a tyrannical
blade stains another with red humor,
lying stem intertwined
like jasmine and carnation on her lovely hand.
Beautiful Atropos[1] to the scissors cedes,
piteous execution, if unexpected,
causing pain to her hand;
even though she cannot give a soul with her blood,
instead of death, she gave the jasmine life,
spreading the sweet empire of love.

---

[1] One of the three Fates.

Index of Poems

Introductory Poems to the Collection

A. Décima al autor. / Décima to the Author.
B. A quien leyere estos versos. / To whomever reads these verses.
C. De el [sic] padre Jacinto Quintero de los Clérigos Menores, a estas obras de María de Santa Isabel. Décimas. / By Father Jacinto Quintero of the Clerics Minor, to these works of María de Santa Isabel. Décimas.
D. No elogio sino deuda a estas obras divinas. De Doña Juana de Bayllo, monja en Santa Isabel el Real de Toledo. / Not a eulogy but a debt to these divine works. By Doña Juana de Bayllo, nun in Santa Isabel the Royal of Toledo.
E. Al mismo asunto, si con menos acierto, con más afecto agraviando en la insinuación tanto lo sonorio [sic] relevante de estas obras como lo [inmenso] del sentir de quien los alaba de esta manera. / On the same topic, if with less success, with more affection, offending by hinting at the sonorous quality of these works that merit my tremendous admiration and praise.
F. Elogio de veras en el sentimiento, aunque en chanza al decir al libro y dueño. Del Licdo. Montoya, opositor de los curatos. / True eulogy in sentiment, even though in jest, to the book and its owner. By the Licenciado Montoya, candidate for the exam of curate.
G. A mi Sra. Da. María de Ortega porque me condujo este libro teniéndole yo muy deseado. / To my lady Doña María de Ortega because she sent me this book, since I so desired to have it.
H. A las nunca bien encarecidas ni bastamente alabadas varias poesías de este libro. Soneto. / To the never sufficiently extolled or praised poems in this book. Sonnet.
I. Elogio a lo espirituoso y elegante de los versos de aqueste libro. De un religioso francisco. / Praise for the spirituality and the elegance of the verses of this book. By a Franciscan religious.

Poems by Marcia Belisarda

1. Al evangelista San Juan. Romance que fue el primero que escribí a los 27 años de mi edad. / To the Evangelist Saint John. The first ballad that I wrote when I was 27 years old.
2. A Señor Santiago. Endecha. / To our lord, Saint James. Lament.
3. A Santa Clara. Romance. / Ballad to Saint Clare.
4. A la profesión de Da. Petronila de la Palma, en la Concepción Real de Toledo, siguiendo la metáfora de la palma. Soneto. / To the profession of Doña Patronila de la Palma, in the Royal Conception of Toledo, using the metaphor of the palm. Sonnet.
5. A la misma: décima. / To the same woman: décima.
6. Otra. Dándome que glosar, rimo [sic], pie y el asunto. / Another, charging me with a rhyme scheme and the subject.
7. Décima de Da. Juana de Bayllo, monja de Santa Isabel el Real a otra que le dio un desmayo. / Décima by Doña Juan de Bayllo, nun at Saint Isabel the Royal to another [nun] who gave her a fright.
8. Respuesta mía por los consonantes mismos [sic]. / My answer with the same consonants.
9. Procurad, memorias tristes . . . / Try, sad memories . . .
10. Otro, dándome el asunto. / Another, charging me with the subject.
11. Alabando al Rvo. Joan Peréz Roldán la ciencia de músico compositor. Soneto. / Praising the Reverend Juan Pérez Roldán, a composer of the science of music. Sonnet.
12. Alabanza al Evangelist San Juan. / In praise of the Evangelist Saint John.
13. A Señor Santiago, Patrón de España. / To Lord Saint James, Patron of Spain.
14. Al Santísimo Sacramento. Vejamen. / For the Holy Sacrament. Satire.
15. A San Jerónimo. Romance. / Ballad to Saint Jerome.
16. Villancico a la Natividad de Cristo entre cuatro. / Christmas Carol for four voices.
17. Otro. / Another.
18. Ensalada de Navidad. / Christmas Salad.
19. A Santa Teresa. Romance. / Ballad for Saint Theresa.
20. A la profesión de una monja Bernarda que la hice en día de la degollación del Baptista estando el Santísimo Sacramento descubierto y su nombre Paula. / For the profession of a nun, Bernarda, on the day of the beheading of the Baptist with the Holy Eucharist present, taking the name of Paula.

21. A la Concepción de Nuestra Señora. / To the Conception of Our Lady.
22. Al baptismo [sic] de Cristo. / To the Baptism of Christ.
23. Otro. / Another.
24. Otro. / Another.
25. Soneto trovando uno de Lope de Vega muy celebrado. / Sonnet, imitating a very celebrated one by Lope de Vega.
26. Alabando la fábula de Hércules y Deyanira de D. Jerónimo Pantoja, vecino de Toledo, escrita en octavas elegantes. / Praising the fable of Hercules and Deianira, written in elegant octaves, by Don Jerónimo Pantoja, a citizen of Toledo.
27. Octava. / Octave.
28. Alabando las novelas de D. Pedro de Paz, vecino de Toledo y de ingenio lucidísimo. / Praising the novels of Don Pedro de Paz, a neighbor of Toledo with very lucid wit.
29. Octava a una señora que con pocas razones enamoraba y decía pesares con gran discreción. / Octave to a woman who foolishly fell in love and recounted her woes with great discretion.
30. Soneto de un galán a una dama seglar. / Sonnet by a gentlemen to a lady.
31. Encoméndoseme la respuesta y fue por los mismos consonantes [sic]. / Charging me with the response using the same consonants.
32. Soneto a consonantes forzosas sobre que habían escrito sonetos con asuntos diferentes, diferentes personas, dieronme por asunto no desmayar a vista de un desdén. / Sonnet with pre-ordained consonants used by various people to write about different topics, taking as my subject not despairing when one encounters an affront.
33. A la Asunción de Nuestra Señora. / For the Assumption of Our Lady.
34. A la misma fiesta de la Asunción de Nuestra Señora, otra. / For the same festival of the Assumption of Our Lady.
35. Otro a San Francisco de Paula. / Another to Saint Francis of Paola.
36. A San Clemente entre dos. / For Saint Clement, in two voices.
37. Décima. / Décima.
38. Descripción del martirio de San Vicente mártir. / Description of the martyrdom of Saint Vincent.
39. Al sudario de Cristo. Romance / Ballad to Christ's shroud.
40. A la soledad de Nuestra Señora. / Ballad to the loneliness of Our Lady.
41. Al expirar Cristo en la cruz. / Ballad to Christ expiring on the cross.
42. A Santa Catalina de Sena. / To Saint Catherine of Siena.

43. Glosa. / Gloss.
44. Décimas a instancia de una monja toledana cuyo amante dejaba un amigo por guarda de su dama. / Décimas requested by a Toledan nun about a lover who left his lady in the care of his friend.
45. Dándome por asunto el sentimiento de una persona a un desdén que la hicieron después de una ausencia grande. Soneto. / Taking as my theme the feelings of a person who is disdained after a long absence. Sonnet.
46. A instancia de una dama. Sentimiento de ausencia por ironía que le escribe a una persona por mí. / At the request of a lady. Writing ironically about feelings of absence.
47. De Navidad. Romance. / Ballad about Christmas.
48. A la Purificación de Nuestra Señora. Romance. / Ballad for the Purification of Our Lady.
49. Al Señor Santiago, patrón de España, villancico. / Carol to Saint James, the Patron of Spain.
50. Décimas a un sujeto bizarro que perdió una canonjía de Toledo por oposición teniendo el día antes de votarse grandes esperanzas de conseguirla. / Décimas about a gallant subject. How a Canon of Toledo lost an election when only the day before he had great hopes of winning it.
51. Romance de un cortesano. / Ballad of a courtier.
52. Mi respuesta por curiosidad por los asonantes [sic]. / My response out of curiosity about the assonant rhymes.
53. Romance que se cantó entre dos en la Concepción Real de Toledo, al Rvmo. P. Fray Baltasar Fernández, su Provincial de la provincia de Castilla, entrando a visitar el convento. / Ballad to be sung by two voices in the Royal Conception of Toledo for the most Reverend Father Balthazar Fernández, the Provincial of Castile upon the occasion of his visit to the convent.
54. A Santo Domingo. Villancico. / Carol for Saint Dominic.
55. A la muy venerable Sra. Doña Beatriz de Silva, fundadora del Real de la Concepción de Toledo. / To the most venerable Lady Beatrice of Silva, founder of the Royal Convent of the Conception in Toledo.
56. Romance melancólico. / Melancholic ballad.
57. Romance burlesco. / Burlesque ballad.
58. Otra a petición de un músico. / Another at the request of a musician.
59. Un estribillo de un tono decía. / A refrain said in one tone.
60. A una gran señora casada a quien aborrecía su marido. / To a great lady married to a man who detested her.

Index of Poems 375

61. Romance en el certamen del Evangelista San Juan que se inventó en el convento de San Pablo para su fiesta de mayo de 1642 años. El asunto que dieron fue que el relámpago es vapor sutil inflamado, que brevemente se desvanece en el aire, que al que mejor relampague [sic] hace chistes introduciendo el Cerro del Búho y la Peña del Rey Moro que iban a dar la norbuena a las religiosas de la fiesta se le daría premio y yo, sin esa golosina, dije por obedecer a las religiosas / Ballad for the contest of the Evangelist Saint John, invented in the Convent of Saint Paul for his festival in May of 1642. The subject they gave was a lightning bolt that is subtle, inflamed vapor that quickly disappears in the air and makes a flash, by making jokes introducing the Owl's Hill and the Rock of the Moorish King. To congratulate the nuns in the festival and to win a prize and I, without that incentive, said in order to obey the nuns.

62. Glosa que dieron en el mismo certamen. / Gloss that they gave in the same contest.

63. Soneto del mismo certamen. El asunto dar la razón de no morir el evangelista ni con el fuego de la tina ni con el veneno del vaso. / Sonnet in the same contest. My topic is to testify that the Evangelist does not die even from the flames of the vat nor from poison in the cup.

64. Al evangelista en la isla de Padmos. Romance. / Ballad to the Evangelist on the Isle of Patmos.

65. Romance. / Ballad.

66. Terceto o redondilla que me dieron a glosar. / Tercet or quatrain that they gave me to gloss.

67. Otra glosada. / Another glossed.

68. Al Santísimo Sacramento en metáfora de la jornada que hace el Rey este año de 1642 para cobrar a Portugal y quietar a Cataluña. / To the Most Holy Sacrament as a metaphor for the effort that the King made in 1642 to recover Portugal and pacify Cataluña.

69. Al Santísimo Sacramento. / To the Most Holy Sacrament.

70. Otra. / Another.

71. A nuestro patrón San [sic] Santiago. Villancico entre dos. / To our Patron, Saint James. Carol in two parts.

72. Burlesco soneto. Alabáronme un soneto tanto que le pedí con instancia aunque después de leído, no entendí nada y respondí el siguiente confesando mi poco saber. / Burlesque sonnet. I heard of such an admired sonnet that I asked to read it and when I did, I did not understand a word of it and I responded, confessing my ignorance.

73. A la venerable señora Doña Beatriz de Silva, fundadora de la Concepción de Toledo, entre dos y en fiesta de Nuestra Señora. / To the venerable Lady

Doña Beatrice of Silva, founder of the Conception of Toledo, for two voices for the festival of Our Lady.
74. A la Magdalena. / To the Magdalene.
75. Otro a San Bernardo. / Another for Saint Bernard.
76. Otro. / Another.
77. Otro. / Another.
78. Otra divina. / Another divine.
79. Otra humana. Para cantada. / Another secular, to be sung.
80. Otra a una religiosa que lloraba sin medida la muerte de otra que la había criado. / Another for a nun who grievously mourned the death of the one who had raised her.
81. A la Natividad vuelto del humano que queda en la plana por lograr el estribillo de batalla. / To the Nativity, based on a secular poem, written so as to maintain its refrain about a battle.
82. Otra. / Another.
83. A instancia de una monja muy evangelista en Día de Todos Santos, se hizo esta letra introduciendo a San Juan por cifra de todos. / At the insistence of a nun very dedicated to the Evangelist on the Day of All Saints, in which I use Saint John as an emblem for all the saints.
84. A San Diego de Alcalá, logrando el estribillo. / To Saint Diego of Alcalá, repeating the refrain.
85. A la presentación de Nuestra Señora, logrando el estribillo. / To the presentation of Our Lady, repeating the refrain.
86. A una copia devotísima del Santísimo Cristo de Burgos. / To a very exact copy of the Most Holy Christ of Burgos.
87. Villancico de Navidad. / Christmas Carol.
88. Para lograr la música de la primera copla y del estribillo (que no escribí yo) me pidieron hiciese a propósito las demás coplas para la Navidad de Cristo, cantóse en la Santa Iglesia, año 1642, en Toledo. / In keeping with the first couplet and refrain (that I did not write), I was asked to write these additional stanzas for the Nativity of Christ, and it was sung in the Holy Church in 1642 in Toledo.
89. Al bautismo de Cristo, año de 1643. / For the Baptism of Christ. 1643.
90. Décimas dándome el asunto. / Décimas, charging me with a topic.
91. Billete en verso de chanza, a una señora que me llamaba su galán. / A joke in verse for a lady who called me her ladies' man.
92. Romance. Al niño perdido. / Ballad for the lost Child.
93. A la Purificación de Nuestra Señora. / To the Purification of Our Lady.

94. A la traslación de una imagen de Nuestra Señora de una capilla a otra nueva en su fiesta de la Purificación, pidiéndome, se hiciese en la forma que el mismo villancico, dirá el que se sigue. / For the moving of an image of Our Lady from one chapel to another on the Feast of her Purification, I was asked to compose a carol and I did so, as follows.
95. Romance burlesco para un billete. / Note for a burlesque ballad.
96. Romance burlesco a instancia de una amiga, cuyo galán pretendía picarla con otra dama, haciendo pruebas en su voluntad. / Burlesque ballad written at the insistence of a friend, whose lover tried to make her jealous with another woman to prove her loyalty.
97. Para una novela. Soneto. / Sonnet for a novel.
98. Décimas para una novela. / Décimas for a novel.
99. Villancico a la entrada de dos hermanas hermosas a tomar hábito en la casa Real de la Concepción francisca. Logrando la música del estribillo, segunda vez. / Carol for the entrance of two beautiful sisters, taking the habit in the Royal Franciscan House of the Conception. With music for the refrain, a second time.
100. Para la misma novela. Romance. Aunque le hice con asunto particular, y no para monja. / Ballad for the same novel. I wrote this for a private matter and not for a nun.
101. A Santa Catalina de Sena. Romance logrando la música del estribillo segunda vez. / For Saint Catherine of Siena. Ballad with music for the refrain, the second time.
102. Al Santísimo Sacramento. Letrilla que se cantó en la santa iglesia de Toledo, año 1643. / To the most Holy Sacrament. Letrilla sung in the Holy Church of Toledo in the year 1643.
103. Al evangelista San Juan, logrando segunda vez la música del estribo. / To the Evangelist, Saint John, with music for the refrain the second time.
104. Décimas escritas muy de priesa [sic], en respuesta de otras en que ponderaban la mudanza de las mujeres. / Décimas written in great haste, in response to other poems that consider the fickleness of women.
105. Dándome el asunto de un alma a quien Dios hacía singulares favores, hice estos versos. / Taking as my theme a soul for whom God did singular favors, I made these verses.
106. Letra humana. / Humane lyric.
107. Elogio a un libro de antinomias que escribió el doctor Alfián en favor de la medicina, de cuyas razones se arguye ser insigne estudiante según ellas mismas lo manifiestan y declaran. / Eulogy to a book about contradictions

that Doctor Alfián wrote in favor of the science of medicine that attests to his eminence as a scholar.

108. Villancico a Doña María de la Puebla profesando en la Concepción francisca de Toledo y estando el Santísimo Sacramento descubierto. / Carol for Doña María de la Puebla professing at the Franciscan Convent of the Conception in Toledo with the Holy Sacrament displayed.

109. A la arrebatada y lastimosa muerte de Doña Ana de Briones, monja de San Clemente de Toledo, de edad de 26. / For the sudden and grievous death of Doña Ana de Briones, a nun of Saint Clement of Toledo, at the age of 26.

110. Letra al Santísimo Sacramento, logrando el estribo humano puesto en música. / Poem for the Holy Sacrament, with a secular refrain set to music.

111. Villancico a Doña Catalina de Molina, profesando en el convento de San Torcuato de la Orden de San Agustín en la fiesta de la Purificación de Nuestra Señora. / Carol for Doña Catalina de Molina, professing in the Convent of Saint Torquatus of the Order of Saint Augustine on the Feast of the Purification of Our Lady.

112. Décimas estrambotadas para una novela. / Extra lines for a song for a novel.

113. A Santa Catalina di [sic] Esena. / To Saint Catherine of Siena.

114. Otra letra a Santa Catalina de Esena. / Another to Saint Catherine of Siena.

115. A la venida del Espíritu Santo. Cantóse en la Santa Iglesia de Sevilla. Año 1644. / To the coming of the Holy Spirit. Sung in the Holy Church of Seville in 1644.

116. Al Santísimo Sacramento. Letra vuelta de la humana que queda escrita. / To the Holy Sacrament. Adapted from a secular theme and written as follows.

117. Celebrando la misa nueva un sacerdote en cuya fiesta escribieron algunos toledanos a ruego de un su amigo, y, yo, diciendo así. / For a priest celebrating his first mass, some Toledans wrote about this occasion on the request of their friend, and I wrote the following.

118. Romance para la novela. / Ballad for the novel.

119. A Santa Teresa, Romance. / Ballad For Saint Theresa.

120. Décimas por cantadas, dándome el asunto al que las había de cantar. / Décimas to be sung, having charged me with the subject about which they were to sing.

121. Vuelta de humana en divina por lograr el tono. / Taking a secular subject and making it divine but retaining the tone [of the original].

122. Romance muy celebrado y cantado con razón. / A very celebrated ballad rightly to be sung.

Index of Poems

123. Mi respuesta, oyendo los últimos versos. / My response after hearing the last verses.
124. A San Vicente mártir logrando segunda vez la música del estribillo. / For Saint Vincent, martyr, with music for the second refrain.
125. Otra, volviéndola de humana, divina, a Santa Catalina de Esena. / Taking a secular song and making a divine one for Saint Catherine of Siena.
126. A la transfiguración de Cristo en el Tabor. / For the Transfiguration of Christ on Tabor.
127. Orta. / Another.
128. Décimas apoyando que los celos declarados son más insufribles que los recelos. / Décimas, supporting that declared jealousies are more insufferable than suspicions.
129. A la Señora fundadora del convento de la Concepción Real de Toledo. Villancico. / Carol to the lady, founder of the Royal Convent of the Conception of Toledo.
130. A Santiago, patrón de España. / To Saint James, Patron of Spain.
131. Persuadiendo a una dama que amase, escribieron cuatro poetas glosando esta copla, y yo respondí sobre la misma glosa por la dama, conforme a su dictamen. / Persuading a lady to fall in love, four poets wrote glossing a couplet and I responded to the same gloss for the lady, according to her dictate.
132. Letra al bautismo de Cristo. / Lyrics for the Baptism of Christ.
133. Esta glosa que escribió una religiosa carmelita de Ocaña, puse aquí por digna de ser celebrada en primer lugar y por leerla yo algunas veces. El asunto fue una pintura de Cristo crucificado de cuyo costado salían dos fuentes, una de sangre, otra de agua, que venían a parar a un corazón que tenía a los pies. Y de él nacían dos pimpollos, uno con tres azucenas y otro con tres rosas y la redondilla que la dieron dice así: / This is a gloss that a Carmelite nun from Ocaña wrote; I include it here because it is worthy of being celebrated, and I have read it several times. It is about a picture of Christ crucified from whose side gushed two springs—one of blood and another of water—that flowed together into a heart at His feet. From the heart were born two buds—one with three white lilies and another with three roses. And the quatrain that they gave her reads:
134. Soneto que hice en alabanza de esta glosa. / Sonnet that I wrote in praise of this gloss.
135. Romance, y el asunto ver un galán que su dama le ofendía y porque se quejaba de ella, darse por agraviada de él. / Ballad about a young man whose lady offended him and because he complained about her, she got angry with him.

136. Letra, para cantada. / Lyrics to be sung.
137. Romance a un retrato de Nuestra Señora de Monserrate [sic] que celebran las devotas religiosas de la Concepción de Toledo. / Ballad to a portrait of Our Lady of Montserrat that the devout nuns of the Conception of Toledo celebrate.
138. Villancico de la Ascensión que se cantó en la Santa Iglesia de Sevilla, año de 1646. / Carol of the Ascension sung in the Holy Church in Seville in 1646.
139. Otro a la venida del Espíritu Santo que se cantó en la misma iglesia. / Another for the coming of the Holy Spirit that was sung in the same church.
140. A San Joseph, letra. / Lyrics to Saint Joseph.
141. A señor Santiago. / To Saint James.
142. Villancico a la profesión de una monja de San Clemente de Toledo, hija de San Benito y San Bernardo, devota del evangelista San Juan, estando el Santísimo Sacramento descubierto en la octava de la Asunción de Nuestra Señora. / Carol for the profession of a nun of Saint Clement of Toledo, daughter of Saint Benedict and Saint Bernard, a devotee of the Evangelist Saint John, with the Holy Sacrament displayed on the octave of the Assumption of Our Lady.
143. A San Bernardo, Romance. / Ballad for Saint Bernard.
144. Al Santísimo Sacramento. / To the Holy Sacrament.
145. Dándome por asunto cortarse un dedo llegando a cortar un jazmín. Soneto. / Sonnet, taking as my theme cutting one's finger while trying to cut a jasmine.

Bibliography

Primary source

BNE ms. 7469. Santa Isabel, María de. *Colección de poesías*.

Secondary sources

Baranda Leturio, Nieves. *Cortejo a lo prohibido: Lecturas y escritoras en la España moderna*. Madrid: Arcos/Libros, 2005.

Befroy, Ann Craig. "The Flesh Made Word: Women in the Poetry and Prose of Late Medieval and Early Modern Spain." Ph.D. Diss. New York University, 2009.

Bibliografía de Escritoras Españolas (Universidad Nacional de Educación a Distancia). www.bieses.net. Accessed 27 Dec. 2015.

Cerezo Soler, Juan. "El *Libro de poesías* de Marcia Belisarda: Notas al ejemplar autógrafo de la Biblioteca Nacional." *Manuscrt. Cao* 13 (2012): n. pag.

Colón Calderón, Isabel. "El linaje de Fabo." *eHumanista* 3 (2003): 91–104.

Conde, Rogerio, OFM. *La beata Beatriz de Silva: Su vida y fundación de la Orden de la Purísima Concepción*. Madrid: Editorial Ibérica, 1931.

Dugaw, Dianne and Amanda Powell. "Baroque Sapphic Poetry: A Feminist Road Not Taken." *Reason and Its Other: Italy, Spain, and the New World*. Ed. David R. Castillo and Massimo Lollini. Nashville: Vanderbilt University Press, 2006. 123–44.

Flores, Ángel and Kate Flores, eds. *Poesía feminista del mundo hispánico (desde la edad media hasta la actualidad): Una antología crítica*. México, DF: Siglo Veintiuno, 1984.

Fox, Gwyn. *Subtle Subversions: Reading Golden Age Sonnets by Iberian Women*. Washington, DC: The Catholic University of America Press, 2008.

Gutiérrez, Enrique. *Santa Beatriz de Silva e Historia de la Orden de la Concepción en Toledo en sus primeros años (1484–1511)*. 3rd ed. Toledo: Convento Casa Madre, 1988.

Herrojón Nicolás, Manola. *Los conventos de clausura femeninos de Toledo*. Temas Toledanos 65. Toledo: Diputación Provincial, 1990.

Janés, Clara, ed. *Las primeras poetisas en lengua castellana*. 2nd ed. Madrid: Endymion, 2000.

Jiménez Faro, Luz María. *Poetisas españolas: antología general. Tomo I: Hasta 1900.* Madrid: Torremozas, 1996. 4 vols.

Kaminsky, Amy Katz, ed. *Water Lilies/Flores de agua: An Anthology of Spanish Women Writers from the Fifteenth through the Nineteenth Century.* Minneapolis: University of Minnesota Press, 1996.

Langle de Paz, Teresa. "Femenismos prevalecientes: hacia una nueva historia del siglo XVII." *Edad de Oro* 26 (2007): 147–58.

Lehfeldt, Elizabeth A. *Religious Women in Golden Age Spain: The Permeable Convent.* Alderhot, UK and Burlington, VT: Ashgate, 2005.

Marín Pina, María del Carmen and Nieves Baranda Leturio. "Bibliografía de escritoras españolas (Edad Media–Siglo XVIII). Una base de datos." *Edad de Oro Cantabrigense. Actas del VII Congreso de la Asociación Internacional del Siglo de Oro (AISO) (Robinson College, Cambridge, 18–22 julio, 2005).* Ed. Anthony Close. Madrid: Iberoamericana/Vervuert, 2006. 425–35.

Martínez Caviró, Balbina. *Conventos de Toledo: Toledo, Castillo interior.* Madrid: Ediciones El Viso, 1990.

Martos Pérez, María Dolores. "Receptores históricos y conciencia autorial en paratextos de impresos poéticos femeninos (1600–1800)." *Criticón* 125 (2015): 79–92.

Mujica, Bárbara. *Women Writers of Early Modern Spain: Sophia's Daughters.* New Haven and London: Yale University Press, 2004.

Navarro, Ana, ed. *Antología poética de escritoras de los siglos XVI y XVII.* Madrid: Castalia, 1989.

Nelken, Margarita. *Las escritoras españolas.* 1930. Repr. La Cosecha de Nuestras Madres. Madrid: horas y HORAS, 2011.

Olivares, Julián and Elizabeth S. Boyce, eds. *Tras el espejo la musa escribe: lírica femenina de los Siglos de Oro.* 1st ed. Madrid: Siglo XXI de España, 1993; 2nd ed. Madrid: Siglo XXI de España, 2012.

Omaechevarría, Ignacio. *Las monjas concepcionistas: Notas históricas sobre la Orden de la Concepción fundada por Beatriz de Silva.* Burgos: n.p., 1973.

———. *Orígenes de la Concepción de Toledo: Documentos primitivos sobre Santa Beatriz de Silva y la Orden de la Inmaculada.* Burgos: n.p., 1976.

Powell, Amanda. "'¡Oh qué diversas estamos, / dulce prenda, vos y yo!' Multiple Voicings in Love Poems to Women by Marcia Belisarda, Catalina Clara Ramírez de Guzmán, and Sor Violante del Cielo." *Studies on Women's Poetry of the Golden Age.* Coord. Julián Olivares. Colección Támesis, Serie A, Monografías 273. Woodbridge, UK: Tamesis, 2009. 51–80.

Ruiz Guerrero, Cristina. *Panorama de escritoras españolas.* Vol. 1. Cádiz: Universidad de Cádiz, Servicio de Publicaciones, 1997.

Sainz de Robles, Federico Carlos. *Ensayo de un diccionario de la literatura. Tomo II: Escritores españoles e hispanoamericanos.* 3 vols. 1949. 4th ed. Madrid: Aguilar, 1973.

Serrano y Sanz, Manuel. *Apuntes para una biblioteca de escritoras españolas desde el año 1401 al 1833*. 2 vols. Madrid: Tipografía de la *Revista de archivos, bibliotecas y museos*, 1903–1905.

Vinatea Recoba, Martina. *María Fernández López (Marcia Belisarda): Obra poética completa*. Colección "Batihoja." New York: Instituto de Estudios Auriseculares, 2015.

Vollendorf, Lisa. "Transatlantic Ties: Women's Writing in Iberia and the Americas." *Women, Religion, and the Atlantic World (1600–1800)*. Eds. Daniella Kostroun and Lisa Vollendorf. Los Angeles: The Regents of the University of California, 2009. 79–110.